PRAISE FOR *STORY B*

"Never underestimate the power of storytelling! If you're in business—and who isn't?—a compelling story can turbocharge your results. Gavin McMahon shows you the power of storytelling in a book that is not only informative and inspiring but also an absolute delight to read! Don't miss it."

—**Ken Blanchard, New York Times bestselling coauthor of** *The One Minute Manager* **and** *The Simple Truths of Leadership*

"With the precision of an engineer and the soul of a poet, McMahon shows that while spreadsheets may capture what happened, stories determine what happens next. *Story Business* is both blueprint and battle cry for leaders ready to wield humanity's oldest and most powerful technology."

—**Jimmy Soni, bestselling author of** *The Founders*

"In a world where ideas compete for attention and outrage passes for dialogue, *Story Business* helps leaders connect through clarity and trust. This book is a vital skillset for meaningful work."

—**Jerry Colonna, author of** *Reunion*, **CEO of Reboot.io**

"McMahon braids history, science, and practical experience to offer actionable tools and essential context. *Story Business* is an immensely readable, jargon-free guide to communicating ideas more effectively—because ideas can change everything."

—**Elise Hu, TED Talks Daily host, award-winning author of** *Flawless*

"By using McMahon's framework, I've become a more effective presenter—someone whose message not only resonates in the moment but nests in the minds of others. That's how transformation happens."

—**Bryce Hoffman, bestselling author of** *American Icon*

"One minute you're reading. The next, you're acting. This book will end up on the desks of leaders everywhere—for good reason. It's the best way to get your boss to understand the why and how of stories."

—**Michael Erard, author of** *Bye Bye I Love You*

"This book offers a blueprint for weaving clarity, authenticity, and strategy into your storytelling—skills essential not just in the boardroom or at the podium, but in classrooms, war rooms, and community halls alike. Richly furnished with fascinating research and examples, *Story Business* belongs on every leader's desk.

It is one of those 'open any page' books with something fresh to offer even the most skilled leader every day. Use it to lead with vision, persuade with integrity, and inspire those you serve."

—Larry Seaquist, retired U.S. Navy Captain and commander of three warships, former Washington State legislator

"Every successful person—whether they realize it or not—is a storyteller. Storytelling is the key that unlocks success, and in this beautifully written, deeply practical book, Gavin hands you that key. Equal parts inspirational and hands-on, this is essential reading for anyone serious about storytelling—and everyone should be, because, as Gavin says, 'stories create value.'"

—Nick Jefferson, CEO of Wylde Market

"Storytelling isn't just a soft skill. It's the sharpest tool in a leader's kit. In *Story Business*, Gavin McMahon doesn't just preach this truth—he proves it. With clarity, humor, and real-world insight, Gavin shows how to turn dry facts into decisions and passive listeners into active believers. If you're leading a team, launching an idea, or trying to move people to action, read this book."

—Kevin Hartman, author of *Digital Marketing Analytics*

"Authentic, insightful, and refreshingly human, this book offers a powerful framework for storytelling that connects people to emotion—not just information. With practical tools and compelling real-world examples, it's a must-read for anyone looking to tell stories that actually resonate."

—Scott McGee, Associate Director of Corporate Communications at Kyndryl, Emmy-winning former journalist and news anchor

"This book earns its keep. It's not just a celebration of storytelling—it's a practical, powerful framework for anyone who's ever needed to convince, clarify, or catalyze. Gavin doesn't just teach you how stories work—he shows you how they work for you. Packed with sharp insight, zero fluff, and just the right dose of wit, *Story Business* is the book I'll be pressing into the hands of leaders, builders, and communicators for years to come."

—Mike Bechtel, Chief Futurist, Deloitte

"A deep dive (and delightful read) on the why, what, and how of storytelling. Readers will come away with the ability to harness the power of story and make change happen—in their work and their world."

—Rob Biesenbach, bestselling author of *Unleash the Power of Storytelling*

"When it comes to the business of storytelling, Gavin McMahon is one of the best in the business. In this engaging and informative work, he walks us through the history of storytelling, makes the case for why storytelling is an essential (if not *the* essential) business skill, and then teaches us how to tell each of the six types of business stories more skillfully. Packed from start to finish with entertaining tales and whimsical illustrations that bring his concepts to life, *Story Business* is a must-read for any business professional who aspires to turn their storytelling skills into a superpower."

—Todd Cherches, CEO of BigBlueGumball, author of *VisuaLeadership*

"In *Story Business*, Gavin McMahon provides practical and powerful tools for identifying and sharing the authentic story behind your organization. This is a valuable resource for any leader looking to bring clarity and cohesion to their business."

—Robert F. Tyson, founding partner of Tyson & Mendes, bestselling author of *Nuclear Verdicts*

"Gavin McMahon's book, *Story Business*, explains and codifies something that good leaders have probably always known: People are motivated by stories. Not fairy tales, not whodunits, but real stories of real people taking real actions and having real results. The author has substantial experience behind him to back up his prescriptions, and he writes clearly and succinctly. In fact, he tells you the story of his recommended stories. It is entertaining, and even better, it is truly helpful."

—Robert Hemphill, former CEO of AES Solar

STORY BUSINESS

Paperback Edition

Creative Director: Saeah Wood
Editorial Director: Amy Reed
Editorial: Amy Reed, Matthew Hoover, Giovanni Olla, Christa Evans
Production Coordinator: Jess Gozur
Design: Ivica Jandrijević
Illustration: Eugene Yoon
Author Photo: Ariane Hunter

Library of Congress Control Number: 2025904022

Hardcover ISBN: 978-1-955671-67-5
Paperback ISBN: 978-1-955671-61-3
E-book ISBN: 978-1-955671-62-0
Audiobook ISBN: 978-1-955671-63-7

OTTERPINE

otterpine.com
Asheville, NC

STORY BUSINESS

WHY STORIES RULE THE WORLD AND HOW THEY CAN REINVENT YOUR BUSINESS

GAVIN McMAHON

OTTERPINE

For my mother, who told me my first stories.

CONTENTS

01 THE WHO, WHAT, WHERE, WHEN, WHY, AND HOW OF STORY

02 THE SIX GENRES OF STORY BUSINESS

07 BRAND STORYTELLING

08 SALES STORYTELLING

PREFACE:
~~THE~~ A GENESIS STORY

Once upon a time, there was...

A man who liked stories. He read a lot. Some stories would keep him reading through the night. He read on planes. He read on trains. He did not read in cars. Turning the page and the wheel simultaneously was a little tricky.

The man was an engineer. He designed and built submarines, sports cars, and steel plants.

Every day...

He read. He liked science fiction stories, mysteries, histories, and thrillers. He didn't really like short stories; he liked long stories. He read fiction and nonfiction; books on business, on strategy, on design, on history.

One day...

He was asked to run a factory in Africa. He'd never done that before. He'd built factories. He'd designed them. But factories had people in them. People had feelings, people had opinions, and people, in his opinion, never stuck to the plan.

He was right.

People didn't stick to the plan. Sometimes it went better; sometimes it went worse. When it went better, it was good. People's ideas, flexibility, willingness to try new things, and hard work meant the factory would make more money than planned.

But when it went wrong, it was bad. The country in Africa was locked in a civil war. Orders ran dry. Union negotiations went badly. The man was locked up in his own factory by the workforce and had to be rescued by the French Foreign Legion.[*]

Because of that...

He left Africa and engineering behind. He went to study at a business school in France. It was dawning on him (slowly) that humans weren't easy to figure out.

How and why companies—and people—did things was a mystery.

Was a company great because of great strategy or great luck? Was it great innovation or great timing? Great technology or great people?

A stint at business school began to unravel the mystery.

Looking back on his time in Africa, he had another slow-dawning revelation: The world wasn't a meritocracy. There were intelligent, hardworking people who never got a shot, who didn't have the privileges he had.

People everywhere had great ideas—but didn't get anywhere if they couldn't get other people to listen, to act. Their work, sadly, didn't speak for itself.

———————————

[*] The detail on this is a whole other story, for a whole other time. Ask me when you meet me.

This is the strange paradox of story and idea. Distinct in theory, but in reality, inseparable. Like avocado and toast, Netflix and chill, phones and doomscrolling. A natural combo—two sides of the same coin.

We speak of ideas and stories separately, yet in practice, they're always intertwined. Like the chicken and the egg, it's impossible to separate one from the other. Stories frame ideas, and ideas give life to the stories we tell.

People, together, build on each other's work. Ideas connect through story.

Playwright George Bernard Shaw said it best: "If you have an apple and I have an apple and we exchange these apples then you and I will still each have one apple. But if you have an idea and I have an idea and we exchange these ideas, then each of us will have two ideas."

The puzzle of why some people—and not others—produce great inventions and great businesses came into focus.

Because of that...

He went to work in the technology industry—the epicenter of the collision of story and idea. At b-school, he'd written a case study on a little company called Netscape. He could spell WWW and was still in his thirties. Prime material for the dot-com boom. He went to America and worked with some like-minded tech nerds at Gartner. He founded the information architecture group, ran requirements engineering, and built an early version of gartner.com.

He was in *management.*

At Gartner, he met his Obi-Wan, and they founded a consulting business together.[*]

The business connected story and idea. It helped others transform their business, lead teams, and shape culture. It grew. The two traveled the world for work and worked with some of the biggest brands on the planet.

The work was challenging. Before a business could move, people had to move. The trick was getting the people to see things differently—to help them execute, help their work life improve, and give them useful tools and practical ways forward.

Clients came in through three different doors: Door #1, the strategy door, Door #2, the leadership door, and Door #3, the capability door.

When they came through Door #1, those clients said, "I have a strategy, but no one's doing it. Can you help?" When clients came in through Door #2, they said, "Er...we just did an employee survey, and we need to work on our leadership and culture. Can you help?" Or they came in through Door #3 and said, "We need to build skills, build a business capability. Can you help?"

The man realized the only way they could help, the only way to move people, was to create and tell stories.

Until finally...

Seventeen years later, he started writing. Not just everyday writing—reports, emails, articles—but a book. A book about stories and business. And this is how it turned out.

---

[*] My partner in business, for over 20 years of my working life, is Rose Fass. She's one of the smartest people I know, smart in a completely different way than me. She's a true entrepreneur, a courageous spirit, and a generous soul. I can't begin to recount what I have learned from her. She will probably hate being referred to as my Obi-Wan, but I hope she secretly loves it.

The end.*

I wish. That's just the story of why I wrote this book. My beginning.

When people say everyone has a book in them, that is probably true. When they tell you about the procrastination, pain, perspiration, and perseverance needed to write a book, that is *most definitely* true.

I hope it was worth it. I hope you like the book.

---

* This storytelling structure, *Once upon a time, there was... Every day... One day...* is from Pixar's 22 Rules of Storytelling, a series of tweets by former Pixar storyboard artist Emma Coates. It's a simple way to organize and structure a story. More on that later.

INTRODUCTION

For over 25 years as a leadership development and organizational transformation firm, fassforward has relied on stories to accomplish our work. That work—driving transformation, shaping culture, translating strategy, building capability—all centers around people. We tell stories to frame how people see the world and move them to action.

I fundamentally believe stories drive business.

Stories create value. The logic is simple: The purpose of a firm is to create value, an idea attributed to management guru Peter Drucker. That value is created—or destroyed—by decisions, large and small, every day.

Take Nvidia, for example. The series of decisions to focus on AI infrastructure propelled its climb to the $1 trillion club, serving as a shining testament to value creation. On the other hand: Boeing. No single decision destroyed value. Instead, a series of choices compromised safety, strained operations, and eroded trust, turning the aviation giant to a shadow of its former self.

Decisions are made by people. And because people are human, those decisions are framed by stories.

The truth is the story we tell ourselves.

What does this mean for you? Simply that *Story Business* is for everyone. Everyone who works in a business, makes a decision, or seeks to influence one.

Stories are big business.

Let's do some back-of-the-napkin math to figure out just how big. (Economists, please look away.)

In 2024, global business revenue hit $140 trillion. The obvious storytellers—media, entertainment, advertising, and PR—account for about $3.4 trillion. But that's the tip of the iceberg. Look deeper: Product development spends $0.4 trillion describing innovations, marketing and sales professionals spend $15.4 trillion persuading customers, and leaders spend $6.3 trillion getting people on board with strategy and culture—all by telling stories. Add it up, and Story Business tops $25.5 trillion.[*]

These numbers tell their own story. Nearly a quarter of the world's GDP is spent on getting people to see and do things differently.

When we think of storytelling as a mechanism that molds decisions, it becomes far more than brand-building or marketing. Story Business applies to various aspects of business, each with special interest groups. Six genres of business storytelling are explored in part II of this book:

> **Value storytelling**—For finance and strategy professionals turning numbers into narrative.

---

[*] This calculation is stitched together from different estimates, research groups and data sources—World Bank Open Data, IBISWorld Industry Market Research, Market Reports World's Entertainment and Media Market Size 2024–2028 report, Deloitte's Global Marketing Trends, and WSJ Market Data. There are rounding errors, and undoubtedly some double counting. I am satisficing to make a point (more about satisficing later).

Product storytelling—For engineers and product managers bringing ideas to market.

Brand storytelling—For marketers and creatives building worlds that captivate audiences.

Sales storytelling—For salespeople and business developers turning prospects into customers.

Leadership storytelling—For managers and executives translating strategy into action.

Culture storytelling—For leaders shaping how organizations think and work.

For each, the theory of storytelling is the same. The practice, different.

How this book is organized

Story Business is divided into two parts, each designed to guide you through the art and application of storytelling.

Part I: The Who, What, Where, When, Why, and How of Story

The history of story and ideas, their role in the human condition, and simple tools to improve your storytelling:

Chapter 1: His·tory of Story

Dives into the spread of stories and ideas—from cave paintings to cuneiform, from the printing press to PowerPoint—showing why storytelling is more crucial than ever in our noisy, digital world.

Chapter 2: The Shoulders of Giants

Unravels the intricate web of stories, ideas, and innovation, proving the victor is not the one who has the best ideas but the one who tells the most compelling stories.

Chapter 3: Synapse and Story

Examines the neuroscience of our narrative networks, challenging us to rethink our understanding of decision-making, and exploring how stories can be used to navigate human perception and motivation.

Chapter 4: The Mathematics of Story

Will teach you how to lift your storytelling, providing practical tools to create memorable stories that connect with audiences on a deep, emotional level.

Part II: The Six Genres of Story Business

Introduces six genres of Story Business: value, product, brand, sales, leadership, and culture.

Chapter 5: Value Storytelling

Value storytelling combines narrative and numbers. From stock valuations to luxury brands, stories are the currency of value creation, underlining the unique relationship between story and business.

Chapter 6: Product Storytelling

Product storytelling is science fiction. It's a story of a future world that is better than today. Go beyond a list of features and benefits, to the rules of *product storytelling* that breathe life into invention.

Chapter 7: Brand Storytelling

Brand storytelling is worldbuilding. Expanding beyond consistency of message, these rules apply to a brand's narrative universe, imbue it with magic and meaning, and turn customers into fans.

Chapter 8: Sales Storytelling

Not just a clever PowerPoint deck, *sales storytelling is personal*— the one-on-one conversations that move people, build relationships, transform skeptics into believers, and turn prospects into customers.

Chapter 9: Leadership Storytelling

Leadership storytelling is shared context. It eclipses command and control. Storytelling amplifies the choices leaders make as they bridge gaps, rally movements, and drive change.

Chapter 10: Culture Storytelling

More than a credo on a wall, *culture storytelling is repeated lore.* Explore how stories shape culture—the invisible machine that creates all future things—and the rules leaders must embrace to craft it.

The Payoff

Read this part last.

A note about style and tone

Grammarly has a field day with my writing.

Sentences are fragments. Paragraphs masquerade as sentences. While I've tried as much as possible to stay near the edges of good grammar, I've opted to write this book the way I speak. This means I try desperately to avoid "corporate pig latin"* and jargon monoxide. Instead, I am going for what a favorite client of ours calls "weekend speak."[1]

I've been heavily influenced by *Why Business People Speak Like Idiots: A Bullfighter's Guide* by Brian Fugere, Chelsea Hardaway, and Jon Warshawsky.[2] It made me a big fan of pithy prose. That means short sentences.

Whenever. I. Can.

---

* This is one of Rose Fass's many vivid phrases I have borrowed. For me, it captures the secret code of corporate jargon, terms of art and acronyms that we all, unconsciously, fall into.

In doing this, I know I am breaking the hearts of high-school English teachers the world over—not in a "matinee idol, pop star" good way, but in a "cringe-inducing, you can't do that, it's against the rules, please-stop" way.

Sorry.

Lastly, I have chosen to write this book in the first person, which feels more straightforward and friendly to me. When I use "I" and "me," I'm talking about my opinion or from my experience and point of view.

When I speak of "we," the "we" I am referring to is either my business partner-in-crime Rose Fass or other frequent collaborators. "We" could refer to my fellow traveler in the storytelling world, Peter Watts. Or it could be some of the frequent thinking partners who are part of fassforward and our extended network of colleagues.

As you will soon see, I have stood on the shoulders of giants.

Where I can, I have footnoted and credited their clever ideas, turns of phrase, or points of view. This book wouldn't exist without them.

The end of the beginning

I can't remember when it happened, just that it did.

One day, sailing along, believing the world is a meritocracy, then another day, suddenly understanding that it wasn't. Despite what self-help books and billionaires might have you believe, success isn't just about working hard or having the best ideas—it's about presenting those ideas in the most compelling way. This realization changed everything for me. It's the heart of this book:

It's not the best idea that wins; it's the best-packaged idea.

If you've ever struggled to persuade a skeptical audience, align a fragmented team, or breathe life into a vision, this book is for you.

This book weaves history, neuroscience, and practical experience to teach storytelling. It's not just a guide, it's a new way to think about stories and decisions. It gives you context and content, and tools and rules, to make you a better storyteller.

By the time you finish this book, I hope you'll see storytelling in a new light—and have the tools to craft narratives that inspire action, direct decisions, and create meaningful change in your business and beyond.

01
THE WHO, WHAT, WHERE, WHEN, WHY, AND HOW OF STORY

I have questions.

Why do some ideas stand out, and others don't?

Why can some people "own the room" and others can't?

Why do some memories echo for years, yet you can't remember where you put the car keys?

The answer to those questions—and others, I suspect—is story.

But when we go to work, when we put on a suit and tie, or when we log in—however we earn our keep—we don't put the words *story* and *business* together. If anyone uses the word *story*, it's usually just those fine folks in marketing. The rest of us don't have time to play with such stuff.

Yet stories, I contend, are fundamental to our decisions. If those decisions are to create value, we should start to figure out how to put our words in a commercially rewarding order—therefore: story.

This leads to more questions:

- Where did stories come from? How did storytelling emerge in society and how has it evolved?

- Why do stories, thinking, and decision-making go together? How do they affect our brain, our biases, and our choices?

- How do ideas spread and gain acceptance? What role do stories play in growth and innovation?

- What makes stories effective? Isn't cold, hard logic better at moving and persuading people?

- What are the fundamentals of story? What should I strive to replicate?

- How can I upgrade my storytelling? What skills can be systematically developed and improved?

Part I will examine each of these questions and more, starting with the history of story.

01 HIS·TORY OF STORY

Those who tell the stories rule society.

—**PLATO**

The invention of storytelling

The first stories were wild.

Those stories were told tens of thousands of years ago, somewhere on the European plain or African savanna.

Someone, the first hero, discovered fire. A second hero, *Somebody*, sharpened a long stick. Somebody didn't name the stick, but they were proud of it and showed it to *Another.* It was Another, the third hero, who used the stick to hunt. Before civilization, humans discovered tools.[1]

Then—the *Storyteller* came along.

The Storyteller told of Someone's discovery. The Storyteller named Somebody's stick and called it a "spear."

The Storyteller thrilled people with tales of Another's hunt.

We don't know the names of the characters the Storyteller spoke of. They come from an era where oral tradition precedes writing. But the fable of the Storyteller contains a permanent truth: Greater than the idea itself is the *spread* of ideas.

Dramatis Personae

Someone
The first hero, who discovered fire

Somebody
The second hero, who sharpened a long stick

Another
The hero and hunter

The Storyteller
Who told the first stories

Someone Else
The inventor who could start fires

As the Storyteller repeated the story of the great hunt, she spread the idea of a magical stick called a spear. More importantly, she laid down the tenets of storytelling.

These tenets have evolved over the years, but the core principles remain the same.

The first tenet the Storyteller discovered: Her stories needed heroes and villains. Characters. In the story of the great hunt, the heroes were Another and his hunters; the villains were the beasts they hunted. As more people joined the hunt, the Storyteller knew her audience was entranced by Another's heroics and wanted to be like him.

The Storyteller cared about order. That was her second tenet. There would always be a beginning, middle, and end to her story. A structure.

The Storyteller kept her stories simple. That was her third tenet. If asked, Another would detail the days-long trek to the hunting ground, but the Storyteller did not. Another was a hunter. He would remark on the shape of rocks, the movement of clouds, and dust on the ground. The Storyteller knew her audience wouldn't be interested, and left that out.

The Storyteller saw the effect of drama. That was her fourth tenet: Make the highs high and the lows low. Some details added drama, while others did not. She kept in the part where Another first picked up the scent. She dwelled on Another's bravery as the beast charged.

The Storyteller loved words. Naming the stick a spear was a particular point of pride. The beast was ferocious and snarling and big and hairy. Rhythm preceded rhyme. Words waxed and waned. She would punctuate her story with staccato sounds, her voice booming then whispering; a rhythm that enraptured her audience. Words, carefully chosen, mattered. They were the little carriers of meaning and emotion. This was her fifth tenet: Words are powerful.

As the crowds gathered—and more people took up the spear—the Storyteller knew that her words inspired. Her audience saw the world through her eyes and thrilled to her voice. This was her final tenet—that stories must move people.

The Storyteller was old now. She had lived through 30 winters, telling tales of the hunt. Her jaw ached from telling stories; her gums bled from chewing the tough hides Another's hunters provided.

Then, a new hero came along.

Someone Else built on Someone's discovery of fire and made it portable. By rubbing small sticks together and adding dry grass, Someone Else could start a fire whenever she wanted. She used the fire to burn the meat. The Storyteller tried the burnt meat and thought it tasted better—she had a new story to tell.

Although her name is lost to history, the Storyteller kick-started civilization.

Of course, none of this is exactly as it happened. But you get the idea.

Storytelling is the engine of human advancement—sharing knowledge, propelling progress, shaping society, and sparking civilization.

Think about that for a moment. Let it settle in.

Without the Storyteller, ideas would never have spread. Without the spread of ideas, we would have no progress. Without progress, we would have no civilization. We would still be hunting and gathering in small clans on the African savanna.

Those who tell the stories rule society.*

In human history, everything that earmarks progress, from the wheel to the automobile, is driven by story. Stories are everywhere. They spread ideas. Any history of invention, from the printing press to the internet, the compass to self-driving cars, religion to democracy, has a story.

Like humankind, those stories have evolved.

From oral tradition to written language

It's a story, Jim, but not as we know it.

If you think you recognize that line, you might be right. *Star Trek*: "It's life, Jim, but not as we know it." Except, not exactly. That dialog never came out of Mr. Spock's mouth. The closest the *Enterprise*'s science officer came was the less snappy: "No life as we know it."[2]

Spock's line, like stories themselves, has mutated. Between the time of the first Storyteller to staples like *Star Trek* to present day, the function of story remains constant—it's the form and format that change.

To understand those changes, consider what happens "if a tree falls in the woods..."

The answer: It depends on the tree. The tree in question: an oak. The *where* and *when*—Nazi-occupied France, September 1940.

The *who*: Marcel Ravidat and three friends, following Marcel's dog, Robot, through the woods.

---

* This is not my line. It's a truism that is difficult to track down. Mostly attributed to Plato, versions of it have been credited to Aristotle, and to a Hopi or Navajo proverb.

The *what*: Suddenly, Robot disappeared. A tree had fallen, its roots pulling up the earth to expose a deep cut in the ground. The boys set about a rescue. Sliding past the tree after the mongrel, Marcel and his friends found themselves in a long tunnel, part of a grand underground cave complex. The boys had stumbled upon the work of the Storyteller's descendants: the Lascaux cave.

On the walls were paintings from prehistory. Imagine a Sistine Chapel of a bygone era, preserved for generations. Art rendered in ochre, red clay, and other minerals. The boys were the first in thousands of years to gaze at a dance of horses, deer, aurochs, ibex, and bison, daubed and engraved by their ancestors under smoky firelight.

Pictures preserved for posterity.

No words. The first Storyteller didn't speak English. At least not as we know it. The human race has been talking and grunting at each other for nearly two million years. Language, tool use, and story developed with each other.[3]

What started as grunts and gestures became words and language. Paintings and pictures symbolized those grunts and gestures—they captured ideas—in the caves of Lascaux and earlier examples in Altamira, Spain, and Sulawesi, Indonesia.[4]

Speech, recorded as pictures. Pictures, turned to writing.

Our first "written" languages were symbols—cuneiform script and Egyptian hieroglyphs. Writing was a natural way to log our stories, our history, a way for us to make meaning, to set down laws, to govern, and to fuel trade.

Kings recorded and published stories

In the history of story, the date is now 640 BCE, or 39,000 years after the Storyteller.

In the largest palace in the largest city of the largest empire of the world sat Ashurbanipal: king, warrior, scholar, librarian—his triumphs on display at his palace in Nineveh. A series of reliefs: sculpted pictures showed the king hunting lions, attended by servants, and relaxing in his gardens. Through the stones ran Assyrian cuneiform, words describing Ashurbanipal's lineage, the extent of his empire, and how he crushed his enemies.[5]

Ashurbanipal's Assyrian reliefs are monumental, over eight feet high, hung on the walls of the imperial palace, designed to impress visitors and glorify the king. The form—words and pictures— would be familiar to a modern audience used to consuming comics, PowerPoint, and memes. But the format—heavy, brightly painted, thin-cut gypsum—would not.

As storytelling has ascended, so has the technology that supports it. What used to be pigment and gypsum are now pixels and pages.

Before his ascent to the throne, Ashurbanipal was his father's spymaster, gathering intelligence from across the empire. He was as proud of his ability to read and write as he was of his ability to fight, depicted holding both stylus and sword in Assyrian reliefs.

So Ashurbanipal commissioned a library.

Two centuries before the great library of Alexandria, Ashurbanipal developed the first systematically collected and cataloged library in the world, made of hundreds of thousands of clay tablets stamped in the small wedges of the cuneiform alphabet.

In the time of Ashurbanipal, the library was a wonder accessible to only a few—most of the world was illiterate. Stories were still told and repeated, not written down.

A blip on the calendar later, in relative terms, the "art" of speaking was codified: rhetoric. By the time of Socrates, Aristotle, and Plato, oral tradition had a system of rules; oratory was a revered skill.

Storytelling was both the human condition and the domain of a privileged few.

The spread of stories

What Ashurbanipal wrote down and the Greeks raised to an art form, the Romans industrialized.

The Roman *Acta Diurna*, literally "daily events," was the *Figaro*, *Tribune*, and *Times* of the Roman Empire. The typical *Acta Diurna* contained news of gladiatorial contests, astrological omens, marriages, births and deaths, public appointments, trials, and executions.[6]

But, like a falling tree in a forest, what use is a story if no one can hear it?

So the Romans developed the postal service, an invention borrowed from other empires: China, Egypt, and Persia all had relay systems of mounted messengers and posthouses. The Romans improved it: The Cursus Publicus used Roman roads, relay stages, and messengers to carry mail day and night.

Stories could now spread across civilization at previously unheard-of speeds. These shared stories didn't just entertain and inform; they bound people and empires together, creating a collective sense of identity and purpose. This shared understanding formed the backbone of cooperation and progress.

By the Middle Ages, artful communication, in the form of pictures and words, was in the hands of the ruling classes. Books were laboriously written and illuminated by religious orders.

Those privileged few in the literate class—the polymaths, the geniuses, and creators like Da Vinci and Galileo—stood out. The rest of us were illiterate, from the wealthiest to the poorest. Literacy wasn't only a rich man's game; it was a specialist's.

~50,000 BCE

The Storyteller emerges, telling tales of Someone's discovery of fire, Somebody's invention of the spear, and Another's great hunt.

~40,000 BCE

Cave paintings appear in places like Lascaux, France, and Altamira, Spain.

~3000 BCE

Development of early writing systems like cuneiform and hieroglyphs.

640 BCE

King Ashurbanipal reigns in Assyria, creating one of the first libraries.

~500-300 BCE

Development of rhetoric and oratory as an art form in Ancient Greece.

~100 BCE-500 CE

In Ancient Rome, the publication of the *Acta Diurna* and the creation of the Cursus Publicus postal system.

~500-1400 CE

During the Middle Ages, illuminated manuscripts were created by religious orders.

1453

Invention of the printing press by Johannes Gutenberg.

1534

Establishment of Cambridge University Press, the first publishing house.

1729

First publication of the *Pennsylvania Gazette*.

1807

Wiley opens its doors.

1821

The Guardian newspaper is founded.

1855

New York & Mississippi Valley Printing Telegraph merge to become Western Union.

1860–1861

The Pony Express operates for about 18 months.

1867

The first stock ticker is introduced.

1874

Bell Patent Association is incorporated (later becomes AT&T).

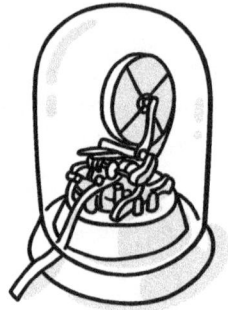

1889

The Wall Street Journal is established.

1945–1960s

Post–World War II era

- The greatest generation returns from service to a postwar boom.
- Influence of military language on business communication.
- Formal business communication methods develop.

1990s–2024

Late 20th/early 21st century

- Rise of digital communication.
- The emergence of new formats: DMs, Slacks, posts, vlogs.
- Generation Z enters the workforce (starting ~2015).
- Data explosion: More information was recorded in the last two years than the previous two million.
- Rise of new professions like data scientists and data visualizers.
- Advent of generative AI, leading to deepfakes and fabulated stories.

But that began to change when we developed tools, which allowed us to apply mass production to writing.

The invention of the printing press in 1453 led to the first publishing house, Cambridge University Press, in 1534. By the 15th century, paper was in widespread use in Europe. Industry joined story. Literacy spread.

The story boom

Ideas and stories spread faster.

Declining costs and wider availability allowed communication and literacy to move from the hands and mouths of specialists to a broader audience. By the 18th century, communication had grown from a cottage industry to a business.

The *Pennsylvania Gazette* first published in 1729, Wiley opened its doors in 1807, the *Guardian* newspaper and *The Wall Street Journal* in 1821 and 1889—all forebears of the media industry today.

Business communicated.

The Pony Express came and went—the Stetson and chaps-wearing version of what the Romans would have recognized as the Cursus Publicus lasted 18 months. Like promising communication ideas that would come later—CD-ROMs, DVRs, and PDAs—it was displaced by newer technologies.

The invention of the telegraph and the telephone, along with the spread of the rail system in Europe and America, meant goods and information traveled faster.

In 1855, the New York & Mississippi Valley Printing Telegraph Company merged to become Western Union. The rail boom quickly followed, connecting metropolitan areas all over the United States. The first stock ticker ticked less than 11 years later.

Alexander Graham Bell's invention of the telephone resulted in the incorporation of the Bell Patent Association in 1874, then turning into AT&T.

While early tools shaped how business communicated, the military shaped the style with which it spoke.

A few years after Robot, Marcel, and the boys discovered the Lascaux caves, the greatest generation returned from service in World War II to a postwar boom that forever changed how we work.

The hierarchical command and control structures in today's large corporations have WWII-vintage military roots. Our language changed, and suddenly we were doing things *ASAP*. We had a *mission* and a *strategy* to go with it. Salespeople had *territories*. *Tiger teams* tackled *snafus* in the *field, headquarters,* or in *war rooms*. Marketing *positioned* products.

In that postwar boom, new tools spread and continued to define how we communicated. Memos were formal, dictated, and typed. Reports were written, white papers authored.

The following generations in business—boomers, X, and elder Ys—prized verbal and written literacy the way Greeks and Romans prized oratory. Advancement and authority depended on a person's ability to write reports and turn a phrase—to be good in a room.

Present day: A revolution is brewing, and stories are everywhere. The form remains steady, but formats abound. Just as emails replaced memos, DMs are replacing emails. Slack, posts, vlogs: Words and pictures mash together.

Surfing a tide of texts, tweets, and TikToks, the first digital natives have entered the workforce. Rules of language have changed and continue changing. Because: internet. Generation Z comes with

Ashurbanipal's Relief

Pictures — Words

Structure

PowerPoint Slides

Pictures — Words

Structure

an affinity for memes and an ability to visually communicate that previous generations left out of their professional personas. And now, AI is changing the rules again.

What the Storyteller did not know and could not predict was this: The stories that came after still followed her tenets. Despite their wildly different forms, there is a common ancestral DNA, a patterned weave of repeating building blocks: *Words*, *Pictures*, and *Structure*. All stories contain these: from Ashurbanipal's reliefs to notices in the *Acta Diurna*, from illustrated manuscripts to the printed tomes that replaced them, from telegraph messages to PowerPoint.

The Words are little carriers of meaning, language that flows with rhythm and hum. Words grab attention. So do Pictures. They stir up experience. The brute-force approach: Show a picture of the king hunting a lion. The subtler one: Use motifs and idioms that paint a picture in the mind's eye. Structure, finally, is the form and format of story. The plot, sequence, and relationship. The scaffolding the story hangs on, whatever the format may be—book, verse, video, sculpted relief, or graphic novel.

The stories have changed, what they are about shifts, the format morphs, but the DNA of story—Words, Pictures, and Structure—remains.

The once and future skill

As media forms explode, so too do the skills to wield them.

Until recently, the ability to draw, capture, or explain ideas visually wasn't in the mainstream of business. Doodling was held as a hobby for the absent-minded. The first computers didn't help; they were word processors. Even the first graphical packages weren't easy on the eyes. But so much communication is visual, from the nonverbal cues in a negotiation to the stock symbol on a dashboard to the billboard of your latest marketing campaign. Mobile technology is accelerating that. Video cameras, the province of well-heeled hobbyists and professionals two decades ago, are in everyone's hands. Virtual reality is moving from game room to boardroom. More people can be moved more quickly by a picture than a book. Speed and virality reign supreme.

Now anyone can be a media creator. Anyone can be a "journalist." Ninety-seven percent of the workforce have smartphones. We are all Googling, Instagramming, X'ing, and Facebooking.[7]

Data is exploding. We've recorded and produced more information in the last two years than the previous two million. We're not just swapping out hard drives and moving to the cloud; we're inventing new words like *exabyte* and *yottabyte* to quantify the amount of information today. As the world swims in and produces more "Big Data," new professions—data scientist, data visualizer—are emerging to make sense of it all.

Next up, generative AI. To quote the famous *New Yorker* cartoon, "On the Internet, nobody knows you're a dog." As generative AI closes in on the Turing test, soon it might be, "On the internet, nobody knows you're a *real* dog."[*]

Generative AI tools will lead to convincing deepfakes, fabulated stories that cross the line from real to fiction and back again. If you remember the promise of the Information Superhighway,[†] and are already reeling from the explosion of information, just wait for the nova that will be (and already is) AI.

---

[*] The Turing test proposed by computer pioneer Alan Turing, is a test to see if a machine can pass as human.

[†] One of the early, now thankfully defunct names for the internet. No joke.

As the tools advance, we are left with a new generation of have-nots. Not the illiterate peasants outside medieval monasteries. Instead, a one-way illiteracy: those who consume stories but cannot create them.

Those who consume stories but cannot create them

We must face a profound truth: A business's value stems from the sum of decisions it makes, large and small. People, coming together, make those decisions—choosing strategies to follow, setting standards for customer service, and adding features to product roadmaps. Individuals make individual choices: how to respond to a particular customer, whether to speak one's mind in a meeting.

Those choices create or destroy value.

These decisions are based on data and experience. Most of all, they stem from the flow of information. Businesses create petabytes of data, yet insight is scarce. Visuals are added to make sense of it all, but, when done poorly, just add to the noise.

Inevitably, that flow of information devolves into parallel, fragmented storytelling formats. One example? PowerPoint and the conversations that go with them. PowerPoint is the lingua franca of business. A patois we all learn to speak.

In business, this is the new illiteracy—speaking to each other in PowerPoint and doing it badly. We misunderstand and are misunderstood. We speak in abstract corporate pig latin rather than concrete, simple English. We dump data, ping, and send emails rather than tell stories.

It is now a personal choice whether to remain a peasant or become a king or queen.

The difference between the PowerPoint of today and the Power-Point of old—Ashurbanipal's reliefs—isn't in form; it's in format. Formats that have the potential to make artful communication the province of everyone, not just royalty.

Some people are trying to fix PowerPoint. Others are trying to fix the people using PowerPoint. So, what do you do if you are semi-literate—an intelligent consumer but not an eloquent creator? What if you must get a message out, but that message is swallowed by all the noise?

First: Make a decision—to be a student of stories. As our ancestors proved, storytelling comes naturally. We must return to our roots, our willingness as children to pick up a pencil or a crayon and draw.

Second: Question your inner critic. Quiet the chorus of "that's not the way it's done" when it comes to how we communicate. Our learned behavior—a "high corporate" dialect of utilizing, empowering, pivoting, and synergy—gets in the way. When you let go of it, you may discover that you have so much more to say.

This takes work—the craft and nuance of Story Business. Part strict law, part ethereal rules of thumb. This is storytelling: the mathematics of the intangible.* The rules that make Words, Pictures, and Structure come together and dance.

---

* Another great phrase I have shamelessly remixed. This one credits to Alexandra McMahon.

YOU KNOW...

...that from cave walls to TikToks, the format of **storytelling evolves,** but its form remains the same. The tenets of the storyteller—heroes, structure, drama, and meaning—are carved in stone.

...that **literacy is a two-way street.** You've got two choices: Stay a consumer, or step up as a creator. The ones who shape stories are the ones who shape their world.

...that stories **help us spread ideas.** Each new idea is a remix that storytelling reforms, mutates, and evolves, turning whispers into movements and sparks into revolutions.

...that **storytelling builds societies.** It has raised armies, molded belief systems, and fueled revolutions. It is how we connect, and sadly, how we divide. It's how we lead, persuade, and disrupt.

...that **Words, Pictures, and Structure** are the DNA of every story, intertwining to create meaning. Own them, and then you won't just tell stories, you'll frame how people feel, think, and act.

...that **storytelling is the once and future skill,** a cheat code that separates forgettable from legendary. Like any craft, it takes effort, creativity, and deliberate practice to master.

You have a choice: Stay a spectator, or step into the arena. Begin the work—take your ideas and package them—wielding storytelling as a tool to frame ideas. Do it well and you inspire action, drive progress, and build lasting connections. With that choice, storytelling becomes the amplifier of your ideas, your decisions, and your leadership.

02 THE SHOULDERS OF GIANTS

Narrative imagining—story—is the
fundamental instrument of thought.

— MARK TURNER

The passing of the creative spark

The Storyteller is not the hero of any story, yet she is a powerful figure. Her power lies in the connection of ideas. Some ideas worth connecting: that story and business come together to sculpt decisions, that story and idea come together to craft invention, that story *is the fundamental instrument of thought*.

We are all receptive to stories.

We learn through story. It's how the creative spark passes from one person to another. In a 1675 letter, physicist Isaac Newton alluded to this movement of ideas. When speaking of his scientific discoveries, he modestly wrote, "If I have seen further it is by standing on the shoulders of giants."

Stories are information conveyors*

Appropriately, describing the spread of ideas with giants and shoulders wasn't a Newton original. The story about the metaphor is a story about how ideas spread.

Twelfth-century philosopher Bernard of Chartres discussed the progress of ideas, noting:

> We see more and farther than our predecessors, not because we have keener vision or greater height, but because we are lifted up and borne aloft on their gigantic stature.[1]

A century earlier, Italian scholar Isaiah di Trani commented on the nature of philosophical thought:

> Who sees farther, a dwarf or a giant? Surely a giant, for his eyes are situated at a higher level than those of a dwarf. But if the dwarf is placed on the shoulders of the giant, who sees farther? Surely the dwarf, for now the eyes of the dwarf are situated at a higher level than those of the giant. So too, we are dwarfs astride the shoulders of giants. We master their wisdom and move beyond it. Due to their wisdom, we grow wise and are able to say all that we say, but not because we are greater than they.[2]

A historical who's-who of scientists, scholars, and philosophers have adopted a version of the giants and shoulders phrase. Some you might recognize: Diego de Estella, Robert

---

* Not my line. I am confident I should credit Peter Watts for this one.

Burton, Blaise Pascal, George Herbert, Samuel Taylor Coleridge, and Friedrich Nietzsche.

Today, the giant's shoulders are everywhere.

Buy a beer with cash in a pub in London, and if you get change, you might spot a two-pound coin engraved with standing on the shoulders of giants. Go to Google Scholar to check some of the citations for this book, and the phrase appears as a quiet nod. Rewatch *The Social Network*, *Jurassic Park*, or old episodes of *The X-Files* and *The Big Bang Theory*, and you'll find direct or oblique references woven in.

We live surrounded by story

Alexander Fleming, a Scotsman, stood on the shoulders of giants—Pasteur, Koch, and Lister—in his discovery of penicillin. A disorganized Fleming, the story goes, noticed mold growing out of a petri dish. That growth inhibited staphylococcus, an infectious bacteria Fleming was working with. The mold was of the Penicillium genus, so he named his discovery "penicillin."

But—no one noticed.[3]

Fleming published his findings, and his peers collectively shrugged. Unable to reproduce his discovery at scale, Fleming abandoned his quest.

Ten years later, in 1937, an Oxford research group led by Howard Florey and Ernst Chain unearthed Fleming's papers. They assembled a team of scientists to work on the "Penicillin Project." Their discoveries paved the way for its commercialization.[4]

By 1941, with clinical trials in hand and a makeshift assembly line in a lab, the pair were ready for production. Chain wanted to patent the process, but Florey refused, insisting their discoveries should serve all mankind.

Wartime urgency meant there were no British facilities available to manufacture the drug, so Florey and his colleague Norman Heatley traveled to the US to find willing manufacturers.

On the basis of one presentation—one story—they convinced Merck, E. R. Squibb & Sons, Charles Pfizer & Co., and Lederle Laboratories to produce the world's first antibiotic.

By D-Day, Allied soldiers carried 2.3 million doses of the "wonder drug."[5]

Mythobiome

More shoulders, and more giants. By the war's end, penicillin had saved millions of lives. Fleming, Florey, and Chain shared a Nobel prize; the drug companies reaped billions.

But imagine if Florey and Chain had not been able to convince, to move people to act. Imagine if they could not tell their story.

Fleming's mold was part of the built biome—the evolutionary biology of our homes, cities, and lives. We live surrounded by such biomes. Phytobiomes enrich soil, zoobiomes produce dairy, and microbiomes aid our digestion. Through biomes, humans have a symbiotic relationship with the world.

So, too, we live in a mythobiome, surrounded by stories making us who we are.

My point: The spread of ideas is part of the human condition. Storytelling is the human condition.

But.

Why could Florey tell the story that Fleming could not?

It's the best-packaged ideas

Ask someone to name the master business storyteller of the modern age, and five out of six people will answer "Steve Jobs."*

Jobs was a superb packager of ideas.

On stage at Macworld in 2007, he told a product story—full of comparison, humor, questions, and emotion. That story introduced the iPhone—an instant status symbol. It put the internet in everyone's pocket, unleashed a zillion selfies, and became an umbilical tether for generations. The device "put a dent in the

---

* That is a completely made-up statistic. I can't say I am proud of it.

universe""* and became a platform for billions of dollars in new products (think tablets, video streaming), businesses (Uber, Grubhub), and industries (podcasting, fintech).

In the days following Jobs's iPhone presentation, Apple's stock surged 16%. Three years later, when he unveiled the iPad, it rose 13%.[6] Steve, the master storyteller, had returned to the company he founded in 1997, a little over a decade after being unceremoniously fired by the board. In his 14-year second run as CEO, Jobs's signature leadership and storytelling bumped Apple's value by 9,000%.[7]

Every time Jobs told a new story, the stock moved.

His not-so-secret recipe: remixing.

Prior to his return to Apple in 1997, Jobs told *Wired*'s Gary Wolf:

> Creativity is just connecting things. When you ask creative people how they did something, they feel a little guilty because they didn't really do it; they just saw something. It seemed obvious to them after a while. That's because they were able to connect experiences they've had and synthesize new things.[8]

Storytellers are shameless remixers and connectors. Steve learned this early. Apple's first successful products, the Apple I and Apple II, were not Jobs originals. They were the brainchild of Steve Wozniak. Wozniak built them; Jobs sold them. Wozniak would speak of video terminals, motherboards, dynamic RAM, and 16-pin chips. Jobs would speak of a computer as a "bicycle for the mind."

---

* Often attributed to Steve Jobs, this is actually a line from the 1999 movie *Pirates of Silicon Valley* with Noah Wyle. But the original source is a 1985 *Playboy* interview with Steve Jobs.

Remixing ideas and weaving them into story were a constant theme. Jobs revealed some of his secrets in a powerful commencement speech at Stanford in 2005, told in three stories. One of these was about connecting dots. He took a calligraphy class before dropping out of college, learning of artistry, fonts and typefaces.

For Jobs, this random course sparked an idea that led to later success:

> None of this had even a hope of any practical application in my life. But ten years later, when we were designing the first Macintosh computer, it all came back to me. And we designed it all into the Mac. It was the first computer with beautiful typography.[9]

Usually, the idea wasn't Jobs's.* In his own words, the iPhone was a combination of three products:

> A Wide-screen iPod with touch controls, a Revolutionary mobile phone, and a Breakthrough internet communications device.[10]

Apple didn't invent the touchscreen or pinch to zoom. That honor goes to two former Disney Imagineers you've never heard of: Danny Hillis and Bran Ferren.[11]

But Apple brought these ideas together and told a story.

Over and over again, it is the combination of remixing ideas and storytelling—not just good product or good marketing—that has led to Apple's success.

Apple may not have invented first, or better, but it owned the story.

---

* This, and storytelling, is a trait he shares with Elon Musk. But that's a subject for a whole other book.

All invention is a remix

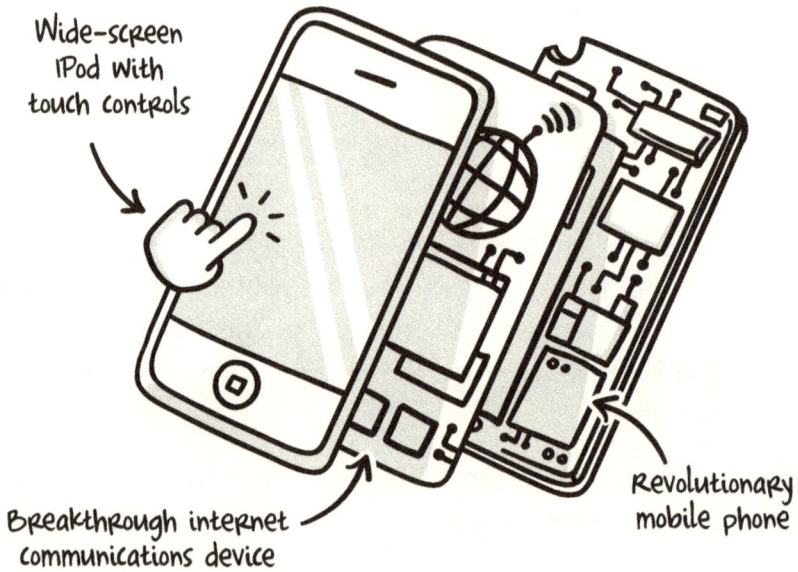

Wide-screen iPod with touch controls

Breakthrough internet communications device

Revolutionary mobile phone

"We stand on the shoulders of giants"

The myth of the lone genius

Story is to idea as chicken is to egg.

As you follow the story of any invention or innovation—Ashurbanipal's library, Newton's laws of physics, Fleming's penicillin, or Apple's iPhone—it's difficult to tease out the founding idea.

There is—literally—no "eureka" moment. Case in point: the epiphany in a bathtub. Archimedes jumps out of his bath shouting "Eureka!" after discovering how to test the king's crown. Great story. But it never happened. Vitruvius wrote it 200 years later. The eureka moment is an excellent, but untrue, origin story of ideas.

We can't help ourselves—idea and story go hand in hand; together, they become truth. Dig deeper, try to separate story from idea, idea from story, and you soon find "There are no truths, just stories. You decide what story you want to tell."*

No invention pops out, fully formed, into the world. Not even for Archimedes. Nothing exists in a vacuum. There is no lone genius. An innovation does not take a market on day one. A movement is not built overnight. They all come from a collision of ideas, big and small, sparking together.

The idea alone is inconsequential. Ideas must connect. And for that, you need story: a carrier of information. A *description* of an idea.

In his excellent book *How to Fly a Horse*, Kevin Ashton dissects the creative process. According to him, ideas come from a series of small steps, not big creative leaps. Those small steps pass from person to person.

Ashton argues against the lone genius archetype:

> The very idea of giving sole credit to any individual is fundamentally flawed. Every creator is surrounded by others in both space and time. There are creators working alongside them, creators working across the hall from them, creators working across the continent from them, and creators long dead or retired who worked before them. Every creator inherits concepts, contexts, tools, methods, data, laws, principles, and models from thousands of other people, dead and alive.[12]

Which brings us back to Newton, giants, and shoulders. Spark. Idea. Story. In all movements, all innovations, and all inventions,

---

* This is translated from the original German, a line spoken by the character Bernd Doppler in *Dark*, which, if you haven't seen it, is one of the best shows on Netflix.

Stories are pathways for ideas

Follow any idea or invention back, and you will quickly find that there is no lone genius. Instead, you will find men and women standing on the shoulders of those who have gone before them—stories of ideas colliding and remixing of disciplines and discoveries that move civilization forward.

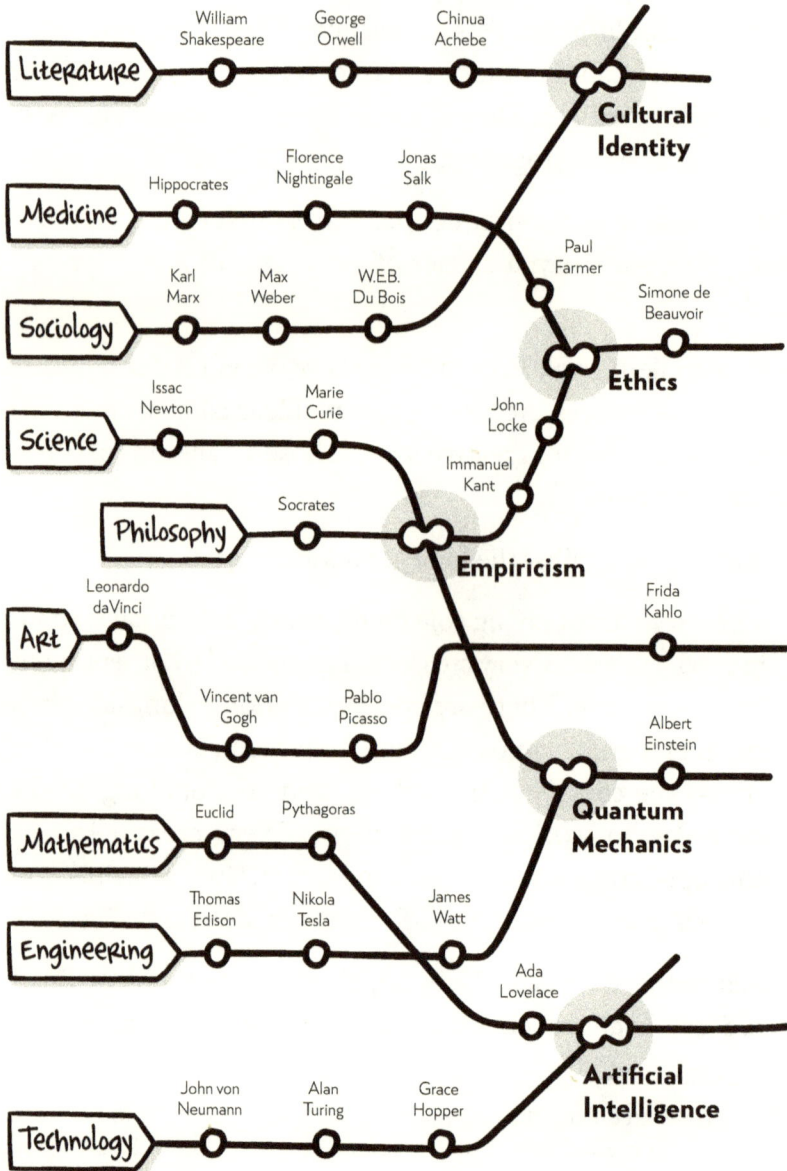

Literature
- William Shakespeare
- George Orwell
- Chinua Achebe

Cultural Identity

Medicine
- Hippocrates
- Florence Nightingale
- Jonas Salk

Sociology
- Karl Marx
- Max Weber
- W.E.B. Du Bois

Paul Farmer

Simone de Beauvoir

Ethics

Science
- Issac Newton
- Marie Curie

John Locke

Immanuel Kant

Philosophy
- Socrates

Empiricism

Art
- Leonardo da Vinci
- Vincent van Gogh
- Pablo Picasso

Frida Kahlo

Albert Einstein

Quantum Mechanics

Mathematics
- Euclid
- Pythagoras

Engineering
- Thomas Edison
- Nikola Tesla
- James Watt

Ada Lovelace

Artificial Intelligence

Technology
- John von Neumann
- Alan Turing
- Grace Hopper

it's difficult to tell which comes first—the description of the idea or the idea itself. One thing is certain: Describing the idea tests it, makes it better, and brings people into the mix. Before people build or buy, they have to believe.

And stories make people believe.

YOU KNOW...

...that **stories spark creation.** They carry ideas forward, shape thinking, and build on what came before—the driving force behind progress, invention, and the spread of human knowledge.

...that **invention is more than ideas.** Storytelling is how creation happens, letting us stand on the shoulders of giants, win attention, gain traction, and inspire action.

...that the world isn't a meritocracy. **An idea alone will not stand.** The best ideas don't always win—the best-packaged, best-told, and best-positioned ideas do. Without a story, even genius is ignored.

...that **stories and ideas are inseparable.** The act of telling a story constructs the idea itself. Each telling sharpens the idea, turning raw potential into something compelling and real.

...that **describing an idea tests it and makes it better.** A well-told story clarifies thinking, refines ideas, invites participation, and turns skeptics into believers.

...that **stories make people believe.** They persuade. They spur action, forge connections, and accelerate progress. They are the foundation of the human condition.

You hold the power to turn ideas into reality. It starts with sharing a story. Frame it, refine it, and share it with conviction. Ideas don't just spread on their own; stories fuel contagion.

By telling your story, you pass a spark that ignites a fire in others' imagination.

03 SYNAPSE AND STORY

The universe is made of stories, not of atoms.

— **MURIEL RUKEYSER**

The universe is made up of stories

As an engineer, I understand that the universe is made up of atoms.

I learned that at school, in chemistry class. Matter is the stuff everything is made of: the water in your glass, the glass itself, the table it stands on. All are made up of matter. For that matter,* so is the building the table is in. So is the planet the building sits on.

And all that matter—water, glass, table, building, planet—is made up of atoms—the stuff of the universe. Because: science. This is the foundation of my inarguable worldview: atoms, matter, science, truth.

But what if I'm wrong?

What if the poet Muriel Rukeyser is right? What if the universe is, in fact, made up of stories? That would explain people. It would explain why every action we take isn't scientific or logical but human and irrational. It would explain why we're supremely predictable in hindsight but not in advance.

It would explain why some ideas flourish and others fade.

---

* I couldn't help it. Puns are very funny.

Our brains run a narrative network

Our minds have a default mode.

A brain idling is much like an engine idling—just ticking over. We haven't pressed go. Psychologists cleverly call this our *default mode network*—a system of connected parts of the brain that lights up when we're awake but unfocused. Activity in the default mode network increases when our mind wanders. This is called *self-referential processing*.

When we pay attention to something, the default mode switches off; our mental apparatus moves from idle and snicks into gear. The imaginatively named *task-positive network* kicks in.[*] We're now focused and consciously engaged in a task.[1]

Noted author of *The Leading Brain*, neuroscientist Friederike Fabritius outlines the default mode network's use for "planning, pondering and daydreaming." According to Fabritius, it's "called the *narrative network* because you take in information through your personal filter and then use its implications to construct your own narrative interpretation of things that have happened and things that you anticipate."[2]

As our minds wander, the narrative network processes the world around us. Input is filtered through a host of *cognitive biases*—features that ease hard thinking and save the brain valuable calories. These biases are mental shortcuts, forged over millennia, bedded in as part of the brain's operating system. You will have heard of some of them before—anchoring bias, availability bias, confirmation bias, the Dunning-Kruger effect.[†] The list goes on.

---

[*] **Task-positive network:** The more studious partner of the default mode (narrative) network. This kicks in when your brain stops noodling around with daydreams and gets focused on solving a problem.

[†] **Anchoring bias:** When we latch onto the first number we hear—which is why car dealers always start negotiations way above sticker price.

These cognitive biases are evolutionary traits. Someone, Another, and the Storyteller all had them and passed them on to future generations. They allowed humans to survive and reproduce. Those routines, whirring in our ancestors' heads, helped them make snap decisions when they needed to and function together as a society. While cognitive biases are mental shortcuts, they are equally blind alleys; as much as they save time, they introduce error.

The Narrative Network

As our minds wander, we are constantly telling ourselves stories—where we are naturally the center of the story.

Availability bias: If you can think of it quickly, you think it happens frequently—which is why everyone's afraid of shark attacks but not falling coconuts.

Confirmation bias: When we eagerly grab onto anything that supports what we already believe—which is why everyone thinks their favorite sports team gets all the bad referee calls.

Dunning-Kruger effect: The less you know about something, the more you think you know about it—which explains about 90% of social media experts.

Input is pre-distorted, filtered through those same biases. When our narrative network confronts that input, it subconsciously seeks to answer the question "What does *this* have to do with me?" The answer comes in the form of a story. One where we are, naturally, the hero. Self-reference writ large: We receive new stimuli, we fit it into *our* world, filtered through our own biases, and fit it to our unique self-view.

Neuroscientists, in seeking to build a theory of the mind, have confirmed Rukeyser's poetry: The universe, at least as we perceive it, is made of stories.

Those stories help us make sense of the world, but equally fool us.

Essayist Nicholas Taleb wrote the book *The Black Swan* to describe how highly improbable events happen. In Taleb's view, these Black Swans—the fall of the Soviet Union, the rise of Google, or 9/11—all have three attributes. They are unexpected, have extreme impact, and, after they happen, require our human nature to concoct an explanation pointing to said event as entirely predictable. "We like stories, we like to summarize, and we like to simplify," Taleb says. This tendency is what he calls the *narrative fallacy*. He goes on:

> The narrative fallacy addresses our limited ability to look at sequences of events without weaving an explanation into them, or, equivalently, forcing a logical link, an *arrow of relationship*, upon them. Explanations bind facts together. They make them all the more easily remembered; they help them *make more sense*.[3]

Humans are sense-making machines. We have an arsenal of cognitive biases that help us sift information quickly and make snap decisions. A narrative network puts us in the middle of the action. The hero of our own story. And we *itch* when the world doesn't make sense. So when we don't understand our part in the world, when we can't see a flow of seeming logic to explain where we are and where we are going, we rely on narrative fallacy to wrap a bow around each beat in a story.

This is *why* story. This is why stories work: Stories exploit the narrative fallacy. Each act feeds our narrative network. Story-telling trips our cognitive biases.

In an article titled "Why Storytelling Is the Ultimate Weapon," American author Jonathan Gotschall elegantly articulates this: "Storytelling is a trick for sneaking a message into the fortified citadel of the human mind."[4]

That's it.

The "it" that describes *why stories work* in 16 words. We hear a story, tuned to slip through our biases, and our narrative network imagines how that story relates to us. We become the hero of the

A story is a trick for sneaking information into the fortified citadel of the human mind.

—Jonathan Gottschall

story. We believe the truth of the story. And if not, we perform an act of narrative fallacy to make the story fit.

All to make a decision.

Why did you do that?

Decision-making: the common thread between business, commerce, and economics.

Codified by Adam Smith in 1776, *The Wealth of Nations* gave us today's foundational business and economic principles—the division of labor (mass production), free markets, and competition as the driver of efficiency and innovation.

Microeconomics, emerging a century later, applies logic to consumer and business decision-making, nibbling at the corners of "Why did you do that?"—looking at how we use resources and set prices. It applies a rational lens to how markets work, how consumers maximize value for their money, and how businesses manage costs.

Where microeconomics pulls on one thread, macroeconomics appreciates the whole tapestry, studying the overall economy and focusing on big trends like GDP, unemployment, and inflation.

Despite their heft, none of them completely answer "Why did you do that?" Because: people. Our irrational decisions are a ghost in the machine. "Why did you do that?" is the existential question of behavioral economics, which remixes mathematics with psychology. The answer, more often than not, involves story.

We make irrational decisions based on whims, habits, and gut feelings. Behavioral economist Dan Ariely argues that we make decisions based on comparisons. In his book *Predictably Irrational*, he starts with "a fundamental observation: Most people don't know what they want unless they see it in context."[5]

Every day, we are nudged to make decisions.

New York City cabbies howled at 2008 regulations forcing them to take credit cards. That howl has turned into a smile. Previously, a rider paying cash would tackle mental arithmetic to tally a tip. In ascending order of difficulty: 1) "Keep the change." 2) Slightly harder, calculating 10%—move the decimal point one to the left. 3) Harder still, 20%—move the decimal point one to the left, then double it. Fifteen percent? Fuhgeddaboudit.

Now we have ubiquitous card readers with tip buttons and choice architecture. Three buttons calculate for us—20%, 25%, and 30%. A combination of inherent laziness and social pressure makes us press the middle button. The result? Average tips for fares moved from 10% to 22%.[6]

Cabbies grin, and Ariely nods knowingly.

Ariely concludes *Predictably Irrational* with a lesson:

> We are pawns in a game whose forces we largely fail to compre-hend. We usually think of ourselves as sitting in the driver's seat, with ultimate control over the decisions we make and the direction our life takes; but, alas, this perception has more to do with our desires—with how we want to view ourselves—than with reality.[7]

Like steak and fine wine, Ariely's observation on comparisons pairs nicely with another theory of behavioral economics, Herbert Simon's Nobel Prize–winning theory of *satisficing*. Simon coined the portmanteau of *satisfying* and *sufficing* in 1956 to describe how humans make decisions. Contrary to prevailing wisdom, Simon argued that we don't "maximize"—make the best possible decision. Nor do we "optimize"—make the best choice for an individual.[8]

We take a shortcut. We satisfice.

Rather than seek the best possible outcome, we operate within what Simon called "bounded rationality." Subconsciously, we are aware of time, our cognitive limitations, and our control over any given situation. Given that, we suffice and satisfy to make a "good enough" decision, one that Ariely would call irrational.

Which bring us back to "The universe is made of stories, not of atoms"—a perfectly poetic description of the field of behavioral economics, of Ariely's irrational comparisons and Simon's satisficing. Rukeyser had another famous quote: "Poetry is, above all, an approach to the truth of feeling." And to find the truth of storytelling, we turn next to Donald Calne and emotion.

Reason, emotion, and decision

Donald Calne is a Canadian neurologist and leading Parkinson's disease researcher. In 1999 he published *Within Reason: Rationality and Human Behavior*.[9] Calne makes a compelling argument: "The essential difference between emotion and reason is that emotion leads to action while reason leads to conclusions." Fit that into your narrative network.

Present a rational argument: Explain why a new basset hound puppy would be too much work, and suddenly your audience becomes a judge and jury. Make an emotional argument: Describe how adorable basset hound puppies are, and you're on the edge of action. Show pictures of that sad, sweet puppy waiting for its forever home, and before you know it, you're in the car driving to pick it up.

Reason leads to judgment. Emotion leads to action. This is the underpinning of behavioral economics: It recognizes that human decisions are influenced by emotion. It is also the missing element in almost all business communication, where everything is posed as a rational argument, devoid of emotion.

Reason leads to judgment
Emotion leads to action

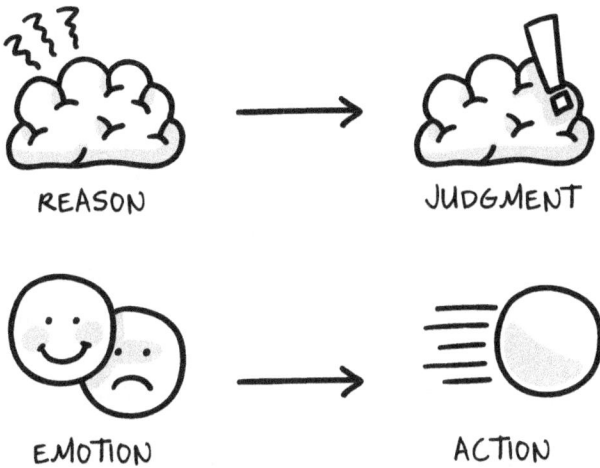

REASON   JUDGMENT

EMOTION   ACTION

Emotion leads us from behavioral economics to neuroeconomics. Out of my depth, I will lean on Jonathan Cohen, Eugene Higgins Professor of Psychology and co-director of the Princeton Neuroscience Institute, to explain:

Neuroeconomics tries to bridge the disciplines of neuroscience, psychology, and economics. I think of economics and psychology as really, in some sense, one discipline...siblings separated at birth. Psychology and economics are complementary disciplines...studying the same phenomena: decision making, value-based judgment, heuristics. One side approaches it from a phenomenological, experiment-driven perspective and the other from an abstract, theoretical perspective.

Cohen goes on to describe how understanding emotions underpins those disciplines:

> Emotions are quick, immediate responses that were developed either through biological or cultural evolution. They are quick and efficient because they are important to survival. If you see a snake ready to strike, you don't want to pause to think, well, is that a toy snake or is that a poisonous snake? You jump— that's the right thing to do—and then think about it later. That emotional fear response to a snake is rational in a world where there are poisonous snakes.[10]

As researchers tease apart a theory of the mind, a new leap looks at how decision-making might happen inside the brain: neurologist Antonio Damasio's somatic marker hypothesis, as put forward in his book *Descartes' Error: Emotion, Reason, and the Human Brain*.[11] Damasio's hypothesis extends into both the behavioral economics of decision-making and Simon's satisficing theory.

Damasio's book begins, appropriately, with a story: the 1848 case of Phineas Gage. The short version: Twenty-five-year-old construction foreman suffers a tragic railroad accident when an explosion shoves a steel spike through his head. Miraculously, he survives. Having lost an eye, he otherwise seems to recover. But friends found him "no longer Gage." With life following fiction, Gage had permanently turned from a Dr. Jekyll to a Mr. Hyde. Previously an upstanding, reliable citizen, he turned into a scurrilous ne'er-do-well who "could not stick to plans, uttered the grossest profanity, and showed little deference to his fellows."[12]

Gage's non-surgical lobotomy removed the part of the brain that dealt with emotions. Without the ability to regulate and control his emotions, he had difficulty making decisions.

Damasio builds on this story with his own clinical research. He postulates that emotions are both a precursor and guide to our decision-making.

Your body remembers. That restaurant where you got food poisoning? Your stomach tightens just thinking about it. First-date jitters? Your palms get sweaty just recalling them. These physical reactions are what Damasio calls "somatic markers"—like little Post-it notes your body uses to flag experiences.

These markers inform our decisions, often before we're even aware of them. When you make a "snap decision," that's your body consulting its collection of sticky notes. Even when you sit down to think things through carefully, these physical memories color your choices.

It turns out "trust your gut" isn't just a saying—it's science. Your grandmother was right all along. Famed psychologist Daniel Kahneman describes this as System 1 thinking—fast, automatic, and, as Damasio explains, rooted in emotion.[13]

Insert emotion here

Imagine you are the CEO of your family. You make a business decision and consult with the CFO. The new strategic direction is a trip to Paris. How do you communicate it?

For Family, Inc., the communication would attempt a clear rationale:

Subject: Project Seine—Enhancing Family Dynamics

Family, Inc. has surpassed quarterly KPIs, demonstrating growth and excellence. We introduce Project Seine to revolutionize our operational paradigm and elevate employee experience.

Project Seine offers solutions to optimize agility, sharpen customer focus, and increase competitiveness. The pilot phase, budgeted for Q3 FY26, aligns with fiscal responsibility.

The objective is to foster synergies, enhance collaboration, and streamline communication. We've allocated a carbon offset for Phase 1 transportation, to be distributed among cooperative families.

Key deliverables include a comprehensive itinerary, logistical support, and post-project impact assessment to measure ROI.

We call upon team members to embrace innovation and rally behind our vision for Project Seine's success. Together, we will redefine excellence in the family dynamics industry.

Sounds insane. Despite the blurred lines between "family" and "business," you just wouldn't, would you? You would speak to your family in the dialect we call "human":

We're going to Paris. The city of lights and romance! We will see the Eiffel Tower by night, with a dinner cruise on the Seine. For the kids—the museums, the Louvre, and the food! OMG.

Realistically, the first passage would have even more jargon, buzzwords, and acronyms. The second, human-speak passage would be even more personal.

This isn't new news. Brian Fugere and company, in the aptly named *Why Business People Speak Like Idiots*, put it like this: "There is a gigantic disconnect between real, authentic conversations and the artificial voice of business executives at every level."[14]

But with a good story, there is no disconnect. Stories reach us. They make us *feel* something. And according to Calne, that feeling makes us do something.

Telling ourselves stories

In our argument so far, we have linked internal monologues—the stories we tell ourselves—to decision. A good example of this is in the stories of what (and how and why) we purchase.

Case in point: I recently bought a new television.

One day, my TV began to fritz. My narrative network sprang into action and confirmed that the hero of my story—myself, naturally—was being affected.

Therefore, I did what most consumers today do and went to the internet. Specifically, Amazon, to look at new TVs—a process fraught with cognitive bias: confirmation bias as I looked at brands I was familiar with, the availability effect of recent glowing reviews, and the herd behavior of social proof.* After a week of watching TV with a shadow, researching TV display technology and pricing on the internet, family discussions about the relative merits of a new TV and how "bad" the shadow was, my wife and I set off to the local Best Buy.

The walls were lined with spectacularly large, spectacularly vivid, spectacularly priced televisions. We made, just as you might, an irrational, satisfied decision fueled by emotion.

Before I finish the story, I'll pause briefly to apologize for the upcoming use of product vernacular. I use it both for veracity and, second, to put you through the painful experience of product-speak over human-speak, an idea I will return to later on.

All set? Let's continue.

First, irrationality and comparison.

---

* **Social proof:** When we trust what others are doing—which is why you're more likely to try a crowded restaurant than an empty one next door.

On the wall are three LG televisions, ranging in size from 83" to 88". Indisputably the best is the *LG SIGNATURE ZX 88-inch Class 8K Smart OLED TV w/AI ThinQ®*. A bargain at only $29,999.99. Not quite as good, but still spectacular, is the *LG C1 83-inch Class 4K Smart OLED TV w/AI ThinQ®*. Clearly it must be inferior, dropping 5" and 4K (the number of pixels, not the number of dollars).

The price? $4,499.99. Perhaps it sounds cheaper if I say "under five thousand dollars." This brings us to the worst of the selection, the *LG NanoCell 90 Series 2020 86-inch Class 4K Smart UHD NanoCell TV w/AI ThinQ®*. The *NanoCell* is thicker and clearly worse in picture quality than its brethren. It's 4K less than 8K —which must be bad. At only $899.99, it's priced as if there is something definitively wrong with it.

Back to Ariely, irrationality, and comparisons.

In this example, the comparison I am making is the wrong one. But it's exactly the one Best Buy likes—to compare the TVs on display on their wall. But shouldn't I be comparing the new TV to our old TV? If I do that, any new TV is thinner, brighter, has 4K more, and has no dark shadow.

Enter Simon's bounded rationality and satisficing.

According to Simon, satisficing depends on my definition of "good enough," the internal trade-off I make between time, mental effort, and control. My internal gauge of when I have enough information to make a decision. For some people, that takes months, for others, moments. For me—in this case—instant gratification beats reasoned resolution.

Next comes a decision.

But first, another story, influenced by those somatic markers we talked about.

This story is the pre- and post-purchase narrative, what we might call the "rationale" behind the decision. Except the rationale isn't rational. It's an edited selection of facts woven into a narrative to justify the decision we have already made. In the case of the obnoxiously large television, that story was as follows:

Our old TV is really old.

We got a lot of mileage out of it—we watch a lot of television. The new one is bigger and better than the old one. I am pretty sure we paid more for the old TV—televisions must have come down in price.

Plus, Best Buy must think I am stupid. No way am I going to pay thirty thousand dollars or even five thousand dollars for a television. I am a smart consumer. OLED, 8K, I see the difference, but I don't need it.

I wasn't born yesterday.

See? A story. A classic example of narrative fallacy, where I rationalized an emotional purchase decision into a logical, predictable, reasonable one. My wife bought it. The television, if not the story.

Hope and Fear in action

The relationship between the rational superbeing we think we are and the emotional, easily led human we actually are is complex. Although we may begin to understand how stories work, and why we need them, wading through a list of cognitive biases and studying a cheat sheet of neuroeconomics is a lot of work.

To shortcut this, for Story Business, we have a *Motive Triangle*.

Like all good triangles, it has three corners—*Hope*, *Fear*, and *Reason*. We move toward Hope. It's the shining city on a hill, the holy grail, the dream we chase. It is our secret wish. Fear, we run away from. It's the shadowy monster under the bed or, in business speak, the burning platform.

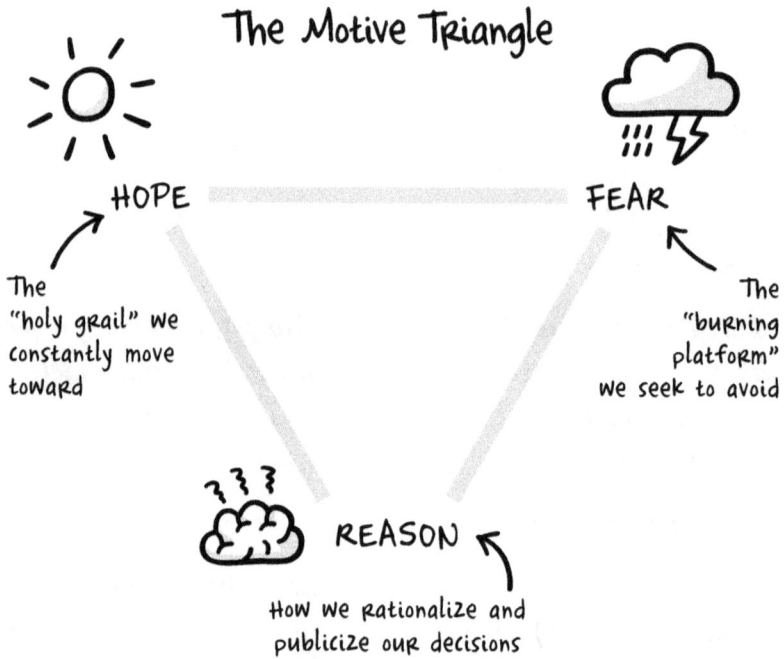

The Motive Triangle

HOPE

The "holy grail" we constantly move toward

FEAR

The "burning platform" we seek to avoid

REASON

How we rationalize and publicize our decisions

But in business, we don't talk about Hope and Fear. We speak of Reason.

Reason is the third corner of the triangle. It's our professional self. It's the rationale that we apply. The ROI. The business case. Reason is what we put on our PowerPoint slides.

Unfortunately, if we apply Reason and ignore Hope and Fear, we will have no action, which is exactly Donald Calne's point. Yet in business, we strip emotion out. It's why *Business People Speak Like Idiots*.

We see Hope and Fear outmaneuver Reason time and again.

For over 50 years,* climate scientists have built their case—researching, compiling data, and publishing tomes brimming with evidence.[15] Each year, reports like *The State of the Global Climate Report*, *The Emissions Gap Report*, and *The Global Carbon Budget* lay out the facts in dense, data-packed detail.

Yet the response to climate change is, ahem, glacial. Why?

Humans instinctively resist overwhelming logic, often due to *psychological distance*—the mental gap between ourselves and something else, be it a place, a person, a fact, or an idea. The further away *it* feels, the harder for us to care, let alone act.

This is why climate change remains an uphill battle for data and logic—why we instinctively discount Reason. It *feels* distant, not today's problem, so we temporally discount it. A report from the World Meteorological Organization has no personal, immediate impact. It doesn't change our daily lives. So, *meh*.

Spatial distance plays its part too. The Maldives sinking under rising seas? Too far away to *feel* real. Stack it all together, and we illogically assign Reason to the back seat.

Or take the anti-vaccination stance. You see your child cry in pain after a shot, maybe spike a mild fever—an immediate, visible reaction. The real threat—polio, measles, or whooping cough—is distant, abstract, invisible. So people latch onto a story that *feels* right, even if it's wrong: "The vaccine caused harm, and Big Pharma is hiding the truth."

What works? Hope and Fear.

Fear: Wildfires tear through *your* state? Climate change. One-hundred-year storms tear down power lines every handful of

---

*The first discovery of global warming happened as far back as 1938, by amateur scientist Guy Callendar, and in 1968, Dr. John Mercer predicted melting ice caps and sea level rise.

years? Climate change. Disaster and flood insurance going through the roof? Climate change. Reports by scientists are abstract, and the Maldives sinking under rising seas is far away, but when the threat is immediate, local, and personal, Fear takes over.

This triangle of Hope and Fear trumping Reason plays out everywhere.

You are more likely to Facebook than floss. Dentists have mountains of data proving the benefits of flossing, yet behavior barely shifts—only about 30% of US adults floss daily.[16]

Facebook, on the other hand, steadily grows. Meta reported 3.29 billion daily active users—roughly the population of China *and* India combined.[17] Some estimates put daily Facebook usage in the US at 67%.[18]

That's twice as many people thumbing through their feeds as flossing.

Daily flossing: probably good for you, takes only minutes—yet most skip it. Meanwhile, two-thirds of us spend significantly more time scrolling and clicking through Facebook. Sure, Facebook offers social connection, instant communication, and easy access to information. But those broad benefits have been narrowly engineered to exploit our emotions and ego—and growing evidence is showing that Facebook, and social media in general, is in fact bad for our health.[19] In other words, the opposite of flossing.

The dark side of Facebook feeds Hope and Fear, not Reason.

Social connection fractures into echo chambers, while information becomes increasingly balkanized, isolating us in bubbles of Hope and Fear. Look around—it's everywhere. Hope and Fear tickling our brains, drowning out reason.

The essence of story.

Consider Tesla. Why did it take over the EV industry when Toyota and Honda had early breakthroughs with hybrids and alternative technologies? Because Tesla didn't just sell a cleaner future; it sold *today's* luxury, *now's* performance, and *immediate* status.

Owning a Tesla isn't about someday saving the planet. It's about driving a car that turns heads and feels cutting-edge today. Tesla collapsed psychological distance, turning an abstract climate challenge into something personal, aspirational, and urgent. It sold the Hope of a cleaner, smarter future and the Fear of being left behind in a technological revolution.*

Of course, this simplifies a complex topic. But the lessons are clear.

First, we are always the hero in our own story. No one sees themselves as the villain. To us, our actions always have a perfectly logical explanation. Second, to return to a theme: We humans rarely make rational, logical decisions; we make emotional ones.

---

*Whatever you think of them, Tesla is a story brand—polarizing, yes, but undeniably a story. Its rise (and near-falls) are textbook examples of how story can drive, derail, and define a brand. Tesla isn't just a case study. It's an object lesson.

YOU KNOW...

...that the **universe is made of stories.** Science tells us the world is made of atoms, yet how we think, decide, and act are guided by the stories we tell ourselves.

...that our **brains are wired for stories.** A built-in "narrative network" filters reality, guides how we process information, helps us make sense of the world, and casts us—inevitably—as the hero of our story.

...that **we make irrational decisions** based on whims, habits, and gut feelings. Cognitive biases evolved to help us adapt and survive are features—not flaws—in our brain's operating system.

...that **emotion, not reason, drives action.** If emotion leads to action, while reason leads to conclusions, then storytelling is the most powerful tool we have to influence decision-making.

...that **Hope and Fear guide our choices.** Strong emotions trigger physical reactions, making stories—parcels of meaning wrapped in emotion—deeply felt, highly persuasive, and impossible to ignore.

...that great businesses **harness Hope and Fear.** Effective storytelling doesn't just explain or inform—it creates urgency, overcomes resistance, and transforms communication into action.

You have a choice: Let Hope and Fear lead you blindly, or harness them with intent. Understand how stories shape decisions, and you'll wield storytelling to clarify ideas, close gaps, and inspire action.

When you choose this path, storytelling becomes more than a narrative—it's your bridge to influence, leadership, and lasting impact.

04 THE MATHEMATICS OF STORY

Storytelling is the mathematics of the intangible.
—ALEXANDRA MCMAHON

The work of story

Newton's mathematics was geometric, exploring motion and fluids. Rukeyser's poetry was expressive and evocative. Both explored the intangible, the connections between the seen and the unseen. Connecting the word *business* to *story* is connecting commerce to emotion. It's not pure entertainment. It's not free. Business stories have to get paid.

Your story has to earn its keep. Tens of thousands of years after the tale of Another's hunt, you have a story to tell. It's a business story. You arrange your words in what you hope is a commercially rewarding order. You dress the story up in a suit and tie (or whatever passes as "professional") and send it on its way, to earn a living.

The story—your story—has to go to work.

This idea of stories as work came up in conversation with Marc Escobosa. Marc is a self-confessed "product guy" turned storyteller, currently a futurist in the office of the CEO at Salesforce. He has over 20 years of experience in product and design roles, with eight years leading a team of creative storytellers. His background spans neuroscience, interaction design, internet technology, and advising startups.

In the course of our conversation, he asked me, "What is a story?" and "What is telling?" Questions well worth answering if you're writing a book on the subject.

My simple definitions, in the context of Story Business:

"What is a story?" A story is a piece of information wrapped in emotion. That information could be a key piece of data, a unique selling point, or an idea. It doesn't matter what the information is. It's information *you* want to sneak into the fortified citadel of your audience's mind. The emotional wrapper is the stealth component that allows the sneaking. Hope and fear bust through biases, turn them into besties, and, with the brain suitably enchanted, allows your information to sink in. Under this definition, the story format could be almost anything: an anecdote, a text, a meme, a PowerPoint.

The answer to Marc's second question is one I have pondered for a long time.

Storytelling hits the sweet spot of frame and action

FRAME the way people see the world

Move people to ACTION

"What is telling?" My answer: (Story)telling occurs in a sweet spot between framing the way people see the world and moving them to action.

Again, the *form* of telling—whether episodically, a viral ad campaign, through a narrative, live and in person, by email thread, with added emojis, or via Slack message—varies, but the "tell" of good telling is that it hits the sweet spot of frame and action.

Underneath both questions lies the deeper dimension Marc was driving at: **"What is the work a story has to do?"** This is the physics of story. Marc's answer:

> Unless you are talking about teaching new words to babies, there's almost never a moment where your audience has no preconceived framing or understanding of the subject.
>
> You're moving people from frame A to frame B.
>
> You don't know where they are precisely, but you know where you want to get them to. You have to read the room and give the audience a chance to show or tell you where they are.
>
> So that work, that storytelling, is like work in physics. In physics, work has a clear definition. It's the transfer of energy that occurs when you apply force to an object. And usually, the object moves in the direction of that force.
>
> That's what I am doing with story. Putting energy in— emotional energy—to move the room from A to B.[1]

Now there is energy—added by story—in the system.

For your story to earn its keep, it has to work—to inspire action, to get people to *do*. But who does it work for? Who or what has to do the work? If storytelling is the mathematics of the intangible, can we begin to crack the code?

The six rules of Story Business

When the Storyteller told her first stories, she did it the hard way. There were no tools at hand. She made her own. Language was barely formed.[2] There were no examples to build from, no giants' shoulders to stand on, no ideas to remix.

Now we have tools, built around the Storyteller's tenets that were first revealed in chapter 1.

My Story...

> **...has heroes and villains.**
>
> (Use characters people can relate to.)
>
> **...has a spine.**
>
> (Build on order and structure: a beginning, middle, and end.)
>
> **...is simple.**
>
> (Include just enough detail and no more. ~~Remove the rest.~~)
>
> **...is evocative and provocative.**
>
> (Fill the story with highs and lows. Propel with drama.)
>
> **...has vivid words and actions.**
>
> (Love words and use them creatively.)
>
> **...frames how you see the world.**
>
> (Move people and inspire action.)

These tenets are your finish line—what Story Business looks like when you're done. We all start in the same place: a blank page, cursor blinking accusingly. The journey from A to B needs the right map and the right equipment.

If those are the six rules of Story Business, here are the tools that will get you there:

1. **Know your audience: Use the *T-Leaf*.**

2. **Apply the *Hero Formula*.**

3. **Use structure: *Hook, Meat, and Payoff*.**

4. **Ask *questions*, don't give answers.**

5. **Begin with a *Hook*.**

6. **Put *Pictures* between your words.**

Know your audience: Use the T-Leaf

Your story will have heroes and villains. What is essential to understand, and what the Storyteller knew well, is that your audience identifies with both.

You must *know your audience*. But how do you know what appeals to them? What are the right questions to ask? What beginning and Hook (more about that later) will capture their attention? What pictures highlight what they want to know?

To understand how this works, we need to stop talking about you.

Researchers find *me* a treasured two-letter word. Psychologists have a name for putting "me" first: the *self-referential effect*. We pay extra attention to information that relates to us, and we remember it. We're all—at least just a little—narcissistic. We love anything that relates to "me": We hear our own ringtone faster, we pick out our own name over the drone of conversation in a crowded room, we treasure mementos that recall an experience or a milestone, we take time to thoughtfully arrange our background on Zoom calls (and we mostly stare at our own face in that little box during the meeting).

This narcissism has been labeled an epidemic, with social media, selfies, and influencers to blame. Professors Jean Twenge and Keith Campbell found that the number of college students scoring high on the Narcissistic Personality Index has risen by 30% since the early 1980s.[3] But maybe it's not. Maybe narcissism is part of the human condition—one that Facebook and others are engineering to the tune of billions and billions of dollars. This is the central hub of the narrative network. Our brain in default mode asking, "What has this got to do with me?"

In Story Business, this is a question you must answer; to answer it, we have a map that I call the T-Leaf.

Applying the T-Leaf gets you off the start line in your storytelling. It may not put you in the shoes of the hero, but it will give you their shoe size. It clarifies your structure. It's as close as it comes to one tool to rule them all.

First, draw a line down a piece of paper, splitting it into two columns. *I* on the left, *They* on the right. Split the two columns up into three rows: *Feel*, *Know*, and *Do*. This is a T-Leaf.

The T-Leaf is your storytelling best friend. It's your guide to creating an experience. It elevates you from a meh presenter to a storyteller who owns their content. This isn't about memorizing lines—it's about knowing your material so well that it flows naturally, infused with your personal anecdotes and insights.

When you walk through a T-Leaf, you're essentially mapping out the emotional and intellectual journey you want your audience to undertake—in the space of two columns. The *I* column represents what you, the storyteller, want to achieve. The *They* column reflects the audience's perspective—what they feel, need to know, and might do.

Begin with *Feel*. On the left, jot down how you want your audience to feel by the end of your story. On the right, consider their

The T-Leaf

I Want...	They Want...
How do I want them to <u>feel?</u>	How do they <u>feel</u> now?

What do I want them to <u>know?</u>	What do they want to <u>know?</u>
1.	1.
2.	2.
3.	3.

What do I want them to <u>do?</u>	What might they be able to <u>do?</u>

current state of mind. Are they skeptical, curious, indifferent? Understanding their emotional starting point creates a gap for you to bridge—between where they are and where you want to take them. It tells you the *tone* you must set.

Next, tackle *Know*. On your side, list the key messages you need to convey. Limit yourself to three.* On their side, identify what they are curious about or what information they seek. This ensures your content is relevant and addresses their interests and concerns. This allows you to *edit* your story down, sticking, at minimum, to what they need to know. It's how you get to simple.

Finally, focus on *Do*. What action do you want your audience to take after hearing your story? Whether it's adopting a new behavior, making a decision, or simply feeling inspired, being clear about this goal helps define your narrative.

To make the T-Leaf come alive, draw on personal experiences. Recall a time when you were an audience member. Think of a presentation that captivated you and one that didn't. For the engaging one, how did you feel going in? What did you learn? What did you feel compelled to do afterward? Contrast this with the boring presentation. You have now highlighted the importance of emotion and clarity in storytelling.

Using the T-Leaf transforms how you approach presentations. It moves you from simply sharing information to creating an experience that resonates with your audience. By aligning what you want to convey with what they need to hear, you ensure your message is heard, felt, and acted upon. So, next time you prepare a story, remember the T-Leaf. It's your tool to map out a narrative that truly connects.

---

*You may ask, why three? This is a rule born from experience. Most people have a tendency to overfill this box. They want their audience to know everything they know and are excited by about their pet project or better mousetrap. That's a mistake. The audience doesn't want to know all that, and they don't care. Limiting yourself to three here is the first step in editing your story—making it simple, concrete, and, most importantly, memorable.

All these tools, but particularly the T-Leaf, mold the elements of story: *Words*, *Structure,* and *Pictures*. They help the story work. They reflect the tenets of the Storyteller. Most importantly, they help the audience do three essential things: *understand*, *engage*, and *remember*—all so we may breach the fortified citadel of the human mind.

Apply the Hero Formula

We need a tool to cut through the narcissism of our audience's narrative network. We have one: the *Hero Formula*, developed by friend and fellow storyteller Peter Watts.

The Hero Formula, applied to business, states:

We bring X to Y to help them deal with Z.

We is us. The storyteller, the presenter.

X is your product or solution; it's the idea.

Y is your audience. The true hero of your story.

Z is their villain—the business issue Y is struggling with.

All stories have a version of this, where We are the mentor or guide. X is the tool, weapon, knowledge, or skill—the magic beans. Y is the hero. And Z is the villain of the piece.

If you recall the tale of the hunt in chapter 1, the guide is the Storyteller. X is the spear. Y is Another, the hunter. Y is also *everyone in the audience* who can relate to Another and wants to take up the spear. Z is the villain, which could be seen as either the hunger of the tribe or Another's struggle with the snarling beast.

This formula repeats over and over again. In *Star Wars*, for example, the guide is Obi-Wan Kenobi. X is the Force. The protagonist, Y, is Luke Skywalker, and his antagonist, Z, is Darth Vader.

All good stories have heroes and villains, even true-to-life ones.

But beware the story that isn't a story. The wolf dressed in sheep's clothing: the list of selling points disguised as "narrative." This is "We bring X"—an incomplete equation of narcissism and promotion. It's perhaps the number one failing of business communication. The trap of We, with a dense, technical explanation of X.

Consider the following example. It sounds like a cut scene from the satirical comedy *Office Space*. It's not. It's from a large, listed company on the New York and London stock exchanges. A company with thousands of employees, and multiple billions of dollars in revenue.

They should know better.

> *How to Improve Workflow with* ▮▮▮▮▮▮▮ */ Enterprise Service Management*
>
> *ESM draws on ITSM principles from other business areas to help you focus on Business Outcomes. Ultimately improving the employee experience, efficiency, and quality.*
>
> *Proven ITSM capabilities and best practices, such as self-service, knowledge management, workflow or task automation, and reporting and analytics capabilities provide outcome-based improvements to other business functions via a single service management platform.*
>
> *To find out more about* ▮▮▮▮▮▮ *, visit the URL below.*

Huh? Do you understand that? Do you know what any of it means?

This is the business equivalent of being cornered at a cocktail party with the world's most conceited bore. While I am not sure what ESM is, or what ITSM describes, I know one thing: This is not a story. It is full of "what" in the form of a consensus-ed compendium of terms and features, likely haggled over by well-intentioned professionals in engineering, product development, and marketing. The script serves as a cautionary, jargon-filled tale. One where the *audience has to do work*, meaning they have to supply the Y and Z themselves to find the product's relevance—a task they will hardly ever sign up for. It's anti-story-telling. The physics is upside down.

It is upside down *because* it is only the first part of the Hero Formula, the "$\underline{We}$ bring $\underline{X}$." To make meaning of it, you have to supply both Hero and villain. Let's add the missing pieces, the $\underline{Y}$ to help them deal with $\underline{Z}$:

> *Banish bureaucracy. Span silos. Let* ███████ */ Enterprise Service Management get rid of the busywork.*

> *No more endless email chains or ticket transfers. No more frustrated employees hitting dead ends. Instead, one platform to track and manage it all: IT support, HR inquiries, Facilities requests.*

> *Imagine a world where your employees can get help with a single click. Where requests are automatically routed to the right team. Where knowledge is at everyone's fingertips. That's the power of* ███████*.*

> *Unleash your productivity with* ███████*, visit the URL below.*

Let's break it down: $\underline{We}$ (the guide) is implicit in both cases. $\underline{X}$ is the product. The magic bean. In the first case, described in arcana and jargon—*ESM*, *ITSM*, and *best practices*. In the improved version, the technical description has been dropped. Instead, it's said more simply, and with context—*one platform to track and manage it all: IT support, HR inquiries, Facilities requests.* In the original, there is no $\underline{Y}$ or $\underline{Z}$. In the revision $\underline{Y}$ (the hero) is clear—employees and the people who serve them: IT, HR, and Facilities. $\underline{Z}$ (the villain) stands out: Bureaucracy. Silos. Email chains. Ticket transfers and dead ends.

Using the Hero Formula transforms your narrative from technical, self-serving, and feature focused to a clear story with heroes and villains. It encourages vivid language and paints an aspirational picture to connect with your audience's emotions.

The revised story is a clear call to action, creates an emotional connection, and has a rugged narrative arc.

The Hero Formula

Storyteller, mentor, or guide → ↓

Magic beans → ↓

Hero → ↓

Villain → ↓

We bring X to Y to help them deal with Z.

The presenter or business

Your product or offering

Your audience

What your audience is struggling with

Use structure: Hook, Meat, and Payoff

Structure is a splendid thing, but mostly it's hidden from us. We don't appreciate its inner workings—holding parts together, creating a connected system. In the architecture of buildings and public spaces, structure is hard at work raising tons of steel and concrete aloft.

Without it, buildings would fall flat. So too would stories. To see the structure of a building, we can look for girders and brickwork or consult blueprints. To find it in stories, we must look beyond scenes, chapters, and acts. In his book *The Seven Basic Plots: Why We Tell Stories*, journalist Christopher Booker exposes this narrative architecture by describing seven universal storytelling patterns. Deep-seated in the human psyche and mirroring the human experience, each plot contains a fundamental story shape. They are:

Overcoming the monster: The hero defeats an evil or powerful adversary that threatens them or their world.

Rags to riches: The protagonist rises from a lowly position to achieve success, wealth, or happiness.

The quest: The hero embarks on a journey to their goal, facing challenges and obstacles along the way.

Voyage and return: The main character travels to a strange world, experiences adventures, and returns transformed.

Comedy: A light-hearted story involving misunderstandings, mistaken identities, and a happy resolution.

Tragedy: The main character faces downfall or destruction, often due to a fatal flaw or mistake.

Rebirth: The protagonist undergoes a transformation or renewal, emerging with a new perspective or identity.

Of these seven plots, four are useful in business storytelling.

Overcoming the monster can showcase how you will tackle a major challenge or competitor; a David vs. Goliath story.

Rags to riches can illustrate your company's growth journey, from humble beginnings to success, like a startup's rise.

The quest depicts your mission to achieve a significant goal; launching a new product or entering a new market.

Rebirth tells stories of rebranding or fundamental transformations within the company.

Even when clearly plotted, using these tropes can be time consuming. A quicker, more universal approach is a simple *Three-Act Structure*: beginning, middle, and end.

Lewis Carrol captured it in *Alice in Wonderland*: "'Begin at the beginning,'" the King said, very gravely, "'and go on till the end, then stop.'"

"Begin," "Go on to the end," and "Stop" aren't very useful instructions for Story Business...

But Hook, Meat, and Payoff are. This is your story's spine.

The Hook is your first act. Its job is to grab attention and give your audience a sense of what's coming. It gets them leaning forward in their seats. They're engaged.

Writers and creative types spend a lot of time thinking about beginnings. From the first line of a book to the opening of a movie, they know it has to rivet the audience right away. My favorite example is *Star Wars*. I vividly remember queuing up to see what promised to be a great science fiction movie. And then the opening line, "A long time ago in a galaxy far, far away."

Hold on. That doesn't make sense. If it's science fiction, then shouldn't it be in the future? I'm leaning forward. Just then, a huge spaceship rumbles overhead. I've never seen anything like it. Then sounds of gunfire as an even bigger spaceship comes into view. With that opening, George Lucas set a Hook worth billions of dollars. Not everyone is going to cash in like that. But anyone who presents, anyone who tells a story needs to Hook their audience. To get them leaning forward. To get them paying attention.

The Meat is your second act. It's a simple way to organize your content; with it, the audience knows where you are—and can follow you. This is your argument, spiced with emotion and broken into digestible chunks—sequenced to help your audience understand.

You had options in delivering your Hook—now you must deliver the argument. You need a clear structure that walks your audience through your points, one by one, with no confusion. Clear beats clever. You don't want people struggling to keep up.

So how do you organize the Meat? It could be as simple as a list—like, "5 ways to build a better team." It could be a timeline—say, a countdown to a product launch. However you organize the Meat, it must be simple and logical and easy to understand. Bite-sized chunks that people can chew on and swallow.

Last is the third act: the Payoff. Here, you invite your audience to participate. This is your call to action. This is what you want them to do differently. What you want them to remember. The Payoff is your ask. It's part conclusion, part summary, and all about turning your story into their story.

No matter how long your presentation is, you have to think about what you want people to take away. How do you want people to think differently? How do you want people to act differently? What do you want them to *do*? This is your ask and your moment to ask it.

A real-world example of Hook, Meat, and Payoff: A Fortune 500 CIO delivers a message to senior executives and leaders throughout the company. His vision: to transform the way technology builds products and services for the business. His problem: Buy-in—a disconnect between what he saw and what others understood.

His **Hook**: A provocative question. He asks the audience how much the company spends on technology (the answer: billions of dollars).

The **Meat**: An argument that leads the audience through chunks of compelling logic.

1. The premise: If you're spending billions, wouldn't you want to spend it effectively and efficiently?

2. The data: How the company spends today.

3. The possibility: How the company can organize (and spend) in the future.

4. The promise: The benefits of this new organizational strategy to individuals in the audience and the company.

And finally, the **Payoff**: An ask to participate. A call to action.

When the presentation was delivered privately to senior executives, the ask was for them to lend their political capital and support to the endeavor. When delivered to a broader audience, the ask was for team members to lean in, get comfortable with change, and understand that this would be a process of iterative improvement.

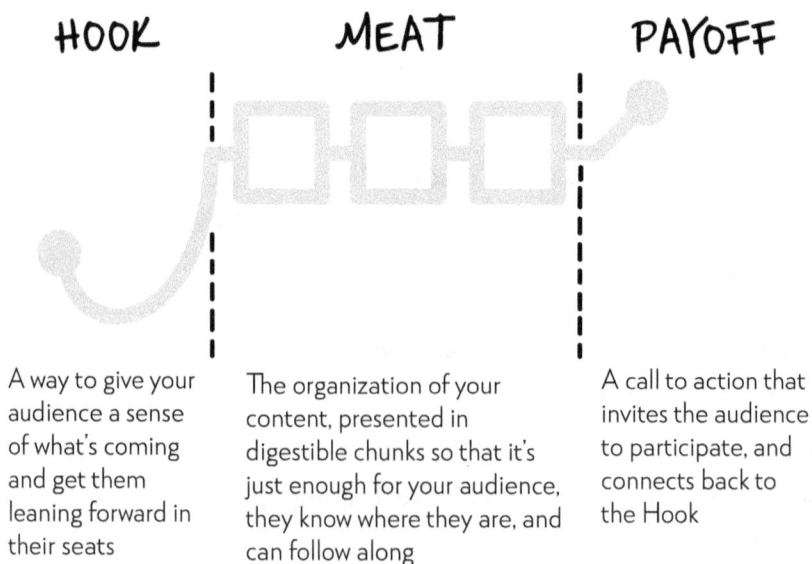

HOOK — A way to give your audience a sense of what's coming and get them leaning forward in their seats

MEAT — The organization of your content, presented in digestible chunks so that it's just enough for your audience, they know where they are, and can follow along

PAYOFF — A call to action that invites the audience to participate, and connects back to the Hook

The power of Hook, Meat, and Payoff is its simplicity and universality. It's easy to apply in almost any business storytelling situation, to almost any message. From an email to a PowerPoint, from an app design to formal address, whether you're pitching a new vision or launching a new product, remember: Hook your audience, chunk your Meat, and push home your Payoff.

Ask questions, don't give answers

Quickly, what's the capital of Brazil?

You think about it. Attention heightens. Distractions fade away. I have hooked you. You are laser-focused on the problem at hand. Rio De Janeiro? No, São Paulo. You're in problem-solving mode, fully alert, critically thinking. The *task-positive network* in your brain has kicked in. Your narrative network—the one that places you at the center of the universe—has quieted down.

By the way, if you thought Rio or São Paulo, you're wrong. Disappointing, I know. But curiously, for learning, very effective. This is the *hypercorrection effect*. Akin to a cognitive bias, it has evolutionary roots, where learning from mistakes gave us a distinct survival advantage. When we're confident in an answer and are proven wrong, we're much more likely to recall the correct answer in the future. Caused by a cocktail of cognitive dissonance, enhanced attention, intense processing, and emotional impact, this hypercorrection increases our ability to learn. By the time you are told the correct answer—Brasília—you're left with a piece of information you're far less likely to forget.[4]

It isn't just your brain's task-positive network that makes questions work. Your ego, curiosity, and the maintenance of your own self-esteem play a powerful role. Somatic markers are laid down from embarrassment and surprise. *Questions work.*

Aristotle learned from Plato. Plato learned from Socrates. The method of teaching: the Socratic method—open-ended questions encouraging deep thinking and dialogue. But what does this have to do with story? And how are questions—not answers—a tool in business storytelling?

The secret lies in negative space. Not what is there, but what is not. Stories are partial creatures. Think of the Storyteller's tenet of simplicity: She leaves details out. You—as the audience—fill them in. In the same vein, questions are directed, forcing your audience to engage in mental exercise or guessing to find the answer. This heightens attention and focus. Ego kicks in (Hope: You want to be right. Fear: You're worried about being wrong). Your audience is engaged and automatically placed at the center of the story.

Storytelling compels your audience to co-create—imagining missing pieces and filling in gaps with their own experiences and knowledge. When questioned, the audience must focus and think critically to provide an answer, heightening their involvement and attention. Storytelling leaves emotional cues for the audience to interpret, which makes the narrative all the more powerful. Subtlety allows for personal connections, as the audience projects their feelings onto the story.

Questions provoke curiosity. Emotional responses arise, along with surprise or satisfaction when the answer is discovered, which enhances learning and memory retention. Asking questions fosters a deeper understanding and encourages critical thinking; your audience explores different perspectives and solutions.

Questions, therefore, are evocative and provocative. Used well, they propel your story forward, introduce twists and turns, and drag the audience with you. Open-ended questions work best, beyond the traditional *what*, *why*, *when*, and *how*. We've found the following to be the most powerful:

Questions to build context and unearth backstory. These are natural Hooks. "Have you ever faced a challenge that seemed insurmountable?" or "How did we arrive at this

Questions can guide your story

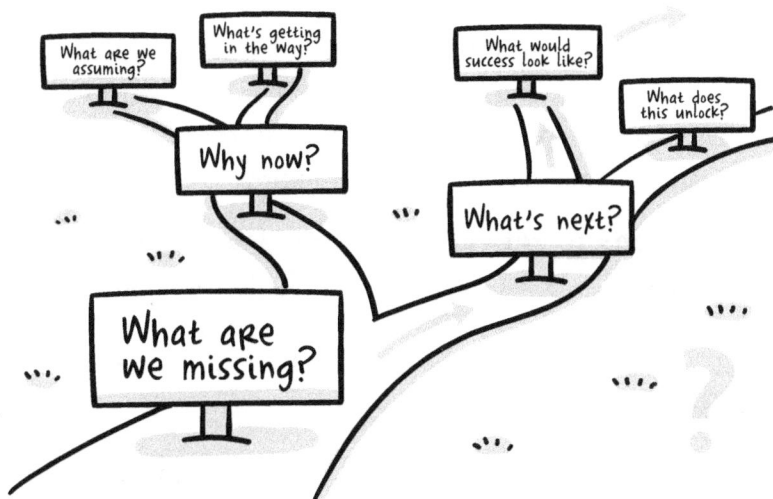

point?" They set the scene, providing necessary background and relatable context.

Questions to introduce key themes and central issues. These are useful pivots between Hook and Meat. "What is the core problem we are trying to solve?" or "How can we address this problem?" They guide the audience through your argument and act as wayposts for the story.

Questions to challenge assumptions and test chains of logic. They force your audience to think critically. "Why do we often choose the safe path over the one that truly excites us?" or "What are we missing?" These questions rail against inviolable beliefs and untouchable standards.

Questions to explore implications and consequences. These encourage systemic and connected thinking. "Implementing this new strategy could significantly increase our market share, but what are the potential risks? How might our competitors react?" You're delving into broader implications and looking for second-order effects.

Questions to foster dialogue and encourage participation. Here you're driving interaction. "What experiences can you share?" or a simple "Say more?" to prompt conversation. You're inviting people to expand their thinking.

Questions to reflect on lessons learned and to plan actions. This is useful in the Payoff. "What lessons have we learned from this story?" or "What actions will you commit to taking based on what you've learned?" The goal: to reflect and encourage practical next steps.

Questions connect. They work like Velcro, attaching story to audience, complementing the narrative network and demanding attention.

Begin with a Hook

"What is my beginning?" isn't a philosophical question, it's a practical one. It's tricky. The beginning is over blisteringly quickly—6.5 seconds—then our minds meander.[*5] In trying to get any message through, we're competing against blinking neural circuits designed to wander. We're competing against noise.

Your Hook has a lot of work to do.

---

[*] The 6.5-second number comes from a client of ours, FCB. Research varies on first impressions, though. From people forming impressions of faces in just 33 milliseconds (A), to judgments on trustworthiness and competence being made within 100 milliseconds (B), to decisions to engage with content happening in 8 seconds (C), to first impressions solidifying in 27 seconds, where smiling and eye contact play a key role (D), and even decisions on romantic compatibility occurring in as little as 3 minutes (E).

So why are most business Hooks boring? Ask yourself if you have done this before: In preparation for the big presentation, you've opened up PowerPoint and started typing. The title slide contains not just the title but, helpfully, your name, the date, and the company you work for. An agenda. The topics you want to cover. Your title and agenda slide then become, inadvertently, your Hook. The worst way to start a presentation.

The exact opposite of George Lucas's stellar *Star Wars* opening.

So how do you start? We analyzed 100 top-rated TED presentations, with reviews such as "Inspiring," "Funny," and "Fascinating." We didn't find any that started with an agenda. But we found six major categories of Hooks, used over and over again.

Anecdote. The most popular Hook is a quick, relevant story. This humanizes you as a speaker and makes you relatable. Even a story of failure can lend credibility and help your message hit home with your audience.

Belief statement or provocative statement. A pithy line capturing your views on the topic. Done well, it entices your audience to join you. It grabs attention by agreeing or disagreeing with their opinions, setting the tone for your presentation.

Video or graphic. Powerful visuals can grab your audience and convey your message instantly. Use them to show rather than tell, making it easier for your audience to understand.

Intriguing structure. Lay out the highs and lows of your story and the path you'll follow. This adds drama and keeps everyone focused. In a business review, it could be "I have a good number, and I'll discuss how we achieved it," and "I have a bad number, and I'll talk about how to fix it."

Humor. Not an easy task, but if you've got a good—relevant—funny story or joke in your arsenal, use it. Warning: It's difficult to pull off. Delivered well, it combines provocation and surprise.

Rhetorical question. Questions always work. If you want your audience to participate, why wouldn't you ask them a question? Isn't it a way to get people engaged from the outset?

Star Wars had a billion-dollar Hook

A long time ago in a galaxy far, far, away...

Put pictures between your words

They say pictures are worth a thousand words. (Ironically, I've rarely seen that concept illustrated—it's always written down.) Humans process pictures incredibly quickly, literally in the blink of an eye.[6] We handle pictures as "conceptual gists," meaning we get the main idea, dealing with context and category, before we get into specific details. In this way, pictures are a unique storytelling tool. Seeing the whole means pictures *are not linear*—there is no beginning, middle, and end.

Pictures, however, are more powerful when they are paired *with* words. This dates back to Ashurbanipal's reliefs with art and cuneiform. Case in point: In 1858, Florence Nightingale returned from the Crimean War and advocated for sanitary reform in military hospitals, making her case with pictures and words—a coxcomb diagram.* Her report *Notes on Matters Affecting the Health, Efficiency, and Hospital Administration of the British Army* used visualized data to show the causes of mortality. Similarly, early users of PowerPoint combined text, charts, and imagery in presentations to communicate business strategy.

Pictures pair powerfully with words

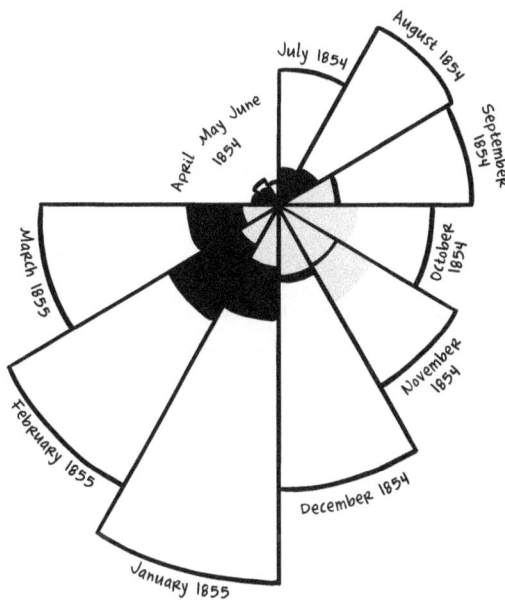

Florence Nightingale's coxcomb diagram powerfully showed mortality rates in the Crimean War

☐ Death from wounds in battle
■ Death from other causes
☐ Death from disease

Based on Florence Nightingale's *Notes on Matters Affecting the Health, Efficiency, and Hospital Administration of the British Army*, 1858.

---

* You've seen these before but probably don't know the name. It's a fancy pie chart, but with elongated wedges like flower petals to show more than just percentages. Florence Nightingale used them to show Victorian generals that their soldiers were dying from filthy hospitals, not enemy fire.

Today, dashboards, memes, technical manuals, instructions, and how-to guides all mix words and pictures. Dual coding theory proposes that we understand and recall information better when our brains process it through two channels—text and visual.[7] Cognitive load theory suggests that a combination of words and pictures reduces our cognitive load; processing in different parts of the brain, in different channels, makes content easier to understand.[8] Educational psychologist Richard Mayer's research on multimedia learning demonstrates that people learn better from words and pictures than from words alone.[9]

There is one catch—the combination of pictures and words must be coherent. For visuals to work—to enhance the story—they must be in sync. Otherwise, the audience feels like they're watching a badly dubbed movie: The words and pictures don't line up, cognitive load increases, and headaches and misunderstandings ensue.

When you use pictures in your story, take a lesson from a trip through the airport. Imagine you're walking past a newsstand. You see a book. From a distance, that's all you see. You know it's a book and think, "Something to read might pass the time on a long flight." As you get closer, you quickly process the picture—the cover. You're still too far away to read the title, but you glean the context and category—a novel, a thriller of some kind—as you walk up to the shelf. Now you can read the title: *The Air Raid Book Club* by Annie Lyons. You're in position to judge this book by its cover. Below the title, the script reads *A Novel.* Your suspicions are confirmed. The picture: a woman in a blue coat, holding a blue umbrella, gazing, as you are, at a bookstore. Her dress and hairstyle hint of the 1930s and '40s. The title font is similar; it looks like the same print as those *Keep Calm and Carry On* WWII motivational posters. You pick up the book and flip it over...

In this imaginary trip through the airport, you have been told a story through words and pictures. Most importantly, you've been on the receiving end of good visual information hierarchy. Step by step, you're exposed to information in a way that prioritizes it for easy understanding and navigation: structure, words, and pictures blended together.

Pictures are powerful tools. Used badly, they overwhelm and distract. Used well, they are percussive beats in your story, allowing you to add layers of meaning, pivot, or add dramatic impact.

"Use pictures well" is similar to "write well"—obviously great advice, but neither one encompasses the thousands of hours required to learn those skills. However, we can begin with an awareness of what types of pictures to use, and what to avoid.

Let's start with what to avoid:

Don't use pictures for minor points. If the information is not central to your main message, don't use a picture. Pictures spotlight content. Reserve them for the good stuff.

Don't add pictures to fill space. Just because you have white space on a slide or page doesn't mean you should fill it. That clutters and detracts from your main message.

Don't use pictures that are out of sync with your message. Choose relevant images. They should support and clarify the point you're making; otherwise, they cause confusion.

Don't use poor or inconsistent images. Images that are low quality or don't match the visual style of your presentation undermine your professionalism and credibility.

Don't use overly complex or busy pictures. Too detailed and too dense is too much. It quickly overwhelms the audience and makes it difficult to quickly grasp the main idea.

Don't use cliché or overused images. Avoid stock photos or common images that your audience has seen many times before; it appears unoriginal and fails to engage.

When you do want to emphasize a point in your story, or reinforce your message, there are useful categories to choose from.

Data visualizations effectively present numerical information. Use *bar charts*, *pie charts*, *line graphs*, *scatter plots*, and *dashboards* to distill complex data into easy-to-understand visuals.

Metaphorical and analogical visuals convey abstract ideas and comparisons. Use *iceberg diagrams* for hidden depth, *tree diagrams* or *funnels* for processes and hierarchies, and *gears* for interconnected systems. Done well, these visuals simplify and clarify complex concepts.

Geographical and spatial visuals are invaluable when location and space matter. Use *maps*, *heat maps*, and *choropleth maps* for geographic trends, and *spatial diagrams* or *floor plans* for physical or conceptual setups. These visuals highlight geographic locations, spatial arrangements, or system structures.

Process and workflow diagrams clarify complex processes. Use *flowcharts* for step-by-step sequences, *process maps* for overviews, *timelines* for chronological sequences, *swimlane diagrams* for roles and responsibilities, and *Gantt* and *PERT* charts for project planning and tracking.

Illustrative and narrative visuals enhance engaging stories and detailed explanations. Use *infographics* for data and narrative, *storyboards* for sequential visuals, *comic strips* for creative storytelling, and *illustrated case studies* or *annotated photos* for in-depth documentation. These visuals make storytelling and explanations more engaging.

Comparative visuals highlight differences and similarities. Use *before and afters*, *side-by-side* bar charts, or *small multiples* for direct comparisons. Photographs or illustrations comparing old and new, size, effect, etc. clarify relationships and distinctions, making it easier to understand and analyze comparative data.

The right pictures at the right time makes your idea more engaging and more memorable, and deepens the power and impact of the story you tell.

YOU KNOW...

...that **everything starts with your audience**. The T-Leaf maps their emotional and intellectual journey—through Feel, Know, Do—helping you craft a story that resonates and moves them.

...that **storytelling needs heroes and villains**— without them, it isn't a story, it's just information. Now you have an equation—the Hero Formula—to create tension and stakes.

...that **stories need structure**. Without a structure, your story won't work. Hook, Meat, and Payoff create a spine that engages, ensures clarity, and compels action.

...that **questions are more powerful than answers**. Asking the right ones captures attention, sparks curiosity, and deepens connection—making your audience lean in.

...that **beginnings matter**. Hooks—crafted with anecdotes, provocative statements, or rhetorical questions—set the stage, grab attention, and pull people into your story.

...that **Words and pictures work together.**
Combined intentionally, they simplify complexity, capture attention, and make your ideas stick—helping your audience understand, engage, and remember.

You stand at a crossroads: to let stories merely entertain, or to make them work for you. It is time to equip yourself with tools to elevate your storytelling.

When used with precision, storytelling transforms from an information dump into a powerful instrument for persuasion.

02
THE SIX GENRES OF STORY BUSINESS

All stories share general truths.

Common elements, if you will. Any movie has plot, characters, conflict, and theme. But different genres have unique elements. Fantasy has mythical creatures, epic quests, and good vs. evil. Horror is often based in the supernatural or psychological. Rom-coms have meet-cutes, love stories, and happy endings.

These stories exist in different genres, appealing to different audiences.

So, too, there are genres of storytelling in Story Business. Communication is commerce. We tell stories to persuade, influence, and make decisions. How and where we do that falls into six genres of business storytelling:

1. **Value storytelling:** the mix of numbers and narrative that propel stock valuation, price, or perceived worth.

2. **Product storytelling:** the science fiction that conceives products and brings ideas to life.

3. **Brand storytelling:** the worldbuilding that draws and attracts a deeply invested audience.

4. **Sales storytelling:** the conversations and stories that engage and convert prospects to customers.

5. **Leadership storytelling:** the shared context that inspires and aligns teams.

6. **Culture storytelling:** the history and lore that shapes collective habits and lays the foundation for the future.

We will examine each in turn, starting with the creation of value through stories.

05 VALUE STORYTELLING

What unites people? Armies? Gold? Flags? Stories. There's nothing in the world more powerful than a good story.
— TYRION LANNISTER, *GAME OF THRONES*

Is it worth it?

Worth, currency, value. These are all concepts we, as irrational beings, strive to rationalize. Worth is a judgment, a sense of scale. We shorthand that to a financial weight, assigning a currency to measure it. Value, then, is the importance, usefulness, or worth of something. Those three words—worth, currency, and value—all looping back on each other.

Economically, we ascribe worth through rational forces: supply and demand. Value is determined by what people are willing to pay, tethered by its scarcity, utility, and perceived benefit.

But psychologically, worth is emotional and irrational. It lives in a nest of biases and satisfices, shaped by how something makes us feel and how it fills our inner needs: security, status, or belonging.

Behavioral economics remixes these two definitions, illuminating a more holistic view: that market forces—numbers—are deeply entwined with human whims—narrative.

That, in essence, is *value storytelling*.

And it's worth getting better at it.

Put away childish things

"I am going to study video games at university."

Words, I am sure, to worry any parent. The inescapable conclusion: My son would spend the next few years developing gamer wrist, hours mashing buttons and mastering levels, pushing pixels, and collecting high scores.

I had a story running in my head, rooted in my own adventures with *Space Invaders*, *Defender*, and *Civilization*. The story: Video games are a nice hobby for a small group of people. A real niche. Gamification for learning or product development. Yes. But games? No.

When it came time for my child to choose a college direction, I had stories and comparisons fighting for attention. On the one hand, I was determined to let him find his own path. On the other, my experience told me that computer science, cybersecurity, perhaps even UX design would be safer and more profitable.

Was I happy when he told me he wanted to study video game design? I haven't read the Bible cover to cover, but the verse about putting away childish things came to mind. I was torn.

Then, he hit me with a story in the form of a question. "Did you know the video game industry is worth more than the movie and music industries combined?"

I did not.

Game industry revenue reached $455 billion in 2024, twice the size of the movie industry, and nearly eight times that of music.[1]

Video games are eating the world. ABBA is de-aging and virtualizing the concert experience with ABBAtars powered by video game tech. Fandoms around *Fallout* and *The Last of Us* began in games before becoming TV and film hits.

By 2028, the global video game market will be worth $691 billion.

My son's question—a story about value—stopped me in my tracks. That story, about a booming industry, broke through the biases in my head and cracked my own *narrative fallacy*. So he went on to study video games (and play them) at the University of York. He's doing very well, thank you.

I feel okay, my mind settled with a *value story*.

Buffett's bet

Value stories lift markets.

"Good morning. Thanks for dialing in today to discuss our second-quarter results."

Wall Street hears a variation of those words every day. It's the opening step in a familiar ritual between traders, analysts, CEOs, and CFOs. After the usual "stock" reminders of forward-looking statements, safe harbors, and risk factors, the CEO steps up with a story.

And it's that story, backed by financial evidence of revenues and expenses, that moves a stock. Analysts are human, after all. Despite their training and models, they make the same emotional decisions as the rest of us. They tie numbers to narrative—and from that, decide: buy, sell, or hold.

With brains full of biases, they fall for stories, just like we do.

Legendary investor Warren Buffett proved this point. He made a million-dollar bet. The Oracle of Omaha's premise: Active investment management, run by seasoned professionals, would underperform the quiet returns of rank amateurs who simply sat still. The bet would be a 10-year horse race between human judgment and a passive index fund.[2]

Hedge fund manager Ted Seides took the wager.

Buffett's horse: Vanguard's S&P 500 Admiral fund (VFIAX). Seides's: Five anonymized funds-of-funds, each with investment experts actively buying and selling.

A race between human decisions and no decision at all.

The result? After a slow start, Buffett's index fund pulled away, garnering a 126% increase over 10 years. The five funds-of-funds gained 36%.

More proof, if you needed it, that even the most experienced, highly paid professionals fall for stories.

Stories inform their beliefs. Beliefs drive their actions.

Bulbs and bubbles

Beliefs, spun into stories, can create bubbles.

In 17th-century Holland, two ideas and a virus collided to form a story. That story sparked speculative fever, and eventually, a bubble burst.

Carolus Clusius, a Flemish botanist, introduced the first tulips to the Netherlands, brought from the Ottoman empire. His cultivation of this new and exotic flower in Leiden's botanical garden captured Dutch imagination.

Gardeners and tulip enthusiasts bred new varieties, some infected with a naturally occurring agent: tulip breaking virus (TBV), which disrupted the pigmentation in the flower's petals. These "broken" tulips displayed beautiful and unpredictable patterns, producing visually striking, streaked flowers. The infection, spread by aphids and other insects, also weakened the plants, making them less robust and harder to grow.

The Dutch, a nation of traders with a well-developed banking system, also developed financial instruments. To mitigate risk and maximize profits in their commercial activities, they used futures contracts to lock in prices for goods delivered at a later date.

Tulip mania captivated the nation. The rarity and beauty of the flowers meant only the affluent could afford to buy and display them. They quickly became a symbol of wealth and social status. The uniqueness of broken tulips added to their allure. Bulbs and bulb futures traded at auction and changed hands in taverns and inns. Like art or rare coins, the most prized tulips were chased by collectors and speculators alike, spiking their value.

In the winter of 1637, tulip mania was in full bloom.

Bulbs sold for extraordinarily high prices, one worth more than a house. The frenzy intensified. Speculation reached fever pitch. FOMO. Story and belief spread as high returns drew more people into the market, creating a self-reinforcing cycle of rising tulip prices.

Then abruptly, at a routine auction in Haarlem in February 1637, bulbs went unsold. Why? Perhaps hardworking Haarlemmers realized the absurdity of paying a fortune for flowers. Perhaps credit ran thin. Perhaps an outbreak of plague kept punters away. This new story led to sell-off. Alarm. Previous irrational exuberance turned into panic. Speculators rushed to sell, driving down prices. The bandwagon effect stiffened into a rush for cash.[3]

The story of bulb to bubble is a cautionary tale. Markets move—both positively and negatively—because humans fall for stories. And the best stories are ones supported by evidence, not irrationalism or outright lies.

What follows is a sad example of such. A tech unicorn and pseudo-story stock, powered by a heady mix of storytelling, optimism, and fraud.

Belief drives bubbles

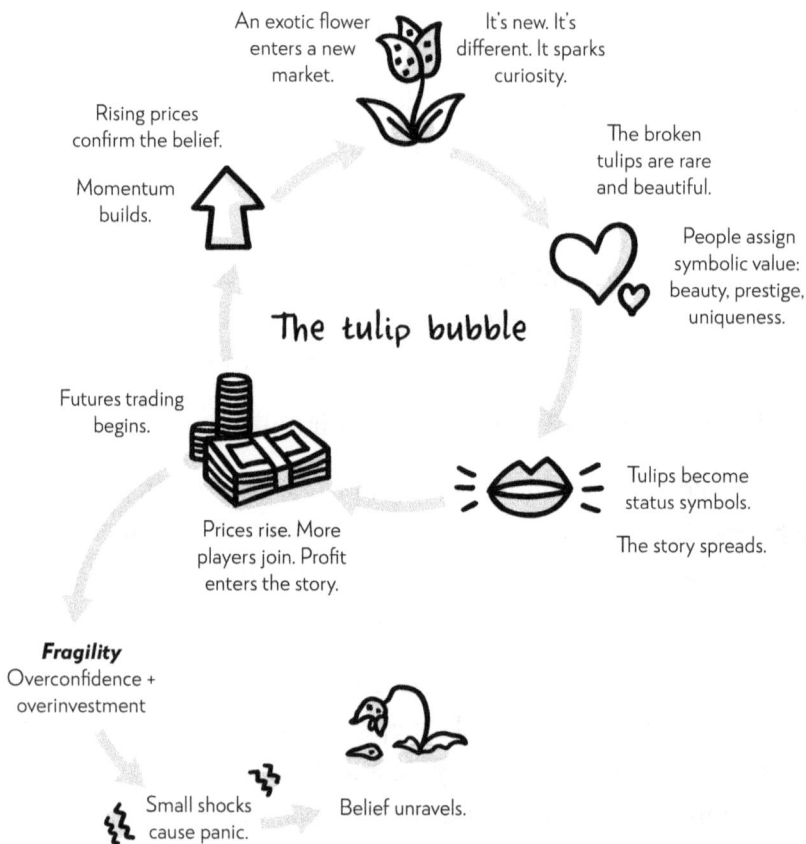

An exotic flower enters a new market.

It's new. It's different. It sparks curiosity.

Rising prices confirm the belief.

Momentum builds.

The broken tulips are rare and beautiful.

People assign symbolic value: beauty, prestige, uniqueness.

The tulip bubble

Futures trading begins.

Tulips become status symbols.

The story spreads.

Prices rise. More players join. Profit enters the story.

Fragility
Overconfidence + overinvestment

Small shocks cause panic.

Belief unravels.

Bubbles and blood

Theranos splashed into the press on the cover of *Fortune*: Elizabeth Holmes, biotech CEO, dressed in a Jobsian black turtleneck with a Mona Lisa smile.[4]

The article spun a classic business fairy tale: the rags to riches startup story. Here was a Stanford dropout with an Archimedean "eureka" moment: pairing blood sampling with wireless telemetry.

The story echoes tenets laid down by the Storyteller. The play on words: Theranos—a portmanteau of "therapy" and "diagnosis." The small details: Holmes laughing as she describes using the technology to observe the difference in her blood makeup after she has eaten broccoli versus a cheeseburger.

Villains add drama. Prescient naysayers say the technology is snake oil and mirrors. They cast doubts: "I don't know what they're measuring, how they're measuring it, and why they think they're measuring it."[5]

The biggest villain of all, the ultimate bogeyman: death.

Here, Holmes taps into those trusty storytelling devices of Hope and Fear, leaning on human optimism: "We're building an early-detection system... I genuinely don't believe anything else matters more than when you love someone so much and you have to say goodbye too soon."

The 2014 *Fortune* feature was followed by a journalistic stampede. Holmes was named one of *Time*'s "100 Most Influential People." Accolades—and money—poured in. Theranos's peak valuation reached $9 billion, crowning Holmes, in a society that cares for these things, the world's youngest self-made billionaire.

The pride before the fall.

The bubble bursts. John Ioannidis, a professor at Stanford University's medical school, singled out Theranos in an article published in the *Journal of the American Medical Association*, questioning the integrity of Theranos' claims, calling out "possibly brilliant ideas, aggressive corporate announcements, and mass media hype."[6]

The first domino fell.

The Wall Street Journal dug further and revealed the emptiness of Holmes's promise. Regulators stepped in.

Holmes countered, but no amount of storytelling could hide the truth: A narrative without numbers is a house of cards. Elizabeth Holmes is currently serving 11 years and 3 months in federal prison for defrauding the investors in Theranos, Inc.[7]

The six rules of value storytelling

In *value storytelling*, narrative validates numbers.

The CFO's domain of financials must now embrace a new frontier: storytelling. Together, they amplify value.

Buffett proved that stories influence perceptions and steer decisions. His million-dollar bet showed the financial world relies heavily on narratives and that those narratives direct investment. Therefore CEOs craft compelling stories, backed with numbers, to sway the opinion of analysts and traders.[*]

Tulip bulbs were the first bubble, boosted by belief. Allure for the exotic, the promise of hefty returns, and a desire to be part of the "in" crowd all tapped into human irrationality and fueled wild speculation.

Theranos' promised future of not having to say goodbye to loved ones too soon was infinitely appealing, but ultimately, Holmes proved herself to be an emperor with no clothes.

These three cautionary tales point to a reality: We believe in stories, and stories magnify value. To avoid the hubris of missing a million-dollar bet, bubbles, and outright fraud, value storytelling should follow six rules:

---

[*] You might wonder, "Doesn't the Buffett story disprove storytelling?" My answer: Yes, if you are a hyper-rational investor like Warren Buffett. But let's face it, there aren't many Warren Buffetts around. The market is made up of those who rely on Story.

1. **Hint at higher purpose.**

2. **Maintain authenticity and truth.**

3. **Support story with evidence.**

4. **Adapt and evolve over time.**

5. **Showcase wins and face challenges.**

6. **Tap into bigger narratives.**

These aren't just guidelines, they're the foundations of effective value storytelling. Each principle builds trust and creates connection. Higher purpose anchors to deeper emotional needs. Authenticity and truth build credibility and long-term trust. Evidence and fact add to this. Ensuring your story grows as the world changes creates value for the long term. Showcasing success punctuates the value story, and facing into difficulties makes it real and relatable. The larger themes resonate with broader audiences.

When story and numbers meet

Blood-red sports cars: Rosso Corsa. The Testarossa. The Ferrari LaFerrari. The Ferrari Monza. Somehow, everything sounds better in Italian.

What doesn't sound as good—even in Italian: *Ferrari, via libera dei soci Fiat al 'divorzio.'* [8] Translation: *Ferrari, Fiat shareholders approve the 'divorce.'*

In 2016, saddled with debt, Fiat Chrysler sold its stake in Ferrari. A financial play set the stage for a new act.

Marked by its sigil of a black prancing horse on a yellow field, Ferrari has become one of the world's most valuable brands—powered by story.

IPO Ferrari, trionfo a Wall Street: raccolti quasi 1 miliardo di dollari. Translation: Ferrari IPO, triumph on Wall Street: nearly $1 billion raised.

The prancing horse's mission: *to win on both road and track.* Its identity—luxury, speed, and exclusivity—stems from decades of dominance in Formula 1, pushing engineering boundaries, and creating handcrafted masterpieces. Limited production enhances Ferrari's mystique. Each road car is a work of art. Through all of this, Ferrari *hints at its higher purpose*: not just selling cars but selling passion and uncompromising performance.

Ferrari follows the Hero Formula:

> <u>We</u> (*Ferrari*) bring <u>X</u> (*passion, exclusivity,* and *racing technology*) to <u>Y</u> (*a limited few—and those who aspire to be one of them*) to help them deal with <u>Z</u> (*mediocrity*).

Every car, every race, and every note of its engines *maintain its authenticity and truth*—Ferrari has never pretended to be for everyone, and that's exactly what drives its value.

But the legend can't live in the past. For every win, *it faces challenges*—regulatory shifts, EV competitors, and changing markets test its dominance.

Ferrari's ability to rise above the fray is what makes it a story stock—a valuation driven more by narrative than traditional financial metrics. A story that captures investors' imaginations.

Aswath Damodaran, New York University professor and author of *Narrative and Numbers*, breaks valuations down like this:

> You have a story, you tell the same story, you act consistently on that story, and you deliver on that story. Very few companies have done that.[9]

Those that do combine story and data, according to Damodaran: Ferrari, Tesla, Amazon, Nvidia. Each rides a potent mix of compelling narrative, high expectations, market sentiment, and an optimistic view of potential. They *tap into bigger narratives*. For Tesla, EVs. For Amazon, e-commerce. For Nvidia, AI. For Ferrari, status.

Crunching the numbers, Damodaran doesn't love the auto business. He calls it "a bad business, where companies collectively earn less than their cost of capital and most companies destroy value." The industry is "cyclical" and "low-growth," with "poor profit margins" and "high-reinvestment needs."[10]

But the Ferrari story is far more glamorous than the numbers:

> I see Ferrari as a maker of luxury automobiles that can charge astronomically high prices for its cars and earn huge profit margins because it keeps its cars scarce and available only to an exclusive club of the very wealthy.

Story *and* numbers, together, create value. Damodaran continues:

> I tie the low revenue growth (4 percent) to Ferrari's need to maintain its exclusivity, with that same exclusivity allowing it to generate its huge profit margins and maintain stable earnings over time, since those who buy Ferraris are so wealthy they are unaffected by the ebbs and flows of the economy that affect other automakers.[11]

The fact that Ferrari sells exclusively to the fabulously wealthy negates the industry's cyclical nature. Rich people spend money regardless of boom or bust. Scarcity brings premium profit margins and stable earnings. This isn't emotion—it's math. IPO figures, earnings, and market performance *support the story with evidence.*

The Ferrari narrative is painted in Rosso Corsa, the numbers written in black—proof that, in value storytelling, story and numbers must meet.

Hint at higher purpose

The father of modern management, Peter Drucker, wrote, "If we want to know what a business is we have to start with its *purpose.* And its purpose must lie outside of the business itself. In fact, it must lie in society."[12]

A "purpose-driven business" is accepted as standard today. That purpose has meaning, not just inside the organization, but outside. It taps into our inherent desire to find connection and belonging, to be part of something bigger than ourselves.

Hint at higher purpose

Think of a purpose-driven business, and my bet is Patagonia pops into your head.

The apparel brand is a classic example. Its mission statement, "We're in business to save our home planet," *hints at a higher purpose*, focusing on environmental conservation. The narrative attracts environmentally conscious consumers and reinforces Patagonia's commitment to sustainability.

Your value story may tap into different motivations. It could be broader societal impact, highlighting how your product or service contributes to a greater good—sustainability, social justice, or community well-being. Think Ben & Jerry's, TOMS, or Bombas.

Purpose can also be personal, with the aspirational ideals of the value story connecting to individual growth, achievement, or excellence. Nike's long-running "Just Do It" campaign is not just about selling shoes; it's about inspiring people to achieve their athletic and personal best.

Like all stories, value storytelling taps into a well of emotion—love, hope, pride, duty—so the audience feels like part of the story, and part of something real. When Dove redefined "Real Beauty," it singled out a villain: traditional beauty standards that disempowered women. The ad campaign gave *all* women a reason to feel confident embracing their natural beauty.

Ferrari's value story is a story of passion. There's a reason avid Ferrari fans are called Tifosi, which translates to "fanatic." They embrace both heritage and future, feeling a collective pride in the racing successes of the marque, and nervous excitement with every turn of a wheel. Fandom is community. Others are inspired by the cutting-edge technology, the unparalleled performance, the appeal of excellence, and the forward thinking.

For those lucky few Ferrari owners, there is an appeal to ego and self. Owning a Ferrari is a symbol of status and achievement, creating a sense of belonging to an elite community of like-minded individuals who share a passion for luxury and performance.

Maintain authenticity and truth

Credibility is fleeting when stories are not grounded in fact. Warren Buffett, famously wary of story stocks, believes intrinsic value and solid fundamentals win out. He has called out this "casino-like behavior," where value has no connection to story. But there is a difference between a meme stock—think GameStop—accelerated by a game of "follow-the-crowd" and speculation—and a true story stock like Ferrari, where narrative *explains* value in a way numbers alone cannot.

Famously, missing authenticity and truth leads to calamity and a speculative bubble collapsing on itself—think Enron, WorldCom, Theranos, WeWork, and FTX, each a house of cards—built on accounting schemes, inflated revenues, deceptive statements, dubious positioning, and outright fraud to sustain false narratives.

Maintain authenticity and truth

Truth fosters trust and trust moves markets, but uncertainty triggers panic. Authenticity—even if it reveals vulnerability or imperfection—matters.

Take Johnson & Johnson's transparent handling of the Tylenol crisis. In 1982, J&J faced a catastrophe when several people died from cyanide-laced Tylenol capsules. The company took immediate action, halting Tylenol production and launching a nationwide recall of 31 million bottles. They openly communicated risks and their response measures, demonstrating an authentic commitment to consumer safety. Their dedication to safety over profit reassured consumers, allowing Tylenol to regain its market leading position within a year.

In contrast, BP's obfuscation during the Deepwater Horizon spill of 2010 led to public distrust and market decline. An oil rig exploded, triggering a catastrophe that led to the largest marine oil spill in history, with significant environmental damage and the loss of 11 lives. BP initially downplayed the severity of the mess and deflected responsibility. Their CEO, Tony Hayward—his narrative network overriding all impulse control—remarked, "I'd like my life back."[13] In one tone-deaf moment, the company's stock plummeted and brand loyalty significantly diminished.[14]

In reputation management, crisis communication expert Howard Waterman advises, "Focus on Job #1. Change the current negative narrative to emphasize what is being done *now* to fix problems, and a timeline for things to return to normal."[15]

When values align—and are authentically communicated—there's a magnifying effect for shareholders and stakeholders.

Ferrari's handling of a cybersecurity breach is a prime example of maintaining authenticity and truth, even when that reveals vulnerability. In October 2020, the Italian supercar manufacturer experienced a ransomware attack. Ferrari took immediate action. In a letter from CEO Benedetto Vigna, the company directly addressed its clients—detailing the extent of the breach, the steps taken to reduce its impact—and the measures taken to prevent future incidents.[16]

This transparency demonstrated Ferrari's commitment to protecting its customers' data and maintaining their trust. Openly addressing the issue and enhancing their security posture, Ferrari reinforced its reputation for integrity and excellence, preserving customer confidence and brand loyalty.

Support story with evidence

Humans are easily fooled. False news travels "farther, faster, deeper, and more broadly than the truth." Fake—at least on X (formerly known as Twitter)—reaches twice as many people, six times faster, than truth. That's according to an MIT study published in *Science* magazine.[17]

Actually, that's not exactly true. I rounded up. Fake reaches 1.7 times as many people. See what I did there?

There are several theories as to why we're more likely to create, share, and consume hyperbolic or false information. We crave the attention generated by novelty and surprise, which feeds our ego and makes us part of the story. Extreme emotional reactions fuel contagion. Social status and influence come with being "in the know" and first to share.

Cognitive biases feed on false evidence: Confirmation bias reinforces pre-existing beliefs, the availability heuristic causes our minds to recall the most sensational stories, and the bandwagon effect makes us believe things because others do.

Dieselgate is one of the most infamous examples of a business falsifying evidence to support a story. The scandal came to light in 2015 when the US Environmental Protection Agency issued a notice of violation against Volkswagen. For years, VW had secretly installed "defeat devices" in over 11 million diesel engines. These contraptions detected when a car was undergoing emissions testing and temporarily adjusted its engine's operating mode to reduce nitrogen oxide emissions, ensuring a pass on the test.

With the defeat device switched off, the engines exceeded legal emission limits by up to 40 times. A toxic corporate culture, immense pressure to meet targets, a lack of accountability, and a top-down management style conspired to exploit a testing blind spot, falsifying data to tell a better story.[18]

The VW emissions scandal destroyed value. The overall financial impact—including lost sales, brand damage, fines, recalls, buybacks, and legal settlements—cost Volkswagen over $50 billion.

Value stories must be *supported by evidence*, but not all evidence is created equal. Simon Levin and Joel Wecksell, founders and managing directors of the firm The Skills Connection, former Gartner analysts, and colleagues of mine, created the evidence stack, a powerful framework to effectively position products and build credibility. The evidence stack outlines the following levels of evidence, listed from strongest to weakest:

Demonstration: Show a working prototype, trial, or proof of concept.

Data/Visualization: Present compelling data points and clear data visualizations.

Given credibility: Share customer testimonials, analyst reports, or validations from third parties.

Borrowed credibility: Associate with well-known brands or use credible-sounding names.

Blinding with science: Use jargon, technical details, and marketing hyperbole without real proof.

Assertion/Claim: Using an unsubstantiated statement or headline (e.g., "The #1 Business Messenger").

The core idea is that the higher up the evidence stack, the more credible and convincing your evidence becomes. The strongest form of evidence is providing a real demonstration or letting a consumer experience the product themselves.

A great example of this is when Impossible Foods introduced its plant-based Impossible Burger in 2016. It had its doubters. To support their claims, Impossible Foods conducted blind taste tests with chefs and food critics (demonstration) and provided scientific evidence about the burger's composition. They showcased the heme molecule, responsible for the meat-like taste, backed by careful research and development (data/visualization). Rigorous evidence and undeniable taste convinced doubters, showcasing the value story of the Impossible Burger.

The Evidence Stack

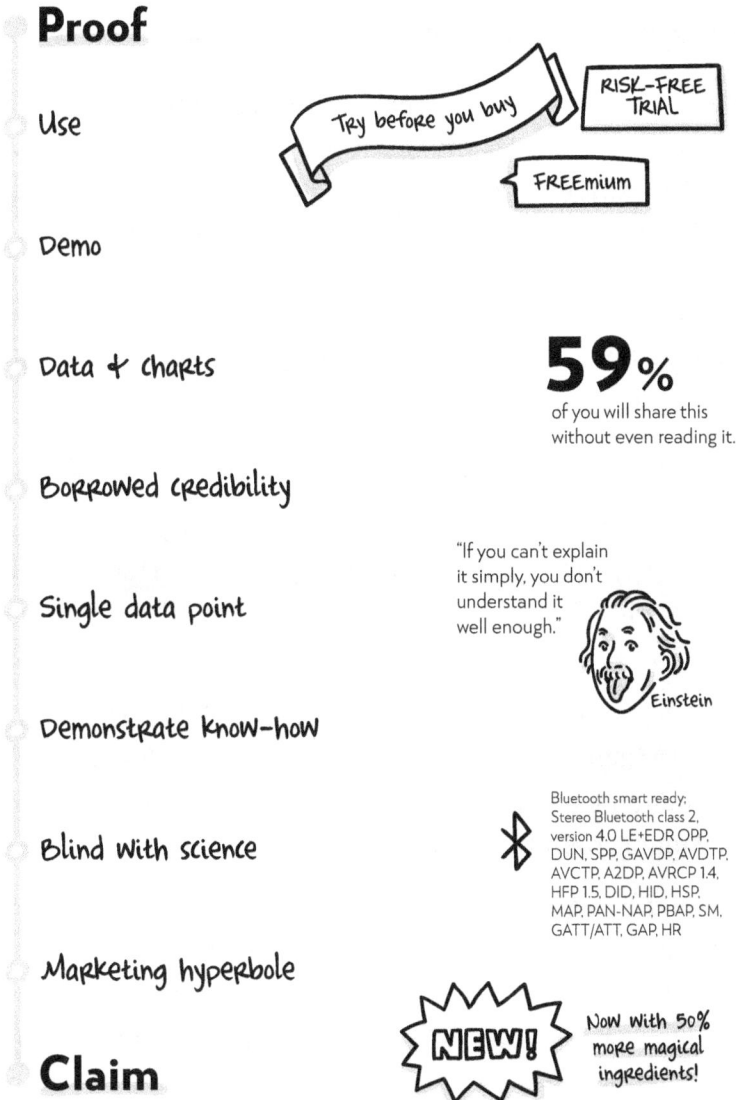

Proof

Use

Try before you buy

RISK-FREE TRIAL

FREEmium

Demo

Data & charts

59%

of you will share this without even reading it.

Borrowed credibility

"If you can't explain it simply, you don't understand it well enough."
Einstein

Single data point

Demonstrate know-how

Bluetooth smart ready:
Stereo Bluetooth class 2,
version 4.0 LE+EDR OPP,
DUN, SPP, GAVDP, AVDTP,
AVCTP, A2DP, AVRCP 1.4,
HFP 1.5, DID, HID, HSP,
MAP, PAN-NAP, PBAP, SM,
GATT/ATT, GAP, HR

Blind with science

Marketing hyperbole

Claim

NEW!

Now with 50% more magical ingredients!

Adapt and evolve over time

Stories are never static. They're retold, reinterpreted, and reshaped by different people and contexts. All business is change business. Businesses must continually adapt to survive, compete, and thrive. So, *value stories must adapt*.

There is a paradox here. Adaptation and evolution have to be gradual; the core DNA of the story must be maintained, not mutated. It's the narrative that adjusts over time.

In the last century, Netflix, the king of streaming, started out as a DVD rental service. Even then it was novel: a convenience with a broad selection of titles, delivered right to your mailbox. An easy alternative to an hour on Friday night spent browsing the partially emptied shelves of your local Blockbuster. Its core DNA: *easy* access to a *wide* variety of entertainment content. That didn't change as Netflix introduced streaming services and evolved its narrative.

Let's focus on two genes in Netflix's DNA—*easy* and *wide*.

Easy: Netflix made movie night more convenient, eliminating the need for a trip to the video store, first by delivering DVDs straight to your mailbox, then the trip became shorter still with the move to streaming.

Wide: When Netflix evolved its business model again in 2013, it began producing its own content, starting with the hit *House of Cards*, building out an ever-broader selection. Again, the narrative adapted around a core DNA.

While Netflix stayed in its lane, Amazon adopted new business models and approached new markets. Starting in 1994 with the ambition to be the largest store on earth, it succeeded by creating a convenient shopping experience and a vast selection. But convenience and selection were not Amazon's core DNA; rather, they were an outgrowth of what was—relentless operational excellence. From its beginnings, Amazon emphasized efficiency. This included optimizing logistics and supply chain management to ensure fast and reliable delivery. A natural outcrop of that was investment in technology. Amazon Web Services started as a solution for Amazon's own needs: to handle its massive e-commerce infrastructure more efficiently, in the cloud.

Credibility, built on Amazon's own DNA, allowed the company to hop between business models. Amazon's value story: Relentless execution in cloud-based internet technology works for us, and it can work for you too.

Adapt the narrative. Keep the DNA.

Easy access   Wide selection

DVD Rentals

Streaming

Originals

Global media platform

Netflix

When Netflix flipped its business model, from DVD delivery to streaming it built on its core DNA: easy access and wide selection.

Ferrari's narrative has adapted and evolved significantly over time as well—from a racing team, to a luxury car manufacturer, to a global megabrand—but its core DNA has never changed. Ferrari continues to balance the paradox of heritage and innovation.

Showcase wins and face challenges

Stories need drama—highs and lows. It's tempting, in business explanation, to be all highs: "We implemented project A, we expect stellar performance B"—the classic hockey stick of growth with little proof. This knee-jerk need to focus exclusively on the positive is a red herring. Challenges and setbacks not only add credibility but also make eventual successes more compelling.

Conflict is central to any story. Blending negative events with positive solutions has been shown to be more effective in enhancing credibility and engagement.[19] Audiences find stories that balance positive and negative more believable.[20] Amazon has lived by this principle. It's a classic story stock, with an optimistic narrative of the future—from how we read, to how we shop, to how we consume—and the infrastructure that supports this brave new world.

While Amazon has a track record of delivering, it's been a rocky road. After IPO-ing in March 1997, the online bookstore turned online everything store ran into a dot-com bubble. The company didn't turn a profit until 2001, much to the chagrin of its investors. Those who looked at the fundamentals, not the story, drove Amazon's value down.

Meanwhile, Jeff Bezos used every cent of cash generated by the online store to invest in expansion. Not all of his bets were successful. But for every Fire phone that failed, there is an Amazon Kindle. We don't just shop on Black Friday, we shop on Prime Day. We ask Alexa. Now more than half of adults in the US start their search for a product on Amazon. AWS, its cloud computing service provider, is set to be one-third of the entire $790 billion global cloud computing industry.

Placing an $18 bet on that story with the purchase of a single share in 1997 would return a value of $33,600 today.

Showcase wins and face challenges

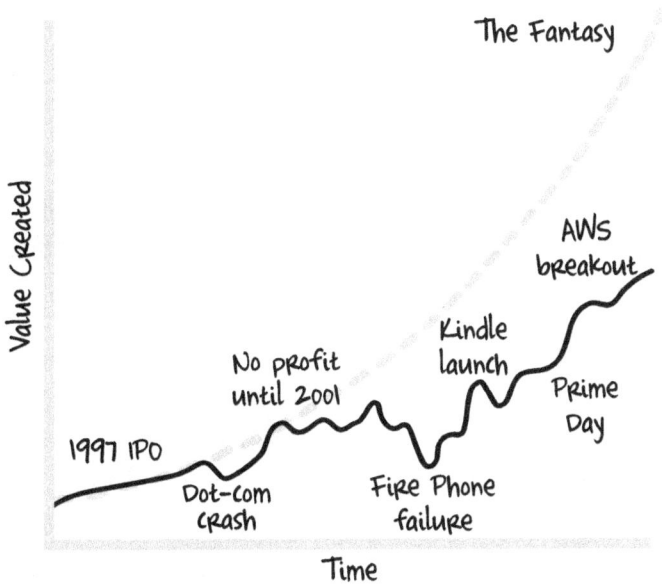

The Fantasy

Value Created

AWS breakout

Kindle launch

No profit until 2001

Prime Day

1997 IPO

Dot-com crash

Fire Phone failure

Time

Resilience, perseverance, and tenacity are natural characters in any value story.

Tap into bigger narratives

Business seems large. Towering office buildings, ticker symbols, billions of dollars of assets—big and business are twins. But story and business are like David and Goliath. Ultimately, stories—words and word-of-mouth—are more powerful.

This is an idea explored by Nobel Prize–winning economist Robert Shiller in his book *Narrative Economics*. "Narratives are major vectors of rapid change in culture, in zeitgeist, and in economic behavior," he writes.[21] They are at the height of their power when they become *narrative constellations*—groups of stories that, while distinct, share common themes and together create a compelling, larger narrative. The intersection of stories adds to their plausibility. If one person says it, it might not be true. But if everyone says it? It must be true.

The *bigger narrative* doesn't just frame economic value, it shifts our perception of value across the spectrum—cultural, social, political, and moral. In this way, the prevailing narrative constructs the *Overton window*—the range of ideas considered acceptable or mainstream. Ideas within the window are considered, while ideas outside it are *radical* or *unthinkable*.

In a 1964 BBC broadcast, science fiction author Arthur C. Clarke made several predictions about the future. One seemed particularly absurd at the time: how future communication technologies would allow remote work and a reduced need for physical offices. In the frame of the Overton window, it was an *unthinkable* idea, outside the mainstream, but one that became more feasible, yet still *radical*, in the 1990s with personal computers and the internet. By the early 2000s through the mid-2010s, remote work became acceptable, bordering on sensible. The infrastructure was in place. When the COVID-19 pandemic struck, work from home flipped from *popular* to *policy*. Prevailing narratives—in a relatively short period of time—had changed. Distributed work, hybrid work, became the future of work.

Some businesses have tried to duck this narrative constellation. But return to office has proved to be a formidable headwind. Frustrated CEOs have issued return to office mandates, snarkily relabeled by employees as "return to the past." Even with firms touting a full five-day return, compliance rates are low. The story is bigger than the business, David has slain Goliath, and a narrative constellation has shifted the Overton window.

Narrative constellations pushing our concept of value, and therefore pushing business, are likely to happen over and over again. As another science fiction author, William Gibson, said, "The future is here—it's just unevenly distributed." Ideas that are unthinkable or radical today—four-day workweeks, universal basic income, personal carbon footprint taxation, lab-grown meat, tax-free zones, crypto as an official currency, privatization of social security—are narrative zephyrs that could become tomorrow's gales.

Stories exist in a narrative constellation

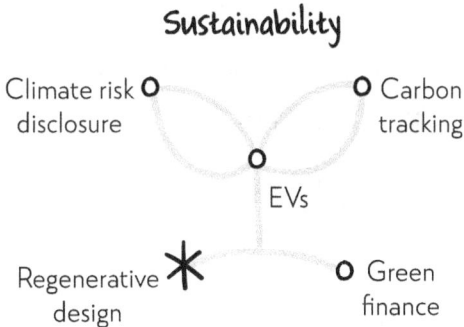

Sustainability

Climate risk disclosure

Carbon tracking

EVs

Regenerative design

Green finance

It's the matching of values that compels these shifts for business. As the broader narrative moves the value set, brands and business must keep up. For Ferrari, narrative constellations of sustainability and digital connection have shifted the supercar manufacturer's focus on innovation toward hybrid technologies and electric vehicles, virtual showrooms, and advanced infotainment systems—all shifts that are necessary for business survival, even at the expense of the "purist."

YOU KNOW...

...that **stories create value.** They magnify worth, direct decisions, and mold perceptions—from stock valuations to luxury brands, stories are the currency of value creation.

...that value storytelling follows six key rules:

1. **Hint at higher purpose.**
2. **Maintain authenticity and truth.**
3. **Support story with evidence.**
4. **Adapt and evolve over time.**
5. **Showcase wins and face challenges.**
6. **Tap into bigger narratives.**

...that **hinting at a higher purpose connects** a value story to deeper emotional needs. It makes the audience feel like part of something bigger, whether societal impact, personal growth, or shared meaning.

...that **authenticity and truth** underpin value. False narratives, hype, or misleading data lead to fraud and a catastrophic loss of trust—a bubble waiting to be burst.

...that **evidence makes value real.** A value story is built through demonstration, data, and credible third-party validation, all of which speak louder than jargon, hyperbole, or empty claims.

...that value stories **must adapt and evolve** while maintaining their core DNA. Markets change. Audiences shift. The strongest stories stay anchored in identity and purpose while adapting to new realities.

...that **showcasing wins and challenges** make the value story more compelling. Focusing only on the positive feels hollow—authentic storytelling acknowledges setbacks, which makes success more believable.

...that value stories **tap into bigger narrative** constellations aligning with broader cultural, social, and economic movements. Those who align their story with the moment form what people see as valuable.

Value isn't just created—it's told. The power of the story changes how we see, measure, and define worth. This was true of the Storyteller's tale of Somebody's spear. It is true today of stocks, products, and brands.

This is value storytelling: From the boardroom to the marketplace, stories are the currency of human connection. They don't just communicate value—they create it. Tell the right story, and you won't only sell an idea, you'll define worth.

06 PRODUCT STORYTELLING

There is only one thing stronger than all the armies of the world, and that is an idea whose time has come.

—VICTOR HUGO

What are we buying?

It's not a product, I would argue, if people don't buy it.

Value stories, ultimately, are validated through purchase: Somebody has to buy something. It's the *stuff* in "sell stuff." That stuff is a product. And because humans do the buying, that product needs a story.

Don't be misled by the name. Product stories are not really about the product, they're about the buyer. For the buyer, the product— no matter how many years it has been on the market, whether it is hardware or vaporware—is new.

The product story, then, is about what this new thing does for them.

We want to buy products we love. Product storytelling is about making your product "wantable." Done well, it turns features and functions into desire and demand. Product leaders and product managers everywhere want to make great products real. They want to turn bold ideas into indispensable essentials. They want to turn their vision into reality.

This is product love. It's a key ingredient in buzz, demand, adoption, use, growth, and loyalty. Product storytelling, in the hands of an expert product manager, awakens that love.

Imagine the future

Step into the Science Museum in London in the summer of 2023, and you could wander through *Science Fiction: Voyage to the Edge of Imagination,* an exhibit about science fiction influencing science—as chickens influence eggs.

The interactive adventure is a journey from *Pan Galactic Starlines* aboard the exploration vessel *Azimuth*. As the AI host and tour guide explains:

> I have discovered that science fiction is a source of human inspiration. Its stories help you believe that science and technology will one day take your species to new worlds.

> Your characters are exciting role models who inspire the next generation of great thinkers, creators, and explorers.

Alongside an exhibit of sleep pods found in the movie *Alien* is a concept from NASA contractor SpaceWorks for a habitat system that induces "torpor sleep":

> Researchers are studying if an existing medical treatment called therapeutic hypothermia could be used for human missions to Mars. It involves sedation to induce a sleep-like state. The body is cooled from its normal temperature of 37°C (98°F) to just 32–34°C (89–93°F). Crew members could spend several days in this torpor state.

For every cyborg movie prop, there is an exploration of science fact about cyborgism and prostheses, such as prosthetic arms made by Open Bionics. Nestling next to movie stills of Frankenstein are exhibits of Micra pacemakers. Alongside the medical tricorder from *Star Trek* is a prototype portable medical scanner.

The *Voyage* exhibition introduces "science-fictional thinking" as a powerful tool for communicating science by sparking curiosity and inspiration. This approach gives researchers and engineers a creative language to challenge conventions and explore the unknown, bridging science and fiction through storytelling.

This isn't a new phenomenon. Wander through the halls of the Science Museum, look at our early attempts at flight, the first steam engines, telescopes, or molecular models, each a marvel of their age, and each surrounded by story.

And in a corner, nestled between one gallery and the next, is a replica of Charles Babbage's Difference Engine No. 2.

The engines of genius

Charles Babbage stood on the shoulders of giants.

In 1812, the Industrial Revolution was in full swing. Luddites raged and Napoleon marched. The seeds of social movements—abolitionism, nationalism, and feminism—took root.

The universe unfolded in numbers.

Mathematical tables—rows of digits—were the paper cornerstone of Britain's imperial might. Numbers steered fleets, built bridges, and expanded humanity's understanding of the heavens.

But mathematics demands rigor—and these log tables were riddled with errors. Charles Babbage, employed by the Admiralty, was tasked to fix this problem.

Back then, the development of mathematical tables carried the same military, political, and economic weight as today's race to develop artificial intelligence. Where AI suffers from hallucination, 18th-century log tables suffered from miscalculation.

If necessity is the mother of invention, frustration is the father. And frustration fueled Babbage's quest.

In 1821, Babbage visited Paris and met Gaspard de Prony, a mathematician with a radical idea: apply Adam Smith's division of labor to arithmetic.[1] He broke down complex calculations into simple steps, then handed them off to an unlikely workforce—hairdressers, jobless after the French Revolution.

"Je ferai mes calculs comme on fait les *épingles*," de Prony said. "I will make my logarithms as one manufactures pins."[2]

Babbage admired de Prony's ingenuity but found his process flawed: slow, error-prone, human. This became his life's work—a production line not for parts, but for numbers. If human calculators were the weak link, he would replace them with machines.[*]

For this, another shoulder, another giant. Babbage borrowed Leibniz's binary numbers and mechanical calculator, then remixed with differentials—mathematics that calculated change with revolutionary precision.

Babbage called his new product the Difference Engine.

The name was genius—combining the exactness of differential calculus with the industrial marvel of the age: the steam engine. He was building a promise: a world where human error vanished, and calculation kept pace with ambition.

But to bring this vision to life, Babbage needed funding.

---

[*] There is some dramatic license to the story here; there is no historical record of de Prony ever meeting Babbage. Babbage did, however, inspect de Prony's work while in Paris.

In 1822, he pitched Sir Humphry Davy, president of the Royal Society: Imagine a machine, powered by gravity or steam, calculating faster than any human.[3] A machine that freed scientists and engineers from the grind of manual arithmetic. The British government bought in.

The birth of Babbage's Engine was difficult. Precision parts proved a monumental challenge. Costs spiraled. Progress dragged. By 1832, with only a working prototype, frustration mounted and delays piled up.

Yet even unfinished, the Difference Engine captured imaginations.

Babbage didn't describe potential—he demonstrated it. The machine became a star attraction in his London drawing room; scientists, politicians, and socialites came to marvel at the mechanism. Gears turned. Levers clicked. The future whirred before their eyes.

Charles was a masterful communicator. He knew invention needed a story, and he told it well. He used language his audience understood, not technical jargon. Not a central processing unit (CPU)—instead, a "mill." Memory? A "store." These terms were practical; commonplace. Babbage made the revolutionary feel familiar.

But for Babbage, his first machine was just the beginning.

While the Difference Engine solved a specific problem—calculating tables—Babbage's mind ticked forward. He dreamed of more. A future unbound by a single function. A machine adaptable to its user's needs.

He called this the Analytical Engine.

Not just a tool. This was a computer. Babbage envisioned a device that could perform any calculation, guided by instructions. An inveterate magpie, Babbage collected ideas. While touring Lyon, he saw Jacquard looms weaving intricate patterns guided by punched cards. An idea clicked: If punched cards could control threads, why not numbers?[4]

Babbage made the unfamiliar familiar

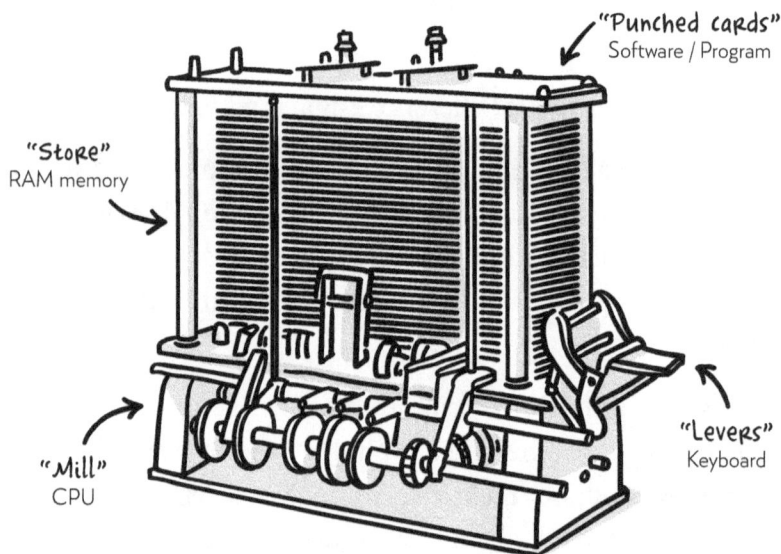

"Punched cards"
Software / Program

"Store"
RAM memory

"Levers"
Keyboard

"Mill"
CPU

Babbage adapted his narrative for different audiences. For funders, he pitched the Analytical Engine as a tool of progress—a machine to keep Britain ahead in the industrial race. For machinists, he offered blueprints and detailed designs. For the public, he delivered dazzling demonstrations, making the complex seem approachable.

During this time, Babbage collaborated with Ada Lovelace, the daughter of poet Lord Byron. Ada combined a brilliant mathematical mind with her father's flair for prose. Her metaphors turned gears and levers into poetry, revealing a vision beyond arithmetic. "The Analytical Engine weaves algebraic patterns just as the Jacquard loom weaves flowers and leaves," she wrote, giving Babbage's invention a new layer of meaning: programming.

Charles died just short of his 80th birthday. The great mechanisms fell silent. Yet Babbage's legacy is vast: the great-great-grandfather of modern computing, a giant for others—and the product stories that followed—to stand on.

The six rules of product storytelling

Product storytelling is the engine of innovation.

It's the collision of ideas, big and small, sparking together. Those sparks are stories.

They're born in people's heads. They pop up in garages, showers, and on long walks. They emerge in conversations. The spark takes root before writing the first line of code or building the first prototype. It breaks conventional thinking and ignites innovation.

Product stories are, by necessity, a science fiction.

They are stories of a future world—better than today. A world where the buyer is the protagonist, the hero of the story. The product is a magic bean, a device that propels the hero forward and gives them special powers.

Visionaries like Babbage are product storytellers—their minds wandering, creating, sparking ideas, and rallying others to turn vision into reality.

When product stories work, products sell. So if you're an entrepreneur or an intrapreneur, a marketer or an engineer, if you're building anything, you want to crack this particular code.

Over and over again, the following six rules of product storytelling repeat themselves:

1. **People don't buy products; they buy better versions of themselves.**[5]

2. **Use old words to describe new things.**

3. **Craft stories for backers, builders, and buyers.**

4. **Demonstrate, don't declare (if you can).**

5. **Adapt and grow your stories over time.**

6. **Product stories fit into a world.**

These rules echo through Charles Babbage's life and work. His computing engines promised to remove the drudgery from mathematical labor. He offered a future of efficient, error-free calculation that captivated the scientific community. Babbage was a master at describing his instruments—not for Babbage words like "arithmometer" or "ratiocinator," but simple, familiar terms like "mill" and "store" to make the complex understandable. Time and again, he demonstrated his machines' potential with prototypes, illustrations, and working models. The evolution from Difference Engine to Analytical Engine showed how he adapted and grew his story as he labored to bring it to fruition. All his inventions were deeply rooted in the Industrial Revolution, addressing the challenges of his world.

Those rules still apply today. The Storyteller would be proud of them. One of the clearest examples comes from an industry founded on Babbage's engines—an industry that has changed how we communicate today—computing.

The backstory of Slack

200 years after Babbage's engines.

2012: Glitch shut up shop.

2021: Slack sold to Salesforce for $27.7 billion.

What happened in between is an object lesson in product storytelling.

Glitch was a whimsical online game that never caught on. A small team of coders labored over it for years. Their startup, Tiny Speck, was spread across Canada and the US. And to communicate, the developers built a home-grown tool called "linefeed."

As the game stalled, Tiny Speck pivoted.

Under Stewart Butterfield, the creator of Flickr, the team went into stealth mode with a clear focus: creating a "team communication tool for the post-email era."[6]

From the ashes of Glitch, Slack emerged.

Slack was the "Searchable Log of All Communication and Knowledge" (a Slackronym, if you will)— an easier, centralized way to collaborate and communicate.[7] At its 2013 launch, Slack and Butterfield had a singular villain in their sights: email glut.

Billed as "your searchable, infinite brain" and "zero-effort knowledge management," Slack ran a successful six-month beta while searching for its voice. It quickly landed on a simple mission: helping people "be less busy."[8] One early tester summed it up:

We were looking for something to help with team communication, and nothing really stuck until we started using Slack. It looks good, feels right, and search just works: being able to trust that I can find things again when I need them is good peace of mind.[9]

Slack was not universally understood at first.

Often compared to Twitter, LinkedIn, Facebook, and Yammer, Slack was dismissed by some as just another "enterprise social network." But early users quickly saw its value and explained it to the world.

By launch, Slack gathered user tweets into a wall of love:

@fanuneza: *It's officially the best tool for team communication I've ever used. Period.*

@kazarnowicz: *Pro tip: @slackhq is like @yammer and @skype without the bad parts. Best communication tool for teams so far! Slack.com*

Months after the launch, Slack reached half a million users, describing itself simply: "Team messaging that works."

By the end of 2016, Slack had five million users. Among them—NASA. Slack was "a messaging app for teams who put robots on Mars."

But then Microsoft launched Teams, and Slack faced competition.

In response, Slack's CEO Stewart Butterfield penned a "Dear Microsoft" letter and published it as a one-page ad in *The New York Times*. Butterfield borrowed credibility from the storied brand and cleverly positioned

Slack as a front-runner: "It's great to have some healthy competition."*[10]

Still, Slack kept growing.

In 2019, the company went public under the ticker symbol WORK. Its advertising proclaimed, "Whatever work you do, you can do it in Slack." Two years later, with 15 million active users, Slack was acquired by Salesforce for $27.7 billion.

This is a product story—and a valuable one.

People don't buy products; they buy better versions of themselves

Modern product development starts with jobs to be done, wicked problems, use cases, or user stories—variations on Ted Levitt's insight: When hanging a painting, "People don't want a quarter-inch drill. They want a quarter-inch hole!" This truth reveals that customers desire outcomes, not the product itself.[11]

Wicked problems have evolved from recognizing individual challenges may, in fact, be interconnected issues. Solving one aspect often causes ripple effects, creating unintended consequences elsewhere. Addressing this demands systemic thinking.

Use cases and user stories codify jobs to be done in granular detail. The use case is a step-by-step dissection of tasks, whereas the user story puts those steps into a context—a real or imagined scenario someone faces.

---

* If an open-letter-as-advertisement in *The New York Times* sounds familiar, it's because you've seen it before. Don Draper pulled a similar stunt in *Mad Men*, itself based on real-life Mad Man David Ogilvy's letter for Hathaway Shirts.

Together or alone, none of these are the product story.

Rather, use cases and jobs to be done are data in the story, but they lack emotion. To tell the product story is to understand the psychology of the buyer. It's to understand that *people don't buy products; they buy better versions of themselves*. That better version is found within the Motive Triangle (see chapter 3): Hope, Fear, and Reason.

People don't buy products; they buy better versions of themselves

Products hold transformative potential. Narrative brings it to life.

We surround ourselves with products that enhance our self-image and social status. They make us more effective or reduce risk—whether you're running a household or a company. Products fulfill emotional needs. A weighted blanket provides comfort; a fitness tracker feeds our desire for progress. The things we use become part of our personal and professional narrative. We're part of the crowd.

Slack tapped into this ethos:

> Who Do We Want Our Customers to Become? ...We want them to become relaxed, productive workers who have the confidence that comes from knowing that any bit of information which might be valuable to them is only a search away....We want them to become masters of their own information [not] overwhelmed by the never ending flow.[12]

This came from a memo titled "We Don't Sell Saddles Here," penned by Stewart Butterfield to the Tiny Speck team—seven months into development and just two weeks before Slack's "preview release."

Butterfield understood what all great product storytellers know: The magic of a product lies in who it helps people become. That's your job as a product storyteller: to recognize—deeply—the better version your customer longs to be. That's the secret wish.

Use old words to describe new things

We like our comfort food. Our go-to traditions. Our favorite playlists.

Human nature prescribes predictability.

Habits and routines save time. We don't have to think too hard. Familiar things trigger comfort, safety, and belonging. Evolution explains this. Better to know which berries are safe to eat. We don't know what dangers lie beyond those mountains.

That doesn't mean humans don't try new things. We do.

But product builders often *overestimate* our fascination with the new and *underestimate* the bundle of biases that make us back off.

Therefore, in product storytelling, we must use *old words to describe new things*. This rule is repeatedly proven in action: Successful product storytellers bridge the gap between the familiar and the unfamiliar. By describing Slack as the "anti-email," Butterfield did just that—positioning it within the category he sought to displace, while framing it as a better alternative. Similarly, Babbage described computer memory as a "store."

What we now call a car was first called a "horseless carriage"—a name with a descriptor and comparator. Meanwhile, the Electrobat, the first commercial electric vehicle, had an impenetrable, nerdy name. No wonder you've never heard of it.[13]

In the pre-dawn of the World Wide Web, the internet went by the moniker Information Superhighway. And when Lee Trevino won the 1984 PGA championship with TaylorMade's "metal wood," golfers rushed to trade in their persimmon wood drivers for metal ones.

Names carry power.

Old words compare and describe new things. The comparator and descriptor work in tandem like a horseless carriage. The order doesn't matter (unlike the carriage). It's a descriptor (metal) and a comparator (wood) plus the promise of a better version of yourself (I will be a better golfer).

You now have a name for your product story.

When innovations aren't accessible, they stall. Think Blockchain, Google Glass, Segways, the Semantic Web, or the Metaverse. Or products like Hadoop or Quipu—niche names you may recognize but remain mostly unfamiliar.

Names can drive or slow adoption

Accessible names	We now call it...	Inaccessible names	Current status
Horseless carriage	Car	Blockchain	Slow adoption
Metal wood	Driver	Google Glass	Defunct
Electronic mail	Email	Segway	Niche product
Ice box	Refrigerator	Semantic Web	Limited adoption
Mobile phone	Phone	5G	Slow adoption
Flying machine	Plane	Metaverse	Emerging

People must have something to latch on to.

Perhaps this partially explains why AI took off in the form of ChatGPT. The "GPT" was—and still is—incomprehensible to most. But the "Chat?" That's something people know how to deal with.

The name has power, but analogies can help, too. You can think of analogies as the verbal art of making the unfamiliar familiar. They can be abstract, like Steve Jobs introducing the computer as "a bicycle for the mind" or an iPod as "1,000 songs in your pocket." Or they can be concrete, like the apocryphal story of Bill Gates demoing Windows to investors by showing them a Mac.

As a product storyteller, you use old words to describe new things. You create vivid, relatable scenarios that showcase your product's benefits in everyday terms. Don't get lost in your own jargon or cleverness; the goal is connection, not confusion.

Use old words to describe new things

COMPARATOR +	DESCRIPTOR +	OUTCOME =	EGO
What do I compare it to?	What is it?	What do I get?	A better version of myself
It's like a ...	We're going to build a ...	So you can ...	Fulfills [HOPE], soothes [FEAR]
Metal	Wood	Hit the ball further.	

Craft stories for backers, builders, and buyers

Every product story has three versions, with three unique audiences: **backers**, **builders**, and **buyers**. Each group has unique wants and needs and buys into your story at different times. That story stays fundamentally the same, but it takes slightly different forms.

Think of this as the book, the movie, and the video game.

The backers: They're investors in the story. Backers buy into the concept and the team, often when the story is a few slides long or just sketches on a whiteboard. Don't think only of VCs or angel investors—backers are anyone who provides the time and resources to build the product's first versions.

For internal products, backers might be your boss or the board of directors—those who greenlight initiatives to reinvent workflows or processes, like an HR learning program or a new call center system. For products to sell, backers could be a group of C's: the CPO, CMO, CFO, and CEO who sign off.

The backers believe in the idea and the capability of the team.

The builders: This is a crucial audience. They turn vision into reality—designers, creators, coders, engineers—whoever is on the team. They'll make thousands of decisions as your product moves from whiteboard to bench to production.

Each of those decisions, you hope, will honor the original spark—or, better yet, improve it. Those decisions build a product that upholds the values, ideas, and aspirations of the original hunch—and bring it to life.

Builders create a product that either lives up to your story or dilutes it. Without a clear narrative to guide them, the original idea gets watered down...and risks becoming a camel—a horse designed by a committee.

The buyers: These are your customers and users. Depending on what you're selling (or giving away), there are people who write the check and people who use the product. It could be the CIO whose budget pays for security software, the CISO who insists on it, the developer who uses it, or the consumer who depends on it.

There's almost always more than one buyer in the loop, even for something as simple as candy: the kid who points to it at the supermarket checkout and the parent who pays for it.

The buyers are the heroes of the product story, even as an ensemble.

The trick is adjusting the narrative to address each one's unique perspectives, interests, and roles. For backers, the story must highlight potential and return on investment; for builders, innovation and the challenge of creation; and for buyers, the practical and emotional benefits of the product. To ensure your story lands, use a T-Leaf (see chapter 4) to understand and align with your audience's needs and perspective.

Message discipline—a stick-to-it-iveness to your central theme—ensures your story stays strong for different listeners.

Craft stories for backers, builders, and buyers

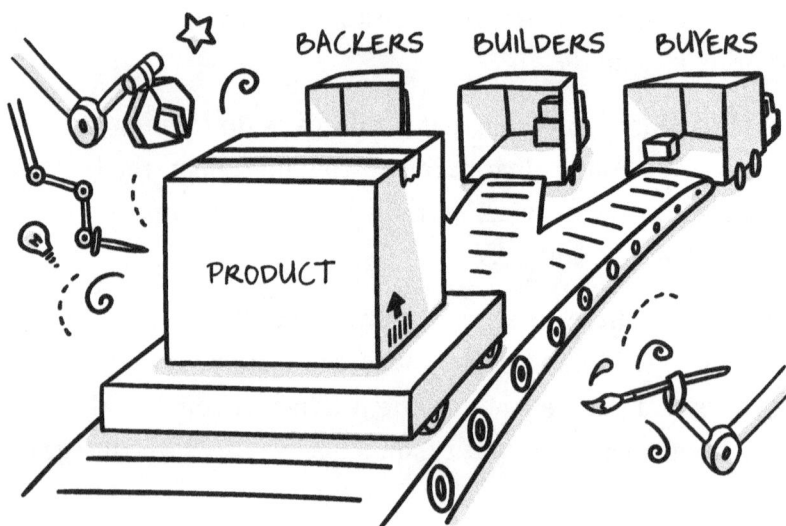

Once again, Slack is a great example. Back in 2013, in a message to Slack's early backers, Stewart Butterfield hinted at what would become a consistent pitch:

> We want to do what Gmail did for e-mail. All your communications just goes into one big place, and you don't worry about it.[14]

The comparison was spot-on—it captured what Slack could be and pointed to a massive addressable market.

Butterfield's 2014 "Saddles" memo adjusted the story for builders:

> We get 0 points for just getting a feature out the door if it is not actually contributing to making the experience better for users or helping them to understand Slack.[15]

The buyer version of the product story, in many ways, was written by those users. Slack didn't even hire a CMO until June 2019, instead, relying on the groundswell of word of mouth to propel growth.

Crafting variations of your product story ensures everyone—from backers to builders to buyers—understands the vision and becomes invested in bringing it to life.

Demonstrate, don't declare (if you can)

Product storytelling is like Aesop's most famous fable.

The tortoise is concrete and tangible. The hare is abstract and hyperbolic. It's tempting to bet on the hare, but the tortoise wins every time. Human nature strikes again. That same tangle of neurological biases steers us—quirks that make us prefer old words for new things and push us to seek a better version of ourselves.

Our brains favor *demonstration over declaration.*

Showing a product in action reduces uncertainty. Seeing, hearing, or touching creates visceral understanding. Stories activate mirror neurons, priming our personal narrative through the reflected experience of others. Testimonials and user accounts add weight and credibility to your product story.

The demo is everything. At product launches, demos surprise and delight. Think of Boston Dynamics' inventive videos of robots breakdancing, performing parkour, or doing backflips—not reasons you'd actually buy a robot, but undeniably impressive.

Demos are also notoriously dodgy. Think Samsung's Galaxy Fold launch, where flip phone screens split and cracked along the crease.[16] Or Tesla's infamous Cybertruck debut, where a metal ball meant to prove the strength of its armored exterior shattered the window, leaving broken glass and awkward laughter.

But it's worth it. Putting the product in people's hands is powerful juju.

Demonstrate, don't declare

The demonstration is a visual and visceral user story. Concrete evidence makes benefits tangible and believable. For the buyer, it creates a sense of sunk cost—they've already invested time and energy through their interaction with the product. It's the foundation of the freemium business model: Use creates a personal and persuasive narrative that increases the likelihood of buying.

Mark Roberge, co-founder and managing director at Stage 2 Capital and senior lecturer at Harvard Business School, has turned the demo into a science. For him, it's a leading indicator of product-market fit. In the case of Slack, if new users in an account send 2,000+ team messages in the first 30 days, they know it's a winner—an objective, data-driven "aha" moment that proves the product will stick.[17]

A great demo—your demo—doesn't show what the product does; it shows what the product can do for the buyer, turning curiosity into commitment.

Adapt and grow your stories over time

The goal of evolving the product story is to power its success.

What constitutes success varies widely.

Android commands 80% of the global cell phone operating system market, four times the volume of Apple's iOS. In credit cards, Visa dominates with 40% of global purchase volume, but Mastercard, at around 26%, is undeniably successful. Tesla holds less than 20% of EV sales but remains the torchbearer for electric vehicles. Ferrari has a fraction of the automotive market but consistently churns out stunning products year after year.

Your product story isn't static. At no stage are you done. The product game is relentless—a lesson learned the hard way by RIM with the BlackBerry and Motorola with the RAZR. Your story must adapt in response to new insights, market changes, and user feedback. Flexibility keeps the narrative relevant and engaging, reflecting your product's evolution and the shifting landscape it inhabits. Miss this evolution, and your product goes from loved to landfill.

The technology adoption lifecycle mirrors that evolution of the product story. In the earliest stages of adoption, it's the innovators who buy in. Representing just 2.5% of the population, innovators are drawn to risk and the allure of the new—a focus on innovation, disruption, and the cutting edge.[18]

After the innovators come the early adopters, who are fractionally more cautious. Representing 13.5% of the population, they will take risks if the benefits are clear. Early adopters buy into early results and case studies, seeking practical solutions to specific problems.

Crossing the chasm to the early majority requires another shift in the story. To reach that 34%, the narrative must amp up social proof and an established track record. This story isn't about being avant-garde—it's about value. The product story quells fears of incompatibility, reliability gaps, complexity, or potential obsolescence.

The story shifts again in the next phase.

This is about FOMO. A product story for the late majority asks "Why aren't you...?" instead of "Why don't you...?" The narrative emphasizes what's essential and what's proven. This is the story for market leaders—about mainstream adoption and the fear of falling behind.

The laggards are natural skeptics.

For every hardcore Slack enthusiast, there's a counter-story: "I already have email, I have messages, I have texts. I don't need another way for people to get ahold of me."

Every product story will face a countervailing one. Laggards are more likely to believe these narratives. They're contrarians who distrust new things and embrace the opposite, however unlikely— whether it's "windmills cause cancer" or "vaccines are tracking you." They're not easily persuaded. If they are to be convinced at all, your product story must remix again.

Adapt and grow your stories over time

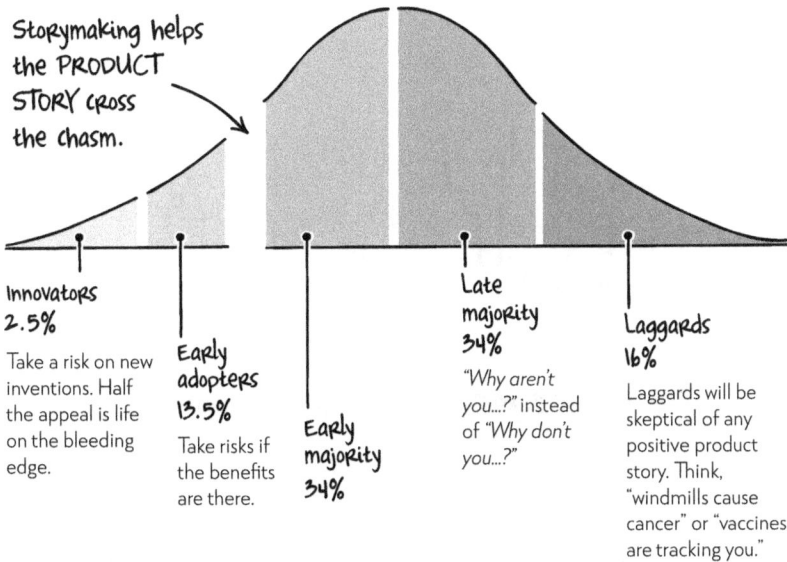

Storymaking helps the PRODUCT STORY cross the chasm.

Innovators 2.5%

Take a risk on new inventions. Half the appeal is life on the bleeding edge.

Early adopters 13.5%

Take risks if the benefits are there.

Early majority 34%

Late majority 34%

"Why aren't you...?" instead of "Why don't you...?"

Laggards 16%

Laggards will be skeptical of any positive product story. Think, "windmills cause cancer" or "vaccines are tracking you."

In the end, *the product story that wins is the one that evolves—* shifting to meet the audience, defusing skepticism, and proving its place in the world.

Product stories fit into a world

This world connects product to brand.

The world is a system: a set of moving parts, interwoven yet interdependent. An intricate web. This web is a narrative network, held together by strings of self-reference, with "I" at the center. At the center of that web sits our hero: the buyer or user.

Into that world pops your product—a relatively stable, relatively simple thing that must function and add value for the buyer. But it's never that simple. The world is an ecosystem, continuously evolving, adapting, and changing.

Product stories fit into a world

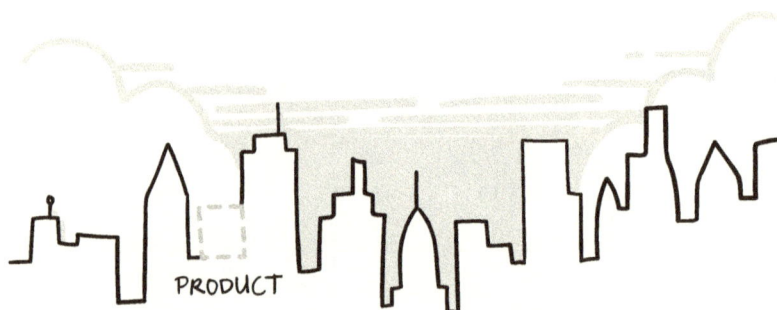

The broader world is a complex ecosystem.

Fitting into a world isn't just a storytelling question—it's a strategic one.

Products exist in what Ron Adner, professor of strategy and entrepreneurship at Dartmouth College and author of the book *The Wide Lens*, calls an innovation ecosystem, which he defines as

> a world in which the success of a value proposition depends on creating an alignment of partners who must work together in order to transform a winning idea to a market success. A world in which failing to expand your focus to include your entire ecosystem will set you up for failure. Avoidable failure.[19]

In development, products are simplified as use cases, user stories, and epics built around personas. These rarely account for the ecosystem—the complex interplay of moving parts where your product will eventually flourish or fail.

In market, products are lifted by tailwinds—zephyrs of random acts or hurricanes of market dynamics. The ones that soar on those winds are Black Swans. The ones battered by them are White Elephants.

Zoom and Tesla demonstrate the power of those gusts. For Zoom, the catastrophe of the COVID-19 pandemic was a random act of chance that transformed its product prospects overnight. Tesla, on the other hand, rides a long tailwind of climate change, positioning its product story as the poster child for a technologically advanced, greener future.[*]

On the flip side, the Segway—a two-wheeled self-balancing technological marvel of personal transportation—arrived with fanfare and left with a squeak. It was a white elephant that seemed poised to revolutionize personal mobility—offering alternative transport for city dwellers. But the Segway story didn't fit the world: The regulatory environment wasn't ready; it was too novel, requiring significant consumer education; and it lacked the ecosystem infrastructure to support it—too clumsy for crowded sidewalks and too fragile for city streets.

To thrive, a product must not just resonate in the world—it must shape it.

Butterfield, Slack's first CEO and co-founder, sensed this. In his "Saddles" memo, he wrote:

> We're selling a reduction in information overload, relief from stress, and a new ability to extract the enormous value of hitherto useless corporate archives. We're selling better organizations, better teams. That's a good thing for people to buy and it is a much better thing for us to sell in the long run.

---

[*] You might be thinking, *I am not so sure about Tesla as an example, given the recent backlash against the brand stemming from its association with Elon Musk.* You may be right. But I would argue that what has promoted the brand so well is story. What is causing the backlash? Also story.

Slack's ecosystem fit was no accident—it came from keen observation of the digital workplace and an understanding that workers needed more than a messaging app. They needed a platform that could help them make sense of their world. Slack succeeded because it integrated a myriad other tools, streamlined workflows, and fostered a sense of community.

The best product stories don't just fit into the world—they bend it around them.

YOU KNOW...

...that **product stories are the engine of innovation.** They are the collision of ideas, big and small, sparking together to turn possibility into reality.

...that **product stories are a form of science fiction,** imagining a future where your buyer is the hero, and your product is a tool that propels them forward.

...that product storytelling follows six key rules:

1. People don't buy products; they buy better versions of themselves.

2. Use old words to describe new things.

3. Craft stories for backers, builders, and buyers.

4. Demonstrate, don't declare (if you can).

5. Adapt and grow your stories over time.

6. Product stories fit into a world.

...that **people don't buy products; they buy better versions of themselves.** The best product stories take root before the first prototype is built, when you're imagining a better you.

...that using **old words to describe new things** bridges the gap between the familiar and the unfamiliar, making new products more accessible and relatable.

...that crafting stories **for backers, builders, and buyers** ensures that the product story resonates with everyone involved in the product's creation and adoption.

...that **demonstrating a product in action** is far more powerful than simply declaring its benefits. Seeing, hearing, or touching something creates a visceral understanding and builds belief.

...that product stories must **adapt and grow over time,** evolving with new insights, market changes, and user feedback. This flexibility allows the narrative to remain relevant and engaging.

...that product stories **fit into a world,** not a vacuum. They fit into larger narratives—of industries, customers, and society—shaping what people see as possible.

From Babbage to Butterfield, Archimedes to Jobs, product storytellers follow these principles—they don't just describe, they create. By standing on their shoulders, you can craft product stories that make your ideas matter.

Whether you're an entrepreneur, marketer, or engineer, how you tell your product story determines if your idea gets traction—or gets ignored.

07 BRAND STORYTELLING

More and more, storytelling has become
the art of worldbuilding.

— HENRY JENKINS

From product to brand

No product story pops out, naked and alone, into the world.

Product storytelling begets *brand storytelling*. There's no chicken-or-egg dilemma—the product story comes first. It's the origin story, the basic building block of value storytelling. Brand comes later.

Author Seth Godin, in *All Marketers are Liars,* writes:

> Stories make it easier to understand the world. Stories are the only way we know to spread an idea. Marketers didn't invent storytelling. They just perfected it.[1]

It's too simplistic to think that your product narrative must be "on brand" with unwavering devotion to select fonts and colors—or that the brand story is simply a curated collection of tales, packaged by marketing pros.

In truth, brand storytelling is a mashup of meaning and emotion. *Brand* is the bond a business builds with its customers and prospects; *Story* is the underlying chemistry that forges that bond.

Done right, it allows a business to stand out in a crowd, spark word of mouth, and build emotional connection—gifting awareness, recall, and loyalty—and filling the coffers of a story stock.

To fully understand what brand storytelling is—and why it matters—we must look to its literary roots. By studying the giants who came before—Hemingway, Tolkien, Lee, Roddenberry, and Le Guin—we uncover a crucial, often overlooked element: worldbuilding.

The writer's war

1917: The United States enters WWI.

Rejected by the military, Ernest Hemingway volunteered as an ambulance driver for the Red Cross. Wounded in a mortar attack, the young journalist saved a soldier's life and earned Italy's Silver Medal of Military Valor. Recuperating in a converted monastery, Hemingway fell in love with his American nurse.

A decade later, he distilled that time of chaos, war, love, and heroism into his second book—*A Farewell to Arms*.

Written with straightforward, unadorned prose, *A Farewell to Arms* put its author on the world stage as a literary phenomenon. Hemingway described his unique voice through the "theory of omission," or *iceberg theory*:

> If a writer of prose knows enough...he may omit things that he knows, and the reader...will have a feeling of those things as strongly as though the writer had stated them. The dignity of movement of an iceberg is due to only one-eighth of it being above water.[2]

Hemingway trusted his readers to imagine the unsaid, letting implied content add depth and complexity—inviting their participation in creating meaning.

The iceberg is a cold lesson brands often miss: Less tells more.

Hemingway's Iceberg Theory

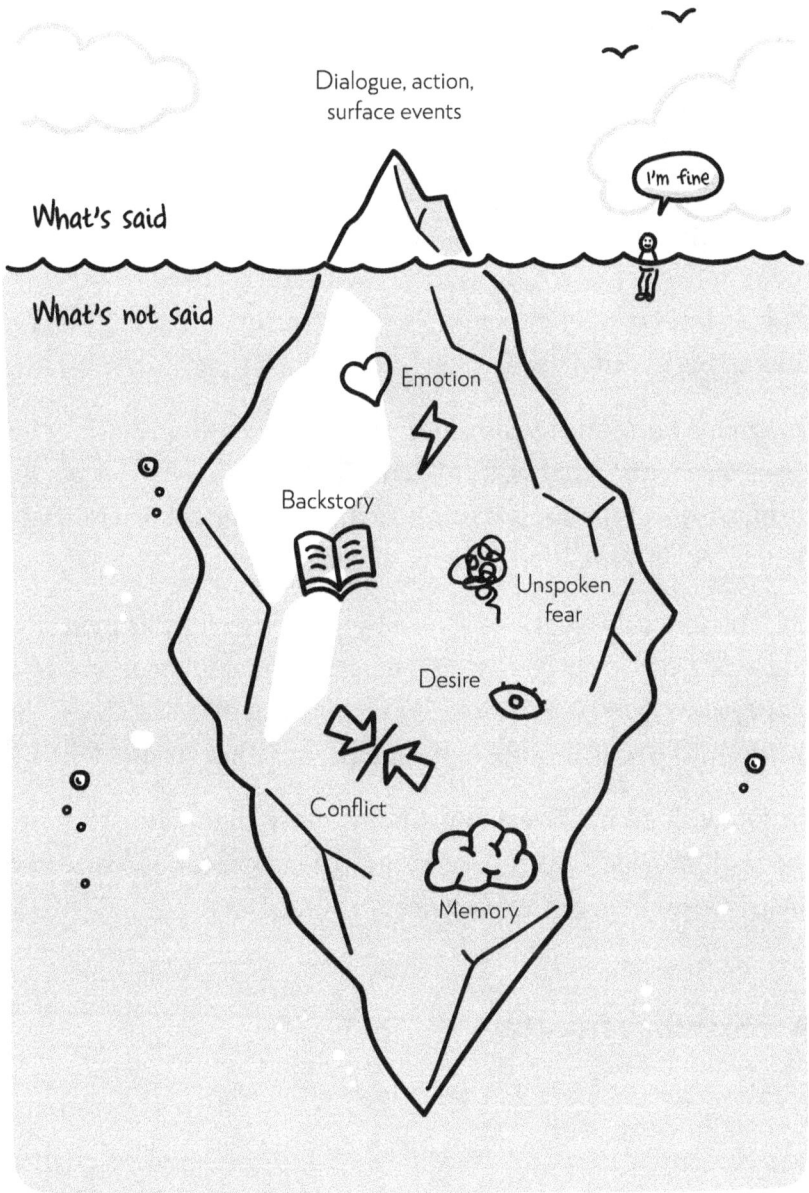

Dialogue, action,
surface events

What's said

I'm fine

What's not said

Emotion

Backstory

Unspoken
fear

Desire

Conflict

Memory

While Hemingway served on the Italian front, J. R. R. Tolkien served at the Somme: part of an ill-fated assault on the German-held village of Beaumont-Hamel.

Recovering in England, Tolkien began *The Book of Lost Tales*, the foundation for Middle-earth's mythology and languages, including *The Hobbit* and *The Lord of the Rings*. His imagined worlds drew heavily on wartime trauma: The Dead Marshes mirrored the desolation of the Somme. Samwise Gamgee embodied the spirit of the English soldier, and the siege of Minas Tirith echoed the grim reality of trench warfare, with hurrying orcs "digging, digging lines of deep trenches," and setting up "great engines for the casting of missiles."[3]

Imagine a bookish signals officer quietly inventing Elvish in his spare moments—that was Tolkien. His method: *sub-creation*, his term for worldbuilding. It was a form of mythmaking: crafting a believable, internally consistent, alternate reality.

For Tolkien, sub-creation required a world to follow its own laws and logic—an "inner consistency of reality" that felt true, *even if it was different from the real world.* "The moment disbelief arises," he warned, "the spell is broken; the magic, or rather art, has failed."[4]

So too with brand. Every touchpoint must align with story—or the spell breaks. This is consistency of concept, not just color: ideas, messaging, and experience working as one.

A marvelous frontier

Stanley Martin Lieber had a relatively quiet war.

Born after Tolkien and Hemingway had returned to civilian life, Stanley grew up during the Great Depression, hustling as a Broadway usher, sandwich delivery boy, and obituary writer. At

17, he landed a job at Timely Comics, running errands and refilling inkwells. By 19, he was interim editor.

Then came Pearl Harbor. Like Tolkien, Stan enlisted in the Army's Signal Corps, serving as a "playwright," where he wrote training materials alongside Frank Capra, Dr. Seuss, and Charles Addams. After the war, he returned to Timely Comics and reinvented himself as Stan Lee.

What followed was a revolution. Lee, with artists like Jack Kirby, created heroes who were flawed, relatable, and grounded in messy, real struggles—Spider-Man navigated high school, Iron Man battled alcoholism, Daredevil patrolled Hell's Kitchen. But Lee's real magic lay in worldbuilding. He crafted an interconnected universe—webs of stories and characters where everyone played a part.

These interconnected worlds didn't just tell stories—they created opportunities.

Crossovers like *Secret Wars* encouraged readers to invest in the larger Marvel world, not just one hero. Lee's approach had a brilliance brands can learn from: scalability. By building a cohesive world where each character fits into a larger narrative, Marvel gave fans endless reasons to engage—and the business endless opportunities to upsell and cross-sell. Every story or new product wasn't an isolated transaction—it was part of an ecosystem that rewarded loyalty and exploration.

By the time *Avengers: Endgame* hit theaters, Marvel had become a $4.24 billion juggernaut, proving a timeless truth: Worldbuilding doesn't just tell stories—it builds a narrative ecosystem that endures for generations.[5]

Strange new worlds

As the Silver Surfer flew through the pages of comic books, millions tuned in to the voyages of the starship *Enterprise*.

Earth date 08.19.1921. A new life-form enters the world in a place called El Paso, Texas—Eugene Wesley Roddenberry.

Legions of fans revere Roddenberry for his iconic creation, *Star Trek*. He described his show as "Wagon Train to the stars," remixing sci-fi and western elements, with worldbuilding resting on consistent internal logic, detailed timelines, iconic characters, and expansive storytelling.

Roddenberry immortalized his approach in *The Star Trek Guide*, a 53-page "show bible," hand-typed on an IBM Selectric. The guide's core test was believability:

> IN EVERY SCENE OF OUR STAR TREK STORY...translate it into a real-life situation. Or, sometimes as useful, try it in your mind as a scene in GUNSMOKE, NAKED CITY, or some similar show. Would you *believe* the people and the scene if it happened there?[6]

Unlike rigid brand guidelines, Roddenberry's show bible balanced structure *and* flexibility. The *Guide* left room for invention within the rules of the universe. He championed relatable language— what he called "audience terminology" (e.g., "That alien ship is more than a mile in diameter!").

Show bibles' rich backstories provide a gritty realism; style guidelines feel more corporate and plastic.

Roddenberry's true brilliance is what I will call an *arrow of coherence*—a straight line of narrative logic that provides causality and consistency—deepening the Federation's lore and making *Star Trek* believable. For brands, this is worldbuilding at its best— creating consistent, flexible narratives that resonate and endure.

A world apart

Hemingway and Tolkien established the basic principles of worldbuilding, Lee demonstrated its potential for cross-platform storytelling, and Roddenberry codified the importance of internal consistency and coherence. One more figure completes the picture: Ursula K. Le Guin, who showed how a fully realized fictional world can become a powerful vehicle for exploring complex social, philosophical, and cultural ideas.

Le Guin's sci-fi and fantasy novels are celebrated for their intricately detailed secondary worlds, each with its own cultures, philosophies, languages, ecologies, and political systems.

In *From Elfland to Poughkeepsie*, Le Guin critiqued "blandscaping"—the creation of imaginary worlds with generic, interchangeable medieval European settings. Effective worldbuilding, she argued, weaves together language, culture, and environment—each influencing the other to create a unique, self-contained whole.

Blandscaping could equally critique brands: How different are your differentiators? Is your brand voice distinctive or dull? Is your identity interesting or interchangeable? Do you have a tribe, or is your brand relationship more of a transaction? In branding, as in novel writing, bold stances are hard; it's far easier to be superficial and safe. But that is anti-brand: dull, interchangeable, transactional, superficial, safe; the definition of blandscaping.

Le Guin's most famous works—*Earthsea, The Left Hand of Darkness,* and *The Dispossessed*—showcase her mastery of detailed, socially complex worlds. They light a path, illuminating how worldbuilding can deal with the cultural zeitgeist and collective anxieties—much like brands navigating shifting views on technology, social media, and privacy. *The Left Hand of Darkness* probed questions of gender, sexuality, and identity—a shifting landscape that, for example, beer brands have used as a crutch but now struggle to adapt to.

Ultimately, the goal of a brand and the goal of an imagined world is the same—to envision an alternate possibility.

The six rules of brand storytelling

Brand storytelling is worldbuilding.

I'd quibble with Seth Godin's claim: "Marketers didn't invent storytelling. They just perfected it." The first part? True. Perfection? Not so fast. It lies, I'd argue, in Henry Jenkins's insight from *Convergence Culture*: "More and more, storytelling has become the art of worldbuilding."[7]

The subtitle of Jenkins's book is *Where Old and New Media Collide*; in it, he argued—back in 2008—that the boundaries between old and new media were blurring, disrupting how media is produced, purchased, and consumed. It's prescient.

That collision is everywhere now.

What industry isn't being disrupted? Mash two words together—*fintech*, *healthtech*, *adtech*, *edtech*—and you get venture-capital speak for "let's throw money into this and see what happens." Now add a dash of AI, a splash of cultural and political chaos, and there are no calm waters left for brands to navigate. At best, strong currents; at worst, whirlpools and potential wrecks.

The strongest swimmers will be the brands that can tell stories and build worlds. In that brew, six rules of brand storytelling emerge:

1. **Omission sparks the imagination.**

2. **Establish a right to play in the world.**

3. **Build a world with magic and rules.**

4. **Spur storymaking and fan fiction.**

5. **Ground reality with interwoven stories.**

6. **Escape the blandscape.**

These rules, drawn from master storytellers, allow marketers to pursue perfection. The Storyteller would recognize them: from Hemingway's iceberg theory, where omission sparks imagination, to Tolkien's demand for inner consistency, and Lee's interconnected universes that give fans endless reasons to return. Believability is built into the blueprint, allowing brands to rise above the blandscape.

Bound by rules of magic, a strong inner logic, and consistency, these worlds inspired legions of fans. However fantastical, they were grounded—rich with gritty textures often molded by their creators' experiences. Above all, they stood out.

Everywhere you see a business at the frontier of branding, you see these rules.

The six rules of brand storytelling

Brand	Omission sparks the imagination.	Establish a right to play in the world.	Build a world with magic and rules.	Spur storymaking and fan fiction.	Ground reality with interwoven stories.	Escape the blandscape.
Marvel	◑	●	●	●	◑	●
Apple	◑	●	◑	●	◑	●
Patagonia	◑	●	◑	◐	●	●
Lego	◐	●	◔	●	◑	●
IKEA	◑	●	◑	◑	●	◑
Tesla	◐	●	◐	●	◑	●
Ferrari	◐	●	◑	◑	◑	●
Salesforce	◕	◔	◐	◕	◐	◐

You too can apply these axioms of brand storytelling. Great brands already do—giants that stand out, riding a wave of word of mouth, with every interaction building emotional consumer connection, supporting fandom, and adding value to their story stock.

Pass the Köttbullar

IKEA's iconic meatballs are a cult favorite.

The meaty spheres were long a secret recipe, part of the mystery and magnetism of IKEA. Billions have been served with sauce and scarfed down in restaurants perched above a maze of delightful discoveries—BILLY bookcases, POÄNG chairs, and MALM beds—all arranged in their own rooms-capes like set pieces scattered throughout the store. Shoppers sip from FÄRGRIK mugs and savor the oniony orbs with blue FRAKTA bags at their feet.

The köttbullar are an edible extension of IKEA's world.

So iconic and tasty, you have to have them. During the isolation of lockdown 2020, the Swedish retailer published its secret recipe, helping people recreate a little piece of its world in their lives. From the news release:

> We know that some people might be missing our meatballs, which is why we've released an at-home alternative which, using easily accessible ingredients, will help those looking for some inspiration in the kitchen.[8]

In IKEA world, every detail aligns.

Founded in 1943 by Ingvar Kamprad, IKEA's name came from his life. The I and K are his initials; the E is the farm he lived on, Elmtaryd, and the A is Agunnaryd, his parish.[9] Struggling with dyslexia, Kamprad named products instead of numbering them, giving each an identity.[*]

IKEA's products are central characters in its world.

In 1976, Ingvar Kamprad published *The Testament of a Furniture Dealer*. *Testament* is the equivalent of Gene Roddenberry's show bible—describing, in nine points, how IKEA must act to remain vibrant. The first point encapsulates the product story: *The product range is the company's identity*. Each sofa, frying pan, and mug reflects IKEA—simple, straightforward, hard-wearing, easy to get on with, and unmistakably Swedish. [10]

The products are characters in the brand story. But we—the assemblers—are its heroes.

Flat-pack furniture gives IKEA its edge. Densely packed, stackable boxes are easier to store and ship. More product fits in every container, truck, warehouse, and store; supply chain heaven, savings passed on as lower prices, felt when we lug loaded FRAKTA to the car.

---

[*] Part of IKEA's worldbuilding includes the roughly 9,500 product names, each the essence of Swedishness. According to Åsa Nordin, identity and symbols leader at IKEA:

> Ingvar Kamprad started by putting names on products. He could have decided that this is product 1, 2, 3, 4, 5, and continued....[There is] an anecdote about him being a dyslexic—and it would be difficult with numbers. But I also think he was quite smart at the time. He wanted to give each product an identity, a character. And that was easier to do with a name attached to a product. It adds emotional value. It also adds uniqueness. (IKEA Museum, "Art of Naming IKEA Products.")

Your flat-pack furniture is unlocked by a small yet mighty tool—the Allen key. That key, paired with wordless line drawings, unlocks the *IKEA effect*—a cognitive bias named for the furniture giant. In "The 'IKEA Effect': When Labor Leads to Love," researchers Michael Norton, Daniel Mochon, and Dan Ariely show that people place greater value on things they build themselves, because they're part of the story. Wield an Allen key, pore over pictorial guides, and suddenly that shelf has emotional heft.[11]

Fan fiction takes labor and love even further with IKEA hacking.

IKEA hackers remix products into new creations, from FRAKTA raincoats to dog carriers. Shared on TikTok and Instagram, these hacks turn fans into storytellers, expanding IKEA's world beyond the catalog.[12]

IKEA is a triumph of Swedish design and identity.

Swathed in the colors of the Swedish flag, it escapes the blandscape through clean, uncluttered design that prioritizes practicality; deeply rooted in Kamprad's ideals of efficiency and Folkhemmet—the people's home.

Through brand storytelling, IKEA made Scandinavian style a household staple.

Omission sparks the imagination

Brand storytelling is subtle.

It's not a single, sweeping narrative—it's a thousand points of light. Glittering anecdotes in a constellation. Brand storytellers perfect what Hemingway started: minimal storytelling.

Simplicity. Strip away non-essentials—extra words, extra lines, extra weight. Highlight the brand's essence, and let the audience fill in the gaps. Imagination does the rest. Implied but unsaid: The mind's eye is unpaid media. It's a magical technique that puts readers and viewers at the center of the story.

Ask Ryan Reynolds, investor, chief creative officer, and pitchman who brings his storytelling skills to Aviation Gin, Mint Mobile, and MNTN. For Reynolds, "Commercials are like diet story-telling. Little bite-sized bits of content that are lots of fun."[13]

Omission isn't mindless. The craft lies in knowing what to leave out and what to leave in. Overexplaining is easy; the challenge is to tiptoe on the tightrope of "just enough."

Omission sparks the imagination

In the quiet between headlines and hashtags, a voice rises — not THE loudest, but the one that lingers. Among countless messages, only a few feel real. Only a few earn the title of BEST — not because they shout, but because they stay. A BRAND is not its logo, not its tagline or color scheme — it is a heartbeat in the background, a hum behind the product. The most powerful STORIES aren't scripts, they are echoes—retold, reshaped, remembered. They don't demand attention; they PLAY quietly in the back of your mind. Not to convince, but To connect. Not to push, but to pull. They speak to the part of us that dreams — that believes in something more. And there, in the silent spaces, they awaken THE IMAGINATION.

Brands that fall fail. Focusing on exhaustive detail—TMI about products or services—leaves no room for the imagination. In pursuit of clarity, well-intentioned marketers get technical and factual. All IQ, no EQ. Emotion—the heart of storytelling—fades away. It's a tell-all approach: The message is received but rings off-key. It lacks subtlety. Falling off the tightrope dishonors the audience, leaving them feel talked down to—or worse, utterly confused.

I'm not sure which is harder to forgive.

All of this is compounded by the need for marketing to work. Fill pipelines. Attract eyeballs. Swing doors. That urgency arms the cannon fire of constant messages—the deafening bombardment of content saturation.

What we need now are bite-sized stories that fit seamlessly into the brand world. Enter: the anecdote.

Lou Hoffman, founder and CEO of the Hoffman Agency, a global public relations firm headquartered in Silicon Valley, captures the power of the anecdote perfectly:

> Anecdotes are a kind of magic elixir to really make it real. A lot of times you are communicating to audiences that can be pretty cynical. They certainly have their guard up, and they're not gonna believe everything you say at face value. So, how do you take your communications and make it real? I would argue anecdotal content does that.[14]

IKEA has mastered the art of the anecdote. They are a brand told in brief snippets—a thousand points of light.

Take IKEA's instruction manuals, renowned for their wordless, pictorial format—gaps for you to fill in. This omission of language solves the thorny problem of internationalization and encourages deep engagement. You're not just reading instructions—you're following visual cues in the assembly story of your UPPLAND armchair.

The furniture itself is a form of minimal storytelling. You are an active participant, transforming flat-pack pieces into something useful, something yours.

IKEA's showroom displays are physical anecdotes—minimal visual stories. Real but brief. Illustrative yet incomplete. What isn't there: walls, ceilings, quirks, and clutter. What you provide: human presence and imagination, filling the gaps as you reimagine these spaces in your own home. Brand storytelling as minimal storytelling invites consumers to see IKEA's furniture in their lives—using their creativity to fill the architectural void.

The best brand stories play to the imagination.

Establish a right to play in the world

If a brand is the emotional bond between a business, its customers, and prospects, it is built on a belief system—a narrative running through their heads. What your brand projects must line up with your audience's hopes and fears, giving them a reason to act.

These beliefs unite the tribe; they are their central "why."

Famously, Simon Sinek urges brands to *Start with Why* by communicating purpose and belief:

> People don't buy what you do; they buy why you do it. And what you do simply proves what you believe.[15]

Apple's "why" is to *think different*, Patagonia's is to *use business as a force for good.*

Said differently in mission statements and executive anecdotes, a brand's central belief burns through. It *establishes a larger right to play in the world*, allowing the business to prosper, earn loyalty, and expand into new markets with ease.

In brand storytelling, that belief—your right to play—is not a list. Tolkien understood this: Internal consistency, where every piece connects, is central to worldbuilding. It's the litany of cause and effect—a narrative scaffolding—that makes the mythos so compelling. It's the deeper belief system that holds the brand world together.

Reduce it to a disconnected list of features and benefits and the brand goes bland.

A brand's right to play in the world links cause and effect to every part of the business. It connects the constellation of stories into a thousand points of light. To make it work, you need a strong throughline from purpose, mission, and values to brand activities—just like Roddenberry's *Star Trek* show bible.

IKEA has its own show bible: *The Testament of a Furniture Dealer.* The first page starts with why: "To create a better everyday life for the many people." That belief permeates every aspect of IKEA's way of doing business—in togetherness, simplicity, frugality, and responsibility.

Cause and effect writ large.

Offering low prices (cause) makes well-designed, functional home furnishings affordable to more people (effect). Affordability (cause) demands an obsession with simplicity and design (effect). Efficient flat-pack furniture design (cause) reduces shipping and storage costs, allowing IKEA to offer low prices (effect).

Systems thinking as worldbuilding lifts the brand.

This establishes a right to play in the world. IKEA's beliefs loom large in consumers' minds, giving the brand permission to enter unexpected adjacencies—becoming one of the world's largest restaurant chains and a go-to grocery destination for lingonberry, herring, and meatballs.[16]

A brand earns its place through the story it tells.

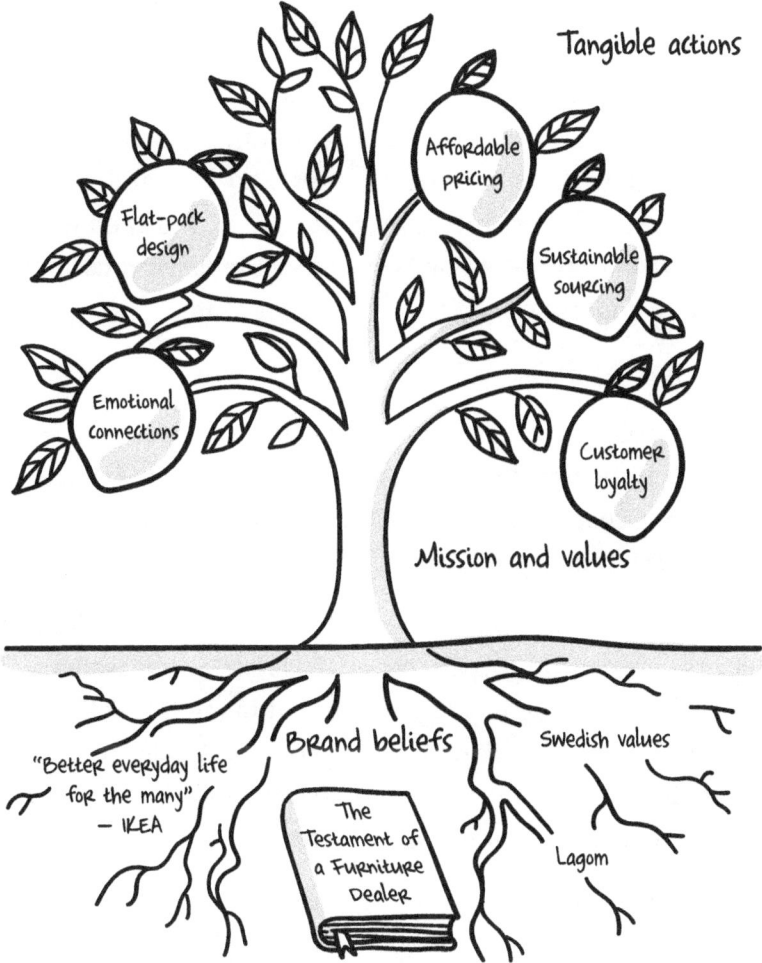

Establish a Right to play in the World

Tangible actions

Affordable pricing

Flat-pack design

Sustainable sourcing

Emotional connections

Customer loyalty

Mission and values

Brand beliefs

Swedish values

"Better everyday life for the many" — IKEA

The Testament of a Furniture Dealer

Lagom

Build a world with magic and rules

Cause and effect develop a canon—a system that binds worlds together.

Rules link action and outcome: consistent laws, logic, and history that govern your brand universe—codified into a show bible. This internal consistency creates a believable foundation for brand storytelling and an escape from the blandscape.

Ironclad rules make your brand unmissable.

Not the weak sauce of differentiators and brand values, but an unerring sense of what is in and what is out. Take two franchises so similar they share half their names: *Star Trek* and *Star Wars*. Both have spaceships and crews, epic battles, and alien worlds— but they're entirely different. Walk into a movie without knowing which one it is and you'd figure it out in seconds.

Can brands say the same?

Can you rapidly figure out who your cell phone provider is? Who adjusts your insurance claims? Which airline you're flying on, or which hotel chain you're staying in? That's what a *world built with magic and rules* does—it grounds you, instantly.

In *Star Trek* you have warp drive, but never hyperspace. You have phasers and photon torpedoes, not blasters or lightsabers. *Star Trek* is all about progress, science, and humanity. *Star Wars* has a pseudo-religion—the Force—and a group of warrior monks who protect it. The Federation is a source of good. The Empire is a source of evil. Different worlds, different rules.

With the right rules, you create a fandom.

These are the laws of magic in your ~~fantasy~~ brand world. What Tolkien started and Le Guin continued was a construct to hold story—a rich backdrop to cast stories in and propel them forward.

Roddenberry fretted over the believability of that backdrop. And believability—realism, even in unreal worlds—comes from rules.

Build a World with magic and rules

Will see	Won't see
Warp drive	Hyperspace
Phasers	Lightsabers
Captain and crew are heroes	Plucky, rag-tag rebels are heroes
Triumph of science	Triumph of religion
Federation as a source of good	Empire as a source of evil

Writers of speculative fiction live by them.

Rules add constraints that dramatize story. Isaac Asimov had his Three Laws of Robotics. J. K. Rowling endowed *Harry Potter*'s wizarding world with Five Rules of Magic. *Star Trek*'s Federation follows the Prime Directive.

Simple rules can equally apply to *brand storytelling*.[*]

Your products are characters in a universe. Customers are heroes. Flawed and human, they have hopes and fears. Their struggles—and the villains your brand helps vanquish—fuel the story. Your brand is their guide in the universe—their Obi-Wan, their Dumbledore, their Gandalf.

---

[*] It's not exactly the same, but it's adjacent. In the excellent book *Simple Rules* by Donald Sull and Kathleen Eisenhardt, simple rules are described as a way to translate strategy to the point of need—the moment a decision is made. That concept carries over well to brand execution.

Rules provide a framework—a foundation, enabling deep, layered creativity, enriching the brand world, not constraining it.

Storytelling brands extend rules into product placement. Rian Johnson, director of *Star Wars: The Last Jedi* and *Knives Out*, revealed:

> Apple, they let you use iPhones in movies, but—and this is very pivotal—if you're ever watching a mystery movie, bad guys cannot have iPhones on camera.[17]

Lego hides easter eggs in its sets. Ben & Jerry's flavor puns are baked into their world. Patagonia weaves hidden environmental messages into its clothing.

Details guided by rules tell the brand story.

IKEA's KALLAX bookcase is a mashup of *kalla* (meaning "beloved") and *hylla* (meaning "shelf"). Naming at IKEA follows a strict but creative canon. Christina Berg-Overgaard, product management leader, explains:

> It has to be somewhere between four and twelve letters. We would love to have it with the Swedish Å, Ä and Ö in it. It must never be a trademark. It cannot be a family name, and of course it has to be a nice word.

Åsa Nordin, identity and symbols leader, adds:

> It's a little bit twinkle in the eye, a little bit fun. It's not taking everything so seriously all the time...It [the product name] also gives that little relaxed feeling about it. Which adds a great deal of value for IKEA.[18]

Rules don't limit creativity, they unlock it, grounding your brand in a world only it can own.

Spur storymaking and fan fiction

The test of brand storytelling is breadth and depth—or, in marketing speak, reach and affinity. But those are sterile descriptions of what brand storytelling really does: Captivate as many eyes and ears as possible, and turn the most mild-mannered consumer into a rabid fan. From Trekkies to cosplayers, Comic-Con shows what happens when fans take matters into their own hands.

Tesla, too, has its army of zealots.

Google "Tesla" and under "video" you will find over 71 million results. Tesla's official YouTube channel: just 351 videos. That's a whopping 200,000x magnification factor—an ant bench-pressing an elephant. This is a company that doesn't rely on traditional media, has no chief marketing officer, and no ad agency. Teslas are fueled by electricity and powered by buzz.[19]

Fan fiction is forged through storymaking and wrought by word of mouth. Ted Wright, CEO of the world's leading word-of-mouth marketing firm, Fizz, explains:

> Eight out of ten of us don't trust brands or organizations. There is less and less trust; more and more demand on your time and money. Which means everybody has moved to the thing that they trust the most—a conversation between two people that know each other.[20]

Word of mouth is minimal storytelling at its finest. It aligns with worldbuilding, creating the perfect conditions for communities to form around shared beliefs—a sense of wonder and belonging within your brand's world. Minimal effort, maximum reward.

This is storymaking, a term coined by Raja Rajamannar, award-winning chief marketing officer of Mastercard's priceless brand. In his book *Quantum Marketing*, he reflects on the shift:

We launched the priceless campaign when the world was much simpler. People sat in front of a TV, with the whole family gathered during prime time. But something dramatic has happened. Today, the world is very different. People still come together in the family room, but it's a collection of individuals who are all in their own private worlds with their own connected devices.[21]

In an interview in CMO Today, Rajamannar notes the transition from traditional advertising-led marketing to experiential marketing:

Consumers don't want to hear brand stories; they want to be part of the story, so we have shifted from storytelling to storymaking. We [need to] enable, create, and curate experiences for consumers; that's the way to connect to them. [22]

Spur storymaking and fan fiction

Cosplay

DIY mod

YouTube channel

Original story

Meme

What you say is just the start.
What they see? That's the story.

Co-creating and curating user stories across brand channels—and building online communities—*spurs storymaking and fan fiction.* Julie Roehm, then chief storytelling officer at SAP, embraced this approach. She expanded beyond traditional case studies by amplifying word of mouth through a curated platform:

> We created a very simple tool on an iPad...In an old-school photo booth with a curtain, and we would ask our customers to sit inside and record their stories.[23]

Roehm continued:

> I fundamentally believe no company is going to be successful unless their customer is successful. And we built around that.

Fan fiction isn't accidental—it's the mark of great brand storytelling.

Ground reality with interwoven stories

Humans are wired for story.

We are social creatures. We connect through telling, sharing, and swapping stories. Place your brand as an ingredient in that mix—the fan fiction that is word of mouth—and your audience makes it their own.

We must recognize two rules of this reality. First: All stories connect. Second: It's impossible to say exactly how.

Take two random, unrelated brands: Stan Lee's Marvel and Salesforce. You might try to concoct a story linking them. You might Google the two and stumble upon an MCU Slack channel. Or you might see no connection at all.

But there is one: *You.*

Even in denial, you are at the center of a thread that loosely connects them. It's Schrödinger-esque. Which proves the second rule—you can't always see how brands connect.

Ground Reality with interwoven stories

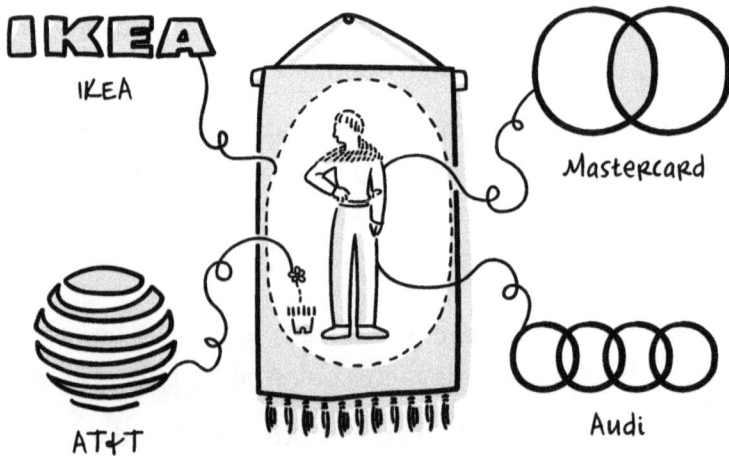

IKEA

Mastercard

AT&T

Audi

You can't predict how a brand worms its way into a billion subconscious minds. But you can shape the stories they tell.

Brands don't control narratives—they intercept them. The goal isn't to dictate meaning but to become an ingredient in fan fiction. First, add *believability*—that frisson of detail that makes a story irresistible. Second, *anchor* those details to stories, places, and experiences that exist in the real world.

Like the novelists, screenwriters, and showrunners you love, you can expand a brand style guide into a living story canon—a deep, layered world where marketers and fans can co-create the narrative together.

Mastercard, under Rajamannar's guidance, keeps adding detail and texture to the brand, weaving more connections to the world we live in. "Priceless" has evolved from a tagline into priceless experiences: exclusive events, celebrity chef dinners, backstage festival access, and VIP sports packages. All designed to forge emotional connections between customers and the brand—and to reinforce what makes Mastercard stand out: priceless moments.

Seeing the rise of audio—podcasts, smart speakers, and voice assistants—Rajamannar met it head-on. His team created Mastercard's sonic brand: a unique identity built on a distinctive melody, sound architecture, and a deep sound library.

You'll hear it across touchpoints—ads, point-of-sale terminals, digital platforms—an earworm designed to enhance emotional consumer connection, boost recall, and build loyalty.[24]

But Mastercard didn't stop at sound. Embracing inclusive design, it created Touch Cards—small notches, big impact. These elegantly sculpted credit, debit, and prepaid cards highlight a level of detail that benefits people with specific needs—and improves the experience for everyone.[25]

The lesson for marketers: Ground your brand in a relatable world. Interconnected stories turn your products into characters in a larger narrative, a flexible tapestry of multi-platform, cross-media experiences.

IKEA does this by being intensely Swedish. Its brand story is woven into the country's national identity. IKEA doesn't just swathe itself in blue and yellow—it embodies Scandinavian design. Simplicity, functionality, and affordability might well be a motto under the Swedish flag.

IKEA is part brand asset, part cultural ambassador—exporting Swedish philosophies, holidays, and traditions. Midsommar is marked and marketed worldwide. Tomte, the Swedish gnome, appears in Christmas decorations. Clean lines, neutral colors, and natural materials reflect the Swedish aesthetic and way of life.

If it were capitalized, LAGOM could pass for an IKEA sofa. A non-Swede might mistake it as a variety of lingonberry—it isn't.

It's a philosophy—the Swedish phrase "Lagom är bast" means "the right amount is best"—a focus on small, thoughtful details that make a product functional, practical, and beautifully simple.

Upcycling and reuse are central to Lagom. IKEA hacking—giving what you already own a new lease of life—embodies the mission of the IKEA-backed Live Lagom community: *Reduce waste, save money, be more sustainable.*[26]

Lagom and Scandinavian design—central to IKEA's brand storytelling—blend beauty with utility to enhance everyday life. It fronts quintessentially Swedish—and quintessentially IKEA—virtues: Good design should be accessible to everyone, no matter their income or status.

The best brand storytellers don't just tell stories—they embed them in the lives we already live.

Escape the blandscape

Ursula K. Le Guin warned of the blandscape—the typical descent of fantasy worlds into predictable Arthurian tropes mixed with a dash of medieval Europe.

Brands, too, must *escape the blandscape.*

In brand storytelling, generic is not the goal. Like a giant striding across a fantasy landscape, brand storytelling must perform a clever trick—fit in with the world, *and* stand out in it.

Look at typical messaging—TV spots, social media. Car ads look like car ads. Beer ads look like beer ads. They carry category codes—visual signifiers that tell audiences exactly what they're looking at. Natural products use the color green. Luxury cars glide down scenic, empty roads. Cosmetic ads feature flawless beauty.

These identifiers anchor brands in their category, cue relevance, and signal "differentiation."

The Catch-22: They are part of the blandscape.

Tide exploited this a few years ago with a traditional, nontraditional Super Bowl ad. As a laundry detergent, it's hard to stand out. But the creative folks behind the "It's a Tide Ad" campaign saw their place in the blandscape and spotted a key insight: what Saatchi & Saatchi Creative Director Daniel Lobatón calls a "brand truth"—every ad is a Tide ad. From this a script was born, with a pitchman who appeared to be hawking various consumer products, only to reveal, again and again, "Nope, it's a Tide ad."

The ad, featuring David Harbour, parodied familiar spots: a sleek car gliding down an empty road in a typical Super Bowl car ad; a bar, full of friends laughing, in a hilarious beer ad. Subverted category codes flashed past—for perfume, insurance, beer, razors, more beer, consumer electronics—each pointing to the immaculately clean clothes each actor wore. Which means every Super Bowl ad was, in fact, "A Tide Ad."[27]

For a brief moment, powered by clever thinking and brilliant execution, Tide escaped the blandscape. Some brands make this break permanent. Many become verbs:

We Google stuff, Photoshop images, Zoom a call, and Uber from the airport.

Some brands are so storied, so dominant, they define the category. In their worlds, they aren't just leaders—they are the *brand*scape: Coca-Cola, Disney, Ferrari, Lego, Rolex.

Through a mix of fortune and bold choices, these blandscape escapees have forged distinct voices and clear identities. They've taken calculated risks in brand storytelling—addressing cultural moments, pushing boundaries, and standing apart.

Take Coke's iconic "I'd Like to Buy the World a Coke" ad. At the height of Vietnam and the Cold War, it didn't sell soda—it sold unity and peace. The ad blurred the line between marketing and entertainment, broke ground with its diversity, and shifted away from the product-centered ads of its time.

In a world where one chair is much like another and a bookshelf is just a bookshelf, IKEA stands apart—both defining the landscape and breaking free of it.

Its minimal storytelling plays out in furniture displays. Its flat-pack model builds cause and effect into the business. Its quirky product names, community building and IKEA hacking, and deep ties to Scandinavian design—all define a personality that feels both universal and unmistakably Swedish.

These worldbuilding elements—woven with IKEA's values and Scandinavian sensibility—create legions of fans and let the company escape the blandscape: holding court as one of the world's most valuable brands, selling everything from meatballs to MALM.

Escaping the blandscape isn't luck—it's worldbuilding.

Escape the blandscape

The Valley of AI Washing

Mount Missionstatement

Our Why

Prompt fog

Now powered by AI!

Machine learning inside

AI-driven Results

Empower

Innovate

Synergize

Maximize value

The Beige Hills

Blando

Neutralia

Tone™

Passionately delivering

Boldly going

Radically collaborating

Values

Mission   Vision

The Gulf of Genericity

Adverbia
(The Capital)

Now entering Spec Swamp. Abandon clarity, all ye who enter.

Unlock potential

Drive impact

Vision

Vibes   Execution

Buzzwords

Acronym alligators

Spec Swamp

Solutions that scale

Here be buzzwords

Unique value prop

Budget blowfish

Scope creeps

For those brave enough to chart their own path

YOU KNOW...

...that **brand storytelling is worldbuilding.** It takes the product's origin story and expands it into a rich, immersive universe that captivates and connects with audiences.

...that **brand storytelling creates an emotional bond.** It sparks word of mouth, builds loyalty, and adds value to a brand's story stock.

...that brand storytelling follows six key rules:

> 1. **Omission sparks the imagination.**
> 2. **Establish a right to play in the world.**
> 3. **Build a world with magic and rules.**
> 4. **Spur storymaking and fan fiction.**
> 5. **Ground reality with interwoven stories.**
> 6. **Escape the blandscape.**

...that **omission sparks the imagination.** It fills the mind's eye, leaves gaps, and invites your audience to complete the story, making the brand feel personal and immersive.

...that brands must earn **a right to play in the world.** This means aligning your brand's values and beliefs with those of your audience, which creates a foundation for trust, loyalty, and expansion.

...that building **a world with magic and rules** creates a cohesive brand narrative—one that stays consistent and makes the brand's universe immersive and believable.

...that spurring **storymaking and fan fiction** turns customers into active participants, storytellers in your brand narrative, deepening connection and amplifying word of mouth.

...that **grounding reality with interwoven stories** creates a tapestry of interconnected narratives that strengthen your brand's relatability, giving it depth and resonance.

...that **escaping the blandscape** means standing out in a crowded market with a unique voice, bold storytelling, and a willingness to take creative risks.

The giants of brand storytelling don't just stand out—they create waves. Every interaction fuels word of mouth, deepens consumer fandom, and adds value to their story stock.

You have a choice: Blend in to the noise, or build a brand story people can step inside. Tell it well, and you won't just attract customers—you'll turn them into believers.

08 SALES STORYTELLING

No, no! The adventures first, explanations take such a dreadful time.

— **LEWIS CARROLL**

We all sell stuff

A product isn't worth much if people don't buy it. A brand has no value if it doesn't sell. And *to sell*, as Dan Pink reminds us, *is human*.[1]

Sales, like storytelling, is both art and science. And we all sell stuff. Click the "abstract" button on any business strategy, and all of them—homegrown or McKinsey-certified—distill down to two words: *sell stuff*. What we sell may differ—cars, insurance, technology, money. How we sell may change—direct, etail, retail, B2B. But the *selling* and the *stuff* are constant. And the same forces animate every decision to buy: Hope, Fear, and Reason.

This holds true even in pure storytelling.

"Commerce is our goal here at Tyrell."

Those are the words of Dr. Eldon Tyrell to Harrison Ford's Deckard in *Blade Runner*. In his case, the stuff was replicants—bioengineered humans—sold to corporations, governments, and off-world colonies.

Even in a dystopian future, sales is a currency. Tyrell wasn't just selling units. He was selling the future. A vision. A necessity. The pitch wasn't about synthetic parts; it was about upgrading humanity.

The opposite of sales storytelling

Not all sales stories work that way. Some don't work at all.

Sales storytelling is personal. We're all selling stuff—whether it's a product manager trying to kickstart an internal project, an HR leader reporting to the board, or—more traditionally—a sales team wringing every last drop of revenue from a territory.

And here, we run into some barriers.

The first is what is sometimes known as the *dark funnel*—the part of the buyer's journey happening without the seller ever knowing. Prospective buyers research, compare, and frame their decisions—what to buy and who to buy from—without ever speaking to a seller.

They Google, they scroll, they ask around. Up to 70% of the buyer's journey is spent in the shadows.[2] By the time they reach out, they're not looking for options—they're looking for confirmation. The classic sales and marketing funnel is mostly invisible.

The second barrier is old: We all love to buy, but no one likes to be sold to.* The resistance lives in our heads. A host of psychological quirks kick in: reactance theory, confirmation bias, authority bias, scarcity mindset, and loss aversion.

Reactance theory explains our need for freedom of choice. Pressure triggers reactance—resistance to the sale. We dig in our heels, even if the product is exactly what we need. Confirmation bias

---

* Pretty sure I first heard this phrasing from author and podcaster Joseph Jaffe.

makes it worse. We filter out information that doesn't match what we already believe. If the pitch doesn't line up, we dismiss it without a second thought. Authority bias stacks the deck against the sales rep. We naturally put more trust in more senior figures—"let me speak to your boss"—anyone wearing the badge of expertise. A scarcity mindset plays on our FOMO, as seen in the power of a heavy-handed "limited time offer." Loss aversion doesn't trade in hope. It trades in fear.

70% of the buyer's journey is spent in the shadows

By the time they reach you, they already know the way.

The third barrier is the monologue.

As the Gryphon tells Alice in Wonderland, "No, no! The adventures first, explanations take such a dreadful time." We should apply that to sales—but we don't. The buyer—who is both audience and hero in sales storytelling—wants information on their terms, at their pace, in their order. That's why they live in the dark funnel. They don't want a lecture. They want an adventure.

Yet sales pitches are invariably presentations—narratives enshrined in PowerPoint by marketing departments. And PowerPoint is a monologue.

Conversations go in different directions; PowerPoint marches in a straight line. Selling is a nonlinear conversation between at least two people. Monologues are all tell; dialogues are give and take. That's the central difference between a sales *pitch* and sales *storytelling*.

In what could be a scene between seller and buyer, two animated superheroes from *The Incredibles*, Bob (Mr. Incredible) and Lucius (Frozone), are sitting in a parked car reminiscing, and they break down the monologuing trap:

> Lucius: So now I'm in deep trouble. I mean, one more jolt of this death ray and I'm an epitaph. Somehow I manage to find cover and what does Baron von Ruthless do?
>
> Bob: [*laughing*] He starts monologuing.
>
> Lucius: He starts monologuing! He starts like, this prepared speech about how *feeble* I am compared to him, how *inevitable* my defeat is, how *the world will soon be his*, yadda yadda yadda.
>
> Bob: Yammering.
>
> Lucius: Yammering! I mean, the guy has me on a platter and he won't shut up![3]

This is death by PowerPoint: a droning list of features, differentiators, and benefits captured by marketing, delivered by sales, and dumped on an unsuspecting audience.

Sales needs a story, but marketing made a deck. A carefully crafted, locked-down, 40-slide "narrative" for customers—maybe they even trained salespeople to deliver it, one slide at a time.

This is the opposite of sales storytelling.

Yet those same marketers howl in anguish when a salesperson skips the script, pulls out their three favorite slides, and tells a sales story.

I have a bridge to sell you

Bait and switch. Bunco. Con. False advertising. Flim-flam. Fraud. Grift. Hoax. Hustle. Peddle. Pyramid scheme. Racket. Rip-off. Scam. Shady. Shell game. Sleazy. Smoke and mirrors. Snake oil. Swindle.

Shades of sales.

Since antiquity, selling has ranked among the lowest of human achievements. Caveat emptor—literally, buyer beware—was enshrined in Roman law. It probably earned the odd mention in the *Acta Diurna*, in the classified section.

All why we love to buy, but mistrust being sold to.

The legend of George C. Parker reflects the dark side of sales, and is the origin story to the phrase "I have a bridge to sell you." Parker, the charming son of Irish immigrants, was born in New York in 1860. His entrepreneurial spirit intersected with good old-fashioned fraud.

The Brooklyn Bridge opened in 1883 as an engineering marvel, a towering symbol of New York and the new world. The span connected the two great cities of Manhattan and Brooklyn as a toll bridge.* Tens of thousands crossed every day—Parker's "prospects."

---

* A little-known fact, even to most New Yorkers: Today's boroughs of Brooklyn and Manhattan were separate cities before they were chartered together in 1898.

Brooklyn Bridge circa 1883

His scam was simple: Find wide-eyed marks—usually newly arrived immigrants—convince them he owned the bridge, and sell them a dream. A new life. A thriving business. A fortune made in tolls on the world's busiest thoroughfare.

The pitch worked. Over and over.

One sale netted Parker $5,000—nearly $180,000 today. He "sold" the bridge twice a week for years. The scam became so common that Ellis Island officials handed out cards warning: *You can't buy public buildings or streets.* [4]

A great sales story tells itself. Parker's did.

But before Parker ever flipped the bridge, someone had to sell it for real.

And it wasn't an easy deal.

The idea to span New York's East River had been floated 70 years earlier, but no one could quite make the case. The engineering wasn't there. The money wasn't there. The political will wasn't there.

Back then, getting from Manhattan to Brooklyn meant a ferry ride—a slow, occasionally hazardous trip at the mercy of tide, weather, and ice. Yet thousands made the daily crossing. It was a necessity.

But necessity alone doesn't close a deal. People had to believe in the bridge before they would back it.

Selling started early. Years before a single stone was laid, *The Brooklyn Daily Eagle* ran article after article shaping public opinion.[5] These were early stars in a narrative constellation—stories orbiting the big idea, designed to make the bridge feel inevitable. It would make Brooklyn important. It would make Brooklyn prosper. Property values would soar. Vacant lots and corn patches would turn to gold.[6]

The soft sell had begun.

John A. Roebling was the bridge's chief engineer, but to get the project greenlit, he had to be a storyteller. He had proof—the Niagara suspension bridge, plus spans in Cincinnati and Pittsburgh. But past success isn't always enough. Investors and politicians needed more than blueprints. They needed to see it.

To lock in final approvals and political goodwill, a tour was hatched.

A "bridge party" set out—Roebling, his son, Washington, along with investors, politicians, engineers, and business leaders.

They toured Roebling's past work: Pittsburgh, Cincinnati, Niagara Falls. Each stop a demonstration. A proof of concept. The message was clear: This wasn't just a bridge—it was a beginning.

The bridge party walked across Roebling's spans and saw the scale, the engineering, the reality. Seeing made believing easier. The tour tipped the scales. It reassured investors, shored up political support, and got the project off the ground.

Money followed. Approvals passed. The bridge had momentum.

Then, disaster.

John Roebling died before construction began. His son, Washington, took over—but was soon bedridden, a victim of caisson disease: decompression sickness brought on after overseeing the brutal construction of the bridge's wooden foundations.[*]

This could have been the end.

But the bridge had one last, unexpected salesperson: Washington's wife, Emily Roebling. She stepped in, not just as a liaison but as the driving force behind the project.

Emily managed contractors, negotiated with suppliers, and oversaw day-to-day operations. She relayed Washington's orders, ensured they were carried out, and handled politicians and VIPs who wanted tours and updates.

A self-taught engineer, Emily was a gifted communicator. She was charming, intelligent, and had a way of putting people at ease. She could talk with anyone—from laborers to politicians—and make them feel important, heard, and respected.

---

[*] Sounds scary. Yes, you read that right, the foundations of the Brooklyn Bridge are partly wooden—yellow pine timber sunk to the bottom of the East River to enable the building of the towers.

She bridged the gap between engineers, investors, and decision-makers. She kept the project moving, the skeptics on board, and the bridge alive.

Most stories about the span highlight John Roebling's engineering genius or Emily's tenacity. What they miss is that the bridge wasn't just built—it was sold, again, and again, and again.

In the Gilded Age, when industry soared and fortunes were made, Emily Roebling understood something essential: An idea alone isn't enough—you have to move people.

Stories do that. They paint a clear vision, create emotional connection, and move others to act. Like in modern sales, Emily's conversations stretched from idea to reality. Without her, the famed crossing between Manhattan and Brooklyn would not exist.

The six rules of sales storytelling

Sales stories are conversations.

Creating space for those conversations creates magic.

Kevin Zavaglia, chief sales officer of Verizon, shared a story from his first quarter in that job. To turn around flagging numbers, he questioned a long-standing assumption: that shorter, more efficient in-store time was always better.

For years, Verizon had pursued operational efficiency—reducing wait times, streamlining service. But that approach missed a precious opportunity: the chance to talk. To connect. To hear the customer's story.

When upgrading phones, a customer wants everything—their apps, pictures, contacts, music—set up just so. Just so—meaning exactly as it was on their old phone.

Verizon calls this service *Setup and Go*. It takes about an hour.

"You are side by side with them," Zavaglia explained. As the rep works with the customer to switch from old phone to new, it's a natural—and unscripted—opportunity for conversations and questions.

> Find out who they are, instead of telling them what we can do....It's a good experience, as long as it's not overkill. We've given reps the freedom to talk about what customers use—and connect. I don't think scripts work. Give them bullets. It's the secondary questions that are important.[7]

The result? Rep interaction scores are through the roof. Accessory take rate is up. Add-a-line is up. Verizon is selling more—all from conversations, and giving salespeople the agency and incentive to have them.

Conversations crush monotonous monologue. Beyond them lie sales stories—bridges that create value, concepts that rise from a tide of ideas, pitches that turn into products. Have enough of them, consistently enough, and you describe a world. You build a fabled brand.

We all have conversations. We all sell. Whether it's convincing your spouse that a new TV is a must-have, pitching a project or an idea to your boss, or in fact trying to sell a bridge to someone, you are selling. But do you sell well? Can you take an idea and insert it into the fortified citadel of another mind?

Crossing the treacherous span between *where someone is* and *where we want them to go* requires *sales storytelling*: a series of conversations that frame the way people see the world and move them to action. In that span, six rules come into view:

1. **Tell tales that tell themselves.**

2. **Paint pictures with words, and use pictures.**

3. **Be a puller of stories, not just a teller.**

4. **Collect a library of love stories and horror stories.**

5. **Remember, Grandma is not a rocket scientist.**

6. **Build a bridge to a better future.**

Most stories of the Brooklyn Bridge celebrate the building of a modern marvel. They dramatize construction more than sale. But without the sale, there would be no bridge.

We don't speak of the conversations that lifted the bridge from idea to blueprint; from drawings to foundation; from pine, concrete, and steel wire to engineering masterpiece. Yet those conversations happened a thousand times.

The concept was a tale that told itself—a bridge uniting two boomtowns, promising economic growth. Evocative language described the work: "an enduring monument," and "the greatest bridge in existence." Drawings painted a picture of what the bridge would be.

Emily Roebling, in particular, knew how to connect. She pulled politicians, businesspeople, and engineers into the scheme. For every horror story of loss of life or cost overrun, a host of love stories propelled the project forward. All to usher in a new era—told in ways that entranced specialists and laypeople alike.

In all walks of life and all businesses, sales storytelling builds a bridge to a better future for our hero—the audience.

The worst idea I've ever heard of

"I'll just Uber to my Airbnb."

A sentence that made no sense 20 years ago now defines today's $335 billion sharing economy.

In 2007, two broke industrial designers, Joe Gebbia and Brian Chesky, had an idea—blow up air mattresses in their apartment and rent the space as a bed-and-breakfast. A design conference was packing San Francisco hotels, and they figured attendees might pay for a cheap crash pad. They called it, straightforwardly, "AirBed and Breakfast."

They thought they were onto something. No one else did.

Chesky floated the idea to a well-known designer, who replied: "I hope that's not the only thing you're working on."[8] His mother was harsher. When he said, "I'm an entrepreneur," she shot back, "No. You're unemployed."

Still, they kept going.

Chesky and Gebbia targeted SXSW, figuring the conference would love it. Almost no one booked. Their new tactic: "Just keep launching." Their new tagline: "Forget Hotels." Next stop: the 2008 Democratic National Convention in Denver.

This time, the press bit. "AirBed and Breakfast Takes Pad Crashing to a Whole New Level," declared *TechCrunch*.[9] Traffic surged. The website crashed. Eight hundred people listed rooms. Eighty guests booked. Then: flatline. After the DNC, the lights went out. Airbnb needed what it couldn't have—a political convention every week.

Typical of the sharing economy, Airbnb is a two-sided market with a two-sided problem—double the selling. It needs both rentees (people looking for a place to stay) and renters (micro-landlords to accommodate them).

And Airbnb was difficult to explain. The bizarro idea of opening your home for rent to a stranger was a tough sell, made doubly so by supply. No one wanted to list their home if no one was booking.

A weird, socially awkward Catch-22.

Running out of money, they got desperate, paying their bills by selling leftover Obama O's—repackaged Cheerios from a DNC marketing stunt.

It also saved their bacon at a crucial investor meeting. The pitch had bombed—until they mentioned surviving off over-priced breakfast. Paul Graham, Y Combinator's co-founder, sat back and laughed. "Wow. You guys are like cockroaches. You just won't die."

He funded them on the spot.

Graham wanted them "ramen profitable"—making just enough to eat. His advice: "Go to New York! *Go to your users.*"[10] They did. Door to door, they met hosts and found what to fix. No one knew how to price their homes. Listings had terrible photos.

Chesky, Gebbia, and team refined their platform.

Then came a stroke of luck. Greg McAdoo of Sequoia Capital asked, "What do you know about the $40 billion vacation rental industry?" Their answer? Not much.

Two ideas collided: "Bed" met "breakfast," and now "vacation" met "rental." A spark.

Sequoia invested. A unicorn was born.

The next few years were a roller coaster—with highs and lows, love stories, and horror stories:

> July 2010: "NSFW: Sorry AirBnB Hipsters, I'll Take Health and Safety Over the Cult of Disruption."

> Jan 2011: "Airbnb Tucked in Nearly 800% Growth in 2010."

> April 2011: "You Can Now Rent Entire Villages on Airbnb. Oh, and an Entire Country Too!"

> July 2011: "The Moment of Truth for Airbnb As User's Home Is Utterly Trashed."[11]

Those early trials forged Airbnb.

Chesky and company prioritized. The product had to improve. The brand had to grow. The marketplace had to scale. And to pay for it all, they had to sell.

They were selling a movement.

A world where anyone could belong anywhere. Hosts weren't just renting space—they were creating experiences. Guests weren't just booking rooms—they were stepping into someone else's life. Chesky and Co. sold to builders, buyers, and backers.

To the Airbnbers—employees and hosts who would scale the company—they sold the mission. *Be a cereal entrepreneur. Champion the cause. Be a host. Embrace the adventure.*

These weren't just values; they were Airbnb's collective DNA.[12]

To the buyers, they sold love stories—honeymooners in a Paris loft, backpackers couch-surfing their way across the world. And they sold horror stories—soulless hotels, overpriced minibars, bad service, sterile rooms that all looked the same.

The backers bought resilience. Setbacks and pivots weren't obstacles, they were the story.

Revenue soared to $4.8 billion by 2019. Then, the pandemic. Travel collapsed. Bookings plummeted. Airbnb laid off a quarter of its workforce.

And months later, Airbnb went public at a $100 billion valuation.[13]

Tell tales that tell themselves

Sales stories must be repeated—and not just by salespeople.

Everyone sells. To sell is human. We know buyers don't like to be sold to and spend much of their time in a dark funnel beyond a salesperson's reach.

So the work of selling falls to something else: a narrative constellation of self-repeating stories. These are sales stories: *tales that tell themselves*. This is social proof, activated—not just the act of someone buying, but word of mouth snowballing.

That story becomes common ground. Everybody knows what Ferrari means. It signals wealth, privilege, maybe a passion for racing. It's understood that if you buy Slack, your business is (or wants to be) modern, agile, collaborative—a workplace that sprints. The IKEA story? Thrift and style. You value Scandinavian design and stylish living.

Tell tales that tell themselves

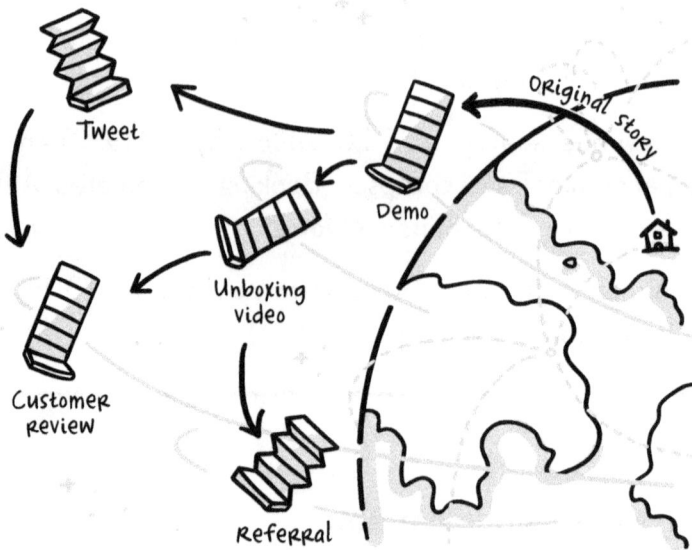

And for every constellation of positive stories, there are counters-narratives: a midlife crisis, an email system we don't need, and cardboard furniture.

The power of self-repeating stories lies in their ability to tap into human cognition and social behavior. Telling tales that tell themselves means creating—and curating—stories so compelling and memorable they spread organically. They carry your message. They fuel word of mouth. This is how you break the dark funnel.

For marketers and sales teams, that means looking for stories that are easy to understand, easy to remember, and easy to repeat. Not an easy task. The goal is to minimize mental effort. The curator—you—faces a two-story barrier: You know too much and are too passionate about it. The solution is to strip a story down to its essence. Then strip it again.

For a story to spread, it must trigger emotion—either hope or fear. You know a story is contagious when hope—or her henchmen: optimism, excitement, anticipation, inspiration, and joy—shows up. Better yet, hope laced with a trace of fear. A whisper of anxiety. A flicker of doubt. A flash of panic.

The story needs a trigger. Selling cybersecurity, it's a failed red team exercise or a competitor hit by ransomware. Triggers are usually part of something bigger, a shift in technology, industry regulation, or business trends. Think of Slack and the agile movement—where one fueled the other.

Concrete details help contagion. The more abstract a story is, the more difficult it is to grasp. Roebling knew this when selling the Brooklyn Bridge—he made it real by pointing to his past work. That's why almost every modern sale includes a demo.

Word of mouth is built into the sharing economy. Customer reviews and five-star ratings are fodder for any market.

Great sales stories don't just sell—they echo. Tell, repeat, resell. If your story isn't being told without you, it isn't selling.

Paint pictures with words, and use pictures

John Roebling, in presentations and proposals, described the Brooklyn Bridge before it existed. He spoke of its majestic stone arches, steel cables stretched taut like sinews, the prodigious span it would support. He *painted a picture* of a future where travel and trade would flourish.

And he didn't stop at words. Sketches, models, blueprints, and site visits—especially to the newly constructed Cincinnati-Covington Bridge—brought his vision to life.

Pictures work. They make the abstract concrete. They pull people into a story. Maps give a sense of place and direction, anchoring narrative. Demos show what could be. Whiteboarding sparks a free-flowing, participatory dialogue—a canvas for ideas, collaboration, and creativity.

Visuals capture what words miss—nuances, subtleties, emotion. They connect dots. Unlike words, illustrations are nonlinear; you see the whole and the parts at once. A gestalt. First the complete picture, then the intricacies within.

When we use language, we tap into specialized regions of our brain. Broca's area forms words and sentences. Wernicke's area deciphers meaning.

Visual language goes further.

Vivid, visceral metaphors pull an audience in. They feed the mind's eye, making stories more engaging, more memorable—evoking sight, sound, smell, touch, and taste. Words with strong associations light up multiple parts of the brain. Read "coffee" and your olfactory cortex—the part managing smell—wakes up.

Metaphors, like "the singer had a velvet voice" or "he had leathery hands," rouse the sensory cortex. Motion-related language activates the motor cortex—when you read "Pablo kicked the ball," the part of your brain controlling your leg fires, as if preparing to kick.[14]

Immersive experiences like these are crucial to sales storytelling.

They are everywhere. Explainer videos fuse words and pictures together—Slack uses them masterfully. Ferrari, like most car companies, leans on imagery to sell sensation.

Paint pictures with words, and use pictures

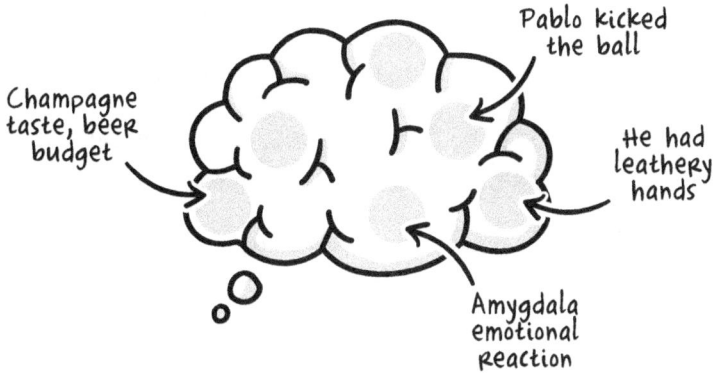

Champagne taste, beer budget

Pablo kicked the ball

He had leathery hands

Amygdala emotional reaction

Some brands push our senses further.

Mastercard is a prime example. CMO Raja Rajamannar champions multisensory storytelling, explaining:

> A normal human being is blessed with five senses. Each sense is a mechanism by which information goes into the individual's brain. They process it, and then they think, feel, act or do something with it.

Mastercard's logo was refashioned, becoming more symbolic by losing the name and subtly repositioning the iconic red and orange circles. In half a dozen Mastercard experience restaurants, those circles reappear as macarons and cocktails. Scent is activated through two fragrances, Priceless Passion and Priceless Optimism, their red and orange perfume bottles evoking the brand. Touch matters too, with cards featuring distinctive notches to help people with visual impairments distinguish between payment types.[15]

Captivating the mind's eye sells.

Airbnb learned this the hard way. Early on, they realized hosts took bad photos. What looked charming in person often appeared drab on the app. At first, the founders rented a wide-angle camera and staged the listings themselves. That experiment turned into a full-blown photography program. Professionally photographed homes generated two to three times as many bookings.

Words followed pictures. Airbnb encouraged vivid descriptions, which helped guests picture themselves in the space.

Remember, in sales storytelling: Show it, stage it, sell it. If they can't see it, they won't buy it.

Be a puller of stories, not just a teller

Sarabeth Stine is a sales leader at T-Mobile. She's led sales teams at Zoom, Trinet, and Verizon. In her view, the best sales storytellers "paint a picture of what could be." To do that, she believes, you have to relate. You have to be authentic. The key is what she calls relationship stories:

> The dad jokes, the show you're binge-watching, or talking about your dog. This loosens the conversation—then asking the right questions helps customers *reveal their own stories*.[16]

These questions uncover needs, desires, fears, and aspirations.

Getting the customer to talk, in Stine's mind, is one of the best things that can happen. This allows a sales storyteller to adapt what they're selling to the person in front of them. The Roeblings did this—Emily best of all. With politicians and business leaders, they knew: Before addressing concerns, before highlighting the bridge's impact, before they could tell their story, they had to pull someone else's.

Kevin Zavaglia, Verizon's chief sales officer, is more specific:

A lot of times salespeople, they over-talk. You often hear selling past the close—it's not even that. Salespeople come in and want to tell you everything they know. But I want customers to tell them everything they care about, and the only way you can do that is by hearing what their needs are.[17]

This is the art of the sales storyteller.

Be a puller of stories, not just a teller

The right questions light the way for someone else's story to unfold.

In his book *Supercommunicators*, Charles Duhigg singles out those who "click" with others more than most. They have learning conversations—where trust and understanding are natural byproducts. Supercommunicators *pull personal stories.* They ask open-ended questions and listen deeply. "What's the best part of your job?" or "If you could wave a magic wand, what would you fix?" They display what Duhigg calls *emotional reciprocity*: "showing others we hear their emotions, which helps us reciprocate." They do this by *looping*—asking open questions, distilling responses in their own words, and working hard to see the other person's perspective.

Sales storytelling as a conversation. A two-way exchange.

Listening and interaction construct the narrative. Sales story-tellers listen beyond words—picking up tone, gestures, and body language. This not only builds deeper relationships, it reveals how your solution fits someone's specific needs.

It's listening for the wish.*

Sales storytellers pull stories; they don't just tell them. Like a character from *Rumpelstiltskin*, they spin this straw into gold. Threading buyer cues into a story that sells.

To thrive as a sales storyteller, invite your audience in. Make it a shared story. Seek their perspective. Listen closely. Weave in their needs, their words, their ideas.

Collect a library of love stories and horror stories

A global services giant (which shall go unnamed) with a centuries-old history was facing a critical problem—a legacy platform built on outdated FoxPro and old Mac tools. Untouched since the 1980s, the system supported a multimillion-dollar business line but demanded constant maintenance.

No one could justify the expense of replacing it. The proverbial can kept being kicked down the road. Then came a radical idea: "Let's crash the system!"—deliberate self-harm as a strategic move. Not literally, but narratively: the horror story of "what if"—the catastrophe of impacted customers, lost revenue, and the

---

* Pretty sure I picked up this gem of "listening for the wish" from Karl Turnbull when he ran strategic planning at DraftFCB.

time needed to recover—spun neatly to the board. And the board, instead of kicking the can, picked it up and invested.

Fear sells. So does hope. The best sales storytellers keep both in their back pocket.

Supercommunicators build rapport by trading stories. Sales storytellers have a *library of love stories and horror stories* to share. Love stories showcase customers who have benefited. Horror stories warn of the risk of *not* buying.

Collect a library of love stories and horror stories

In selling the Brooklyn Bridge, love stories were everywhere: increased commerce, thousands of jobs created, ease of passage for Brooklynders and New Yorkers, and a monument to a new world.[*]

---

[*] **Brooklynders:** the old term for Brooklynites. Manhattanites were called New Yorkers, since it was New York before 1898. In sales storytelling, you want to try and get people's names right.

Every newspaper report of harsh weather, accidents, or delays in ferry crossings would serve as a horror story, pushing the project forward.

Love stories and horror stories are best told as anecdotes. They illustrate hope and fear—giving salespeople a way to shape the conversations and spark emotional connection.

Manoj Nair, chief innovation officer at Snyk, knows this well. A veteran of Silicon Valley, tech startups, and the security industry, he told me of love and horror stories from his time as GM of the data-protection platform Metallic.

The love story:

> Hope you enjoyed that burger on the 4th of July. You almost didn't get one. One of the largest meat-packing companies in the US was crippled by a ransomware attack weeks before. Luckily, they used our software—and were back up in hours.

This contrasted sharply with the horror story:

> Remember the Colonial Pipeline ransomware attack? Desperate drivers hoarding fuel in plastic bags? Gas prices spiking and panic at the pumps? Operations down for a week? They couldn't respond quickly enough.

Unsaid but clear—Colonial Pipeline did not use Nair's software.

Love stories prove what you're selling works. Horror stories prove it's needed. Your job is to collect them and deploy them.

Remember, Grandma is not a rocket scientist

Perhaps the greatest barrier businesspeople have in storytelling is that, to requote Brian Fugere, *they speak like idiots*. To put it kindly, it's a knee-jerk need to obfuscate with grandiloquent discourse bury meaning under jargon and corporate pig latin, acronyms, and terms of art.

There is a simple explanation—expertise.

When selling, in business and not, we have an instinct to prove our aptitude and so establish authority. We operate under the assumption that credibility wins trust. That acumen is attractive. Proficiency is persuasive. It's a confidence play, a way to fit in and stand out, to be part of the club but also a leader. So, we speak like idiots.

This goes against the timeless wisdom of our grandmothers—insights gained through years of experience, distilled into savvy truths, and passed down through generations. Grandma reminds us: Keep it simple, free of jargon, and grounded in clarity. Our grandmas teach us to value common sense, trust our instincts, and prioritize the practical over the abstract.

This is a paradox that sales storytellers master. They are adept at modifying their story to suit any audience, whether a roomful of experts or an outsider. They simplify without dumbing down. They add depth without losing clarity. The story is always relevant and resonant.

My favorite examples are some lines from Commvault CEO Sanjay Mirchandani, as he remembers that *Grandma is not a rocket scientist*—even when he is speaking to a room full of them.

He uses the complex language of his world—SAAS, containerization, virtual machines, and so on—but carefully adds verbal seasoning. When presenting a list of customers, he might say, "I call this our family portrait"—a clever mix of grandma language and credibility language.

In speaking about the increasing prevalence of ransomware attacks, he might say, "This is a new vector for the bad guys." He does not say, "This is a new vector for bad actors." If he did, he would have spoken in the terms of art—the credibility language—of the security industry. Neither does he say, "This is a new way in for the bad guys." If he had, he would have spoken *only* in grandma language.

Instead, he mixes them together, balancing expertise with relatability.

Remember, Grandma is not a rocket scientist

A new vector for the bad guys.

TERMS OF ART
say "I belong"

GRANDMA LANGUAGE
makes it relatable

Airbnb struggled early on because it was hard to explain. But focusing the story on easily memorable taglines and simple themes helped its story spread. Today, Airbnb's platform is built for everyone—from tech-savvy millennials to older generations. The booking process is simple. Listings are clear. Support is there when needed.

The grandma–rocket scientist rule in sales storytelling is about knowing your audience and flexing your narrative, keeping it accessible, engaging, and impossible to ignore.

Build a bridge to a better future

When selling the Brooklyn Bridge, the Roeblings sold progress, growth, and a brighter, better future. The bridge symbolized a new tomorrow, with improved connectivity and economic opportunity. Literally and figuratively, they *built a bridge to a better future*. So, too, did conman George C. Parker. For good or bad, people buy a better version of themselves, a better tomorrow. They buy hope and run from fear.

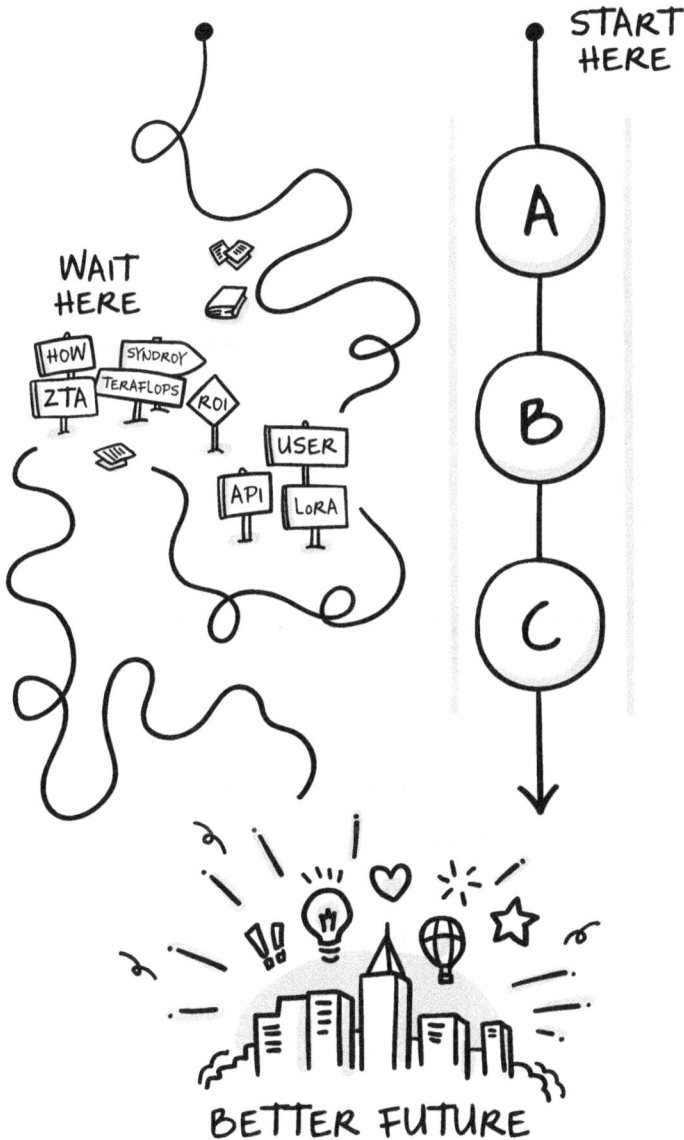

Build a bridge to a better future

START HERE

A

B

C

WAIT HERE

HOW ZTA SYNDROY TERAFLOPS ROI USER API LoRA

BETTER FUTURE

This last rule of sales storytelling is about stories that connect dots from where the buyer *is* to where they *want to go*. It weaves in "what's in the bag" (what you're selling), and "what's in it for me" (the buyer's unmet needs and secret wishes). Most importantly, it's a bridge, not a mountain—an easy crossing, not a treacherous traverse of ice falls, chasms, and crevasses.

The sales storyteller makes the path clear. Again, simplicity is key. It's how you can be up and running tomorrow, not how many hoops you must go through.

The idea of a better future has expanded Airbnb's horizons. In 2024, it launched Airbnb Icons. A next-level leap from "cute cottage" to "once in a lifetime." Icons offers extraordinary experiences: drifting off in a re-creation of the floating house from Pixar's movie *Up*, suspended from a crane in the New Mexico desert; sleeping inside the Museo Ferrari in Maranello, hosted by ex-Formula 1 racing driver Marc Gené; or spending the night in Ted Lasso's favorite pub, pint in hand. These bucket list experiences are unlocked through a Willy Wonka–like golden ticket—a better future on steroids.

Airbnb isn't just selling the destination—it's improving the bridge. It continuously upgrades the website and app for seamless booking. It launched AirCover—a comprehensive protection program with booking guarantees, 24-hour safety support, and verified Wi-Fi quality. Now listings use generative AI to summarize guest reviews, making them clearer and more accessible.

Narratives—sales stories—should guide from now to next, illustrating a path laden with possibilities. They show how every step forward is a step toward becoming, turning aspiration into achievement.

YOU KNOW...

...that **sales storytelling is personal.** We're all selling stuff, whether it's a product, a project, or an idea. To sell is human, and stories are the most powerful tool we have.

...that **the best sales stories are conversations, not monologues.** They involve listening, asking questions, and adapting the narrative to the audience's needs and desires.

...that effective sales storytelling follows six key rules:

1. **Tell tales that tell themselves.**

2. **Paint pictures with words, and use pictures.**

3. **Be a puller of stories, not just a teller.**

4. **Collect a library of love stories and horror stories.**

5. **Remember, Grandma is not a rocket scientist.**

6. **Build a bridge to a better future.**

...that the best sales stories **tell themselves.** They are simple, repeatable, emotionally resonant, and spread organically, breaking through the dark funnel.

...that **painting pictures with words** and visuals makes what you're selling stand out. Vivid descriptions and images bring ideas to life, making abstract concepts concrete and memorable.

...that sales storytellers are adept at **getting others to tell their stories.** They listen for cues and weave them into the story of what they're selling, spinning straw into gold.

...that a library of **love stories and horror stories** is a sales storyteller's secret weapon. These anecdotes illustrate hope and fear, allowing you to tailor your conversations and emotionally appeal to decision-makers.

...that speaking like **a grandmother, not a rocket scientist,** is key to sales storytelling. It's about finding the right balance of credibility and relatability, simplifying without diluting the message.

...that the ultimate goal of sales storytelling is to **build a bridge to a better future.** It's about connecting the dots from where the buyer is now to where they want to go, showing how your solution is the path forward.

These principles aren't just for salespeople—they're for all of us. We all sell.

Sales storytelling isn't merely a technique—it's a competitive edge. Use it well, and you won't just sell, you'll influence, persuade, and change minds.

09
LEADERSHIP STORYTELLING

Either write something worth reading
or do something worth writing.
—BENJAMIN FRANKLIN

To do

Look up the word *leadership*, and you'll quickly run into *inspire*. Dig into *inspire*, and you'll find it's getting people to want to do something. All of that is captured perfectly by Dwight D. Eisenhower:

> Leadership is the art of getting *someone else* to do something you want done because they want to do it.

It's the people—the *someone else*—who connect sales storytelling, brand storytelling, and product storytelling. Sales storytelling falls flat without them. Brand storytelling, without people, is just expensive ad spend. Product storytelling, minus people, is just an idea rattling round your head.

You can't engineer people. You have to *lead* them—and there lies the conundrum. People like to be led—*sometimes*. They want direction, but crave autonomy. They value clear instruction, but love making up their own minds. They want someone to take the risk, but they're just not sure they can trust anyone else to do it. Leadership is both an art and a practice—sometimes subtle and nuanced, sometimes loud and in your face.

Ultimately, leadership is about choice.

It's a personal choice to rise to the occasion and lead. It's everyone else's choice to follow. It's a choice to step up or step back, to go left, right, or straight ahead. It's a choice to control or to delegate. To speak or stay silent. To do—or to do nothing.

Whatever you choose as a leader, storytelling amplifies that choice.

You say you want a revolution

Now recognized as a founding father, gracing the back of $100 bills, we know Benjamin Franklin as a scientist, diplomat, and writer; lesser known is Franklin the entrepreneur and business leader.

Pre-revolution, he was a man of the British Empire—an Englishman among Newton's thinkers and tinkerers at the Royal Society. But Franklin wasn't just a man of invention—he was a man of action. As a leader, he guided businesses, movements, and nations—not through authority, but through storytelling.

His legacy built on his ability to package ideas.

The tenth son of a Boston candlemaker, Franklin was largely self-taught. At 12, he was indentured to his brother's print shop.* By 17, he'd had enough and fled to Philadelphia. There, he plied his trade.

Franklin was affable. A natural networker.

Philadelphia was a boomtown—the colonies' political, economic, and intellectual hub. Its swelling population, new schools, and

---

* An indentured apprenticeship was a legally binding agreement between servant and master—essentially pre-selling labor in exchange for training. For Franklin, it was to last until he reached his majority, at 21.

thriving commerce made it a magnet for innovation, much like Silicon Valley during the dot-com boom 250 years later.

But Franklin wanted more. He set sail for England.

In London, Franklin honed his craft, mastering the latest technological advancements in printing before bringing them back to Philadelphia.

Back home, he took a job working for Samuel Keimer.

Keimer taught a master class in mismanagement. It became Franklin's classroom, and his first real test of leadership. He organized, trained, and stabilized a failing business, then walked away to build his own.

At the same time, Franklin founded his first movement: the Junto—a circle of tradesmen and thinkers debating ideas, building businesses, and kickstarting civic projects. For Franklin, it was a launchpad.

He soon took over the *Pennsylvania Gazette*, turning it into a hub of debate, satire, and influence. His business empire grew—stationery shops, printing innovations, and colonial partnerships. And when Pennsylvania introduced paper currency, Franklin, its most vocal advocate, landed the contract to print it.

Drop Franklin's business beginnings into today's world, and you might call him a new media tycoon—an entrepreneur who built a brand, invested in emerging tech, and pioneered new ways of working. He reimagined a business model to create cross-promotion, content syndication, and cross-media marketing. The 18th-century equivalent of a Musk, Zuckerberg, or Bezos.

Franklin ran his life like a startup—lean, disciplined, and built for growth. His *Thirteen Virtues* were a personal operating system. Some feel old-fashioned (Temperance, Chastity), but others read like a leadership manual:

Order—Prioritize what matters.

Resolution—Do what you say.

Frugality—Spend wisely.

Industry—Work with purpose.

Sincerity—Lead with integrity.

He didn't just list them, he tracked them, improving one each week. A productivity hack, 18th-century style.

Franklin applied the same thinking to *Poor Richard's Almanack*—another piece of his media empire. Part calendar, part wisdom, part entertainment, it became one of the most popular publications in colonial America. *Poor Richard's* offered weather predictions, astronomical data, and practical advice—often in the form of aphorisms that reflected Franklin's personal code for life and work:

"Little strokes fell great oaks."

"He that lies down with dogs, shall rise up with fleas."

"Be slow in choosing a friend, slower in changing."

Franklin understood the language of influence and used it to propel his rise.

By 1736, his stature in Philadelphia led to his election as clerk of the Pennsylvania Assembly. At 31, Franklin made a power move—he was appointed Philadelphia's postmaster. That meant controlling the mail. And controlling the mail meant getting his *Gazette* into more hands, faster. His reach grew. His influence spread.

By 42, Franklin was a wealthy man. He sold his business and turned his attention to building institutions—founding the Academy of

Philadelphia (later the University of Pennsylvania) and Pennsylvania Hospital, the first in the colonies.

Franklin built for the future.

A trip to Boston in 1748 sparked his obsession with electricity. He experimented relentlessly—testing static charges, designing devices, even zapping turkeys. His most famous experiment involved a kite and a key, proving the lightning in the sky and the sparks in his lab were the same.

He published his findings in *Experiments and Observations on Electricity* and sent them to London. The Royal Society awarded him the Copley Medal—its highest honor. Franklin the scientist. Franklin the global figure.

His story as a founding father is well known; his part in the American revolution is history. When he died in 1790 at 84, he left $2,000 each to Boston and Philadelphia, with instructions to invest it for 200 years. By the time the funds were finally distributed, they had grown to $4.5 million.

Benjamin Franklin told a story that kept working long after he was gone. Because leadership is a choice—and storytelling ensures those choices endure.

The six rules of leadership storytelling

Leadership storytelling is shared context.

Stories pass the creative spark between people. They share knowledge and wisdom. They whisper advice. Shared context connects people and ideas. At scale, it creates movements—even revolutions. Ben Franklin—writer, businessman, scientist, inventor, diplomat, and founding father—told stories. In many ways, storytelling was his path to wealth—and his ultimate legacy.

Leadership storytellers—Bezos, Buffett, Nadella—know that leadership isn't just about decisions; it's about the stories that make those decisions stick.*

What Franklin knew—what every leader should know—is this: Storytelling isn't optional. Without stories, leaders lose people. Connection evaporates. Authority and empathy drift apart. Engagement fades. Trust erodes. There is no team. Vision and values become isolated, misunderstood, left unspoken. Change—the currency of leadership—stalls.

Leaders tell stories of value. They tell product stories, sales stories, and brand stories. They shape culture. These stories communicate vision and purpose: *Where are we going, and why?* They communicate self and place: *Who are we, and what do I do?* They communicate reality: *How are we doing, and how do we make money?*

To lead is to choose. To tell stories is to amplify that choice.

Leadership storytelling follows a pattern—timeless principles that form movements, shift perspectives, and turn ideas into reality. These six rules hold true across generations:

1. **Truthtelling, not fabletelling.**
2. **Question the future.**
3. **Preach practical wisdom and simple rules.**
4. **Create a movement.**
5. **Connect people and dots.**
6. **Lead change.**

These are rules leaders live by—just as Franklin did.

---

* You may quibble with my list. Some charismatic leaders are polarizing. I could have chosen others—Obama, Trump, Zelenskyy—who are even more so. What's true of all of them is this: 1) they have a following, and 2) they are, each in their own way, great communicators.

When George Washington wintered at Valley Forge, Franklin offered the great general a blunt truth: Balance strict order with humane treatment. Franklin's life reflected these principles: leading change in calling for the abolition of slavery, bringing people together through the Junto, and fomenting revolution. He was a master of proverbial wisdom. "A penny saved is a penny earned" became a cornerstone of capitalism.

These rules of leadership storytelling, modeled by Franklin, apply everywhere—but especially in business.

The code whisperer

On a clear day in Seattle in April 2019, Microsoft hit a $1 trillion valuation. Two years later, it doubled. By 2024, it broke $3 trillion, locked in a horse race with its old nemesis, Apple, for the title of world's most valuable company.

Numbers tell part of the story. The rest is narrative. And shaping that narrative is Microsoft's CEO—Satya Nadella.

When Nadella took over in 2014, Microsoft was reeling from a series of missteps. It had fumbled mobile, lost the browser wars, and watched its products become punchlines—Zune, anyone? Anyone?

His predecessor, Steve Ballmer, was a sales-driven bulldozer—aggressive, short-term focused, competitive. Nadella was a product guy. He saw Microsoft's challenge not just as a business problem, but as a story problem.

He set out to rewrite that story—starting with a little *truthtelling*.

Nadella's first move as a CEO was to own the past. In an open email to all employees, he acknowledged what many already knew: that Microsoft had "missed the mobile revolution." The PC era was over. He stood before assembled Microsofties with a stark truth:

> Our industry does not respect tradition. What it respects is innovation.[1]

The message was clear: Microsoft couldn't rely on its history. It had to *question the future*.

Nadella is a man full of questions. A lifelong learner, he admits:

> I buy more books than I can finish. I sign up for more online courses than I can complete. I fundamentally believe that if you are not learning new things, you stop doing great and useful things.[2]

To Nadella, learning isn't a hobby—it's a habit. Leadership isn't about having all the answers; it's about asking the right questions.

The future, Nadella reasoned, would be "mobile-first and cloud-first." Not device-first or phone-first. It's a phrase he has since repeated thousands of times. Words matter.

Like all leaders, Nadella distills his experience into *practical wisdom*:

"Make it happen. You have full authority." A mantra for speed, cutting through bureaucracy.[3] "The best code is poetry." A standard for simplicity, software, and creativity.[4]

But culture, more than code, defines his legacy.

A few years before becoming CEO, Nadella had picked up *Mindset* by Stanford psychologist Carol Dweck. The book outlines the concept of a growth mindset, a belief that ability and intelligence can be developed through dedication, hard work, and learning. In contrast, a fixed mindset assumes talent is static and unchangeable. The idea stuck. Nadella later told *The Wall Street Journal*:

> We know how that story ends. The learn-it-all does better than the know-it-all.[5]

That belief sparked *a movement*—to shift Microsoft from a culture of know-it-alls to a culture of learn-it-alls. His ambition: to create an environment where everyone could bring their A game.

This shift *connected people and dots*, swapping internal competition for collaboration. Microsoft had long been divided—teams hoarding information, engineers working in silos. Under Ballmer, it had aggressively fought open-source software. Ballmer had called Linux "a cancer."

Nadella flipped the script. At a press event in 2014, he declared, "Microsoft loves Linux."[6]

It wasn't just words. Microsoft joined the Linux Foundation in 2016, acquired GitHub in 2018, and embraced open-source development.

Nadella's tenure has been one of *leading change*.

His leadership philosophy is formed by his first love—cricket. In his book *Hit Refresh*, Nadella shares lessons drawn from the game he grew up with:

> Compete with passion in the face of uncertainty.

> Put your team first, ahead of personal recognition.
>
> Rally the team around those choices.[7]
>
> That final lesson—make choices, then rally the team around them—is the ultimate remix of leadership and storytelling. Through it, Nadella laid the groundwork for Microsoft to become a trillion-dollar company. He embraced open-source, guided market perception, and led in the cloud—fueled by a learn-it-all culture. Now Nadella faces his next test—to ride the next wave of Microsoft's value story—the AI revolution.

Truthtelling, not fabletelling

In the 1758 edition of *Poor Richard's Almanack*, Ben Franklin wrote, "Half a truth is often a great lie." A half-truth can break trust spectacularly. At Theranos, Elizabeth Holmes told the world, "We're building an early detection system." She told truth and lie. That Theranos was building such a system? True. That it worked? A lie.

Fabletelling isn't just an outright lie or half-truths, both of which break trust; it's a fundamental lack of authenticity. Fogging messages with corporatese. I have sat in senior executive meetings where item one on the agenda covered staff cuts and cost controls. Travel would be severely restricted. Economy class, no exceptions. Item two? The purchase of a new corporate jet. Irony, anyone?

Authentic storytelling builds trust.

Leadership depends on trust—the belief that you are as good as your word. Trust depends on honesty and transparency. But trust itself is abstract—forged one relationship, one conversation, at a time. Clarity, candor, and consistency earn trust. Care, credibility, and capability keep it.

Former Verizon executive and CEO Tami Erwin is a truthteller, known for both care and candor in her communication style. Now serving on multiple boards, she sees integrity as the defining factor in communication. She points to Apple CEO Tim Cook as an example:

> I think Tim Cook is very measured as to what—and when—he tells the world. When you talk about a CEO who's a truth teller, Tim Cook, I believe is a truth teller.

Careful honesty matters. According to Erwin, truthtelling is a duty. Narrative and numbers must "tick and tie."

> You can't just tell a story. If you don't understand the fundamentals of your business, you haven't earned the right to tell an imaginative story—and you mislead your stakeholders.[8]

Satya Nadella, she believes, is another truthteller—known for his concrete, direct style and refusal to hide behind corporate doublespeak.

In early 2023, as tech companies slashed jobs, Microsoft cut 10,000 employees. Nadella didn't deflect. He was candid:

> These are the kinds of hard choices we have made throughout our 47-year history to remain a consequential company in this industry that is unforgiving to anyone who doesn't adapt to platform shifts.

He stayed consistent with earlier messages—Microsoft had adapted before and must adapt again. He didn't shift blame. He didn't sugarcoat. He told the truth:

> Today, we are making changes that will result in the reduction of our overall workforce by 10,000 jobs through the end of

FY23 Q3....These decisions are difficult, but necessary. They are especially difficult because they impact people and people's lives—our colleagues and friends.[9]

Trust in leadership isn't built in good times. It's built when leaders stand in front of hard truths—when they lean into *truthtelling, not fabletelling*.

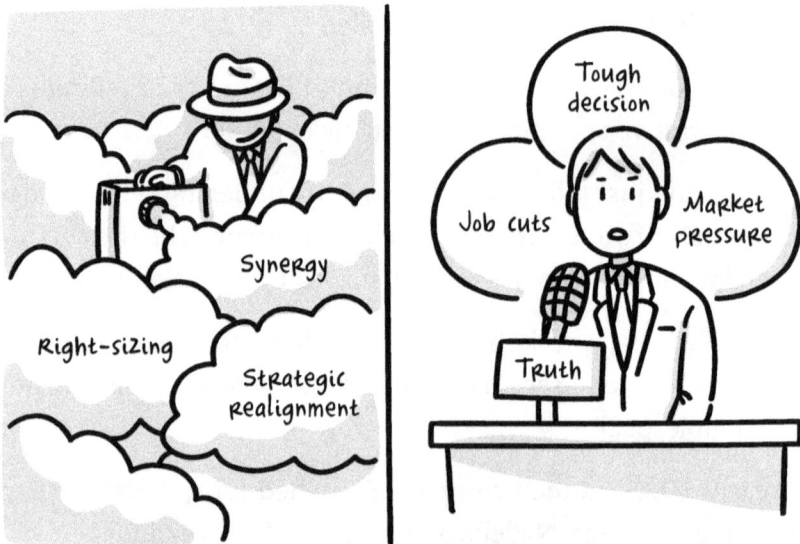

Truthtelling, Not Fabletelling

The best leaders don't spin—they stand in front of hard truths.

Question the future

Brian Chesky and Joe Gebbia, founders of Airbnb, built a business around a question:

What if people could rent out their spare rooms to strangers?

Reed Hastings, founder of Netflix, looked at Blockbuster and said:

What if there were no late fees?

When Glitch morphed into Slack, Stewart Butterfield asked:

What if we could make communication at work better?

Ingvar Kamprad founded IKEA with a question:

What if everyone could afford well-designed furniture?

These are beautiful questions. Leaders ask them. They're ambitious, yet actionable. They shift our understanding. They reinterpret perception.[10]

Questions shape our future.

Ben Franklin asked them too: What is the nature of lightning? How can we create a fair and just government?

Asking questions, as we've previously discussed, is a practice in minimal storytelling. The question is the setup. The answer—the work of the audience—is the punchline.

At its best, leadership means standing in today's reality, having the courage to face the future and the vision to ask a beautiful question—engaging others in the answer. That answer creates common context.

I spoke with Ronan Dunne, chairman of Six Nations Rugby and former CEO of Verizon and O2. He believes questions generate shared understanding:

Insightful leaders ask questions as a way of liberating their talent.[11]

For Dunne, it's all about context:

When people have common context, the opportunities for people as a group, as opposed to as individuals, are markedly different. In fact, they are markedly better.

Question the future

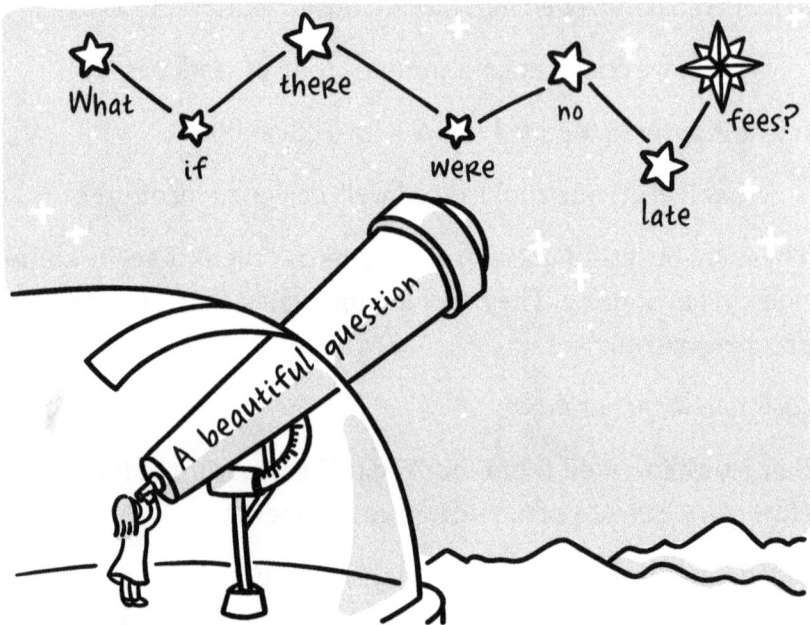

The question, and common context, rallies. A question like "How do I think and operate like a software company?" steers teams toward a digital future.

At Microsoft, Nadella is asking even more pointed questions:

> When we talk about AI, you can distill it into a more natural interface using natural language, a reasoning engine that works on top of all your data, giving you more power...

> The question is, what happens next? With this AI comes more opportunity.[12]

Questioning the future is the ability to look ahead. Preparation is as crucial today as it was in Franklin's time. Leaders must anticipate change, adapt strategies, and guide their organizations—not just to survive, but to grow.

Preach practical wisdom and simple rules

"Anecdotes are a magic elixir to make 'it' real," says Lou Hoffman, CEO and founder of the Hoffman Agency, a global PR firm. He explained why:

> Executives are communicating to audiences, not just journalists, but customers, job candidates, investors, you name it. No matter who those audiences are, they tend to be pretty cynical. They certainly have their guard up. So, how do you make it real? Anecdotal content does that.[13]

Leaders are full of anecdotes—small, distilled stories sculpted by experience. Frank Slootman, former CEO of Snowflake, tells a tale of cleaning toilets in his book *Amp It Up* (his chapter title: "My Journey from Teenage Toilet Cleaner to Serial CEO").[14] Jensen Huang, CEO and founder of Nvidia, scrubbed away any sense of entitlement when speaking at Stanford's Business School:

> To me, no task is beneath me because, remember, I used to be a dishwasher...I used to clean toilets. I've cleaned a lot of toilets.[15]

Toto Wolff, CEO and principal of the Mercedes-AMG Petronas F1 Team, shares a similar story. Why all the toilet-related anecdotes?

They *preach practical wisdom*—pay attention to details, do the hard work, and stay humble. Leadership advice in a small story.

Anecdotes are short, memorable stories. Aphorisms are cleverly worded statements. Axioms are established truths. All three are vehicles for leadership storytelling. And the best ones boil down to simple, repeatable rules.

Ben Franklin was full of them—sharp truths distilled into a single line. His take on actions over words: "Well done is better than well said."

Preach practical wisdom and simple rules

Well Done Is Better Than Well Said

— Wisdom for everyday leadership —

Do the work.
Stay humble.

Prepare.
Don't wish.

Rule No.1:
Never lose
money.

Executives today do the same—packing their leadership philosophies into small, potent phrases. Snowflake's Frank Slootman emphasizes focus and accountability with lines like, "The best way to build a brand is to get more customers" and "Hope is not a strategy." These succinct axioms become guiding principles—setting clear boundaries and expectations. Some, like Warren Buffett's famous rule—"Rule No. 1: Never lose money. Rule No. 2: Never forget rule No. 1."—are framed as nonnegotiable laws.

Others, like "Inspect what you expect," a memorable Denny-ism from former Verizon Wireless CEO Denny Strigl, embed operational rigor into a company's culture.

Over time, these phrases are repeated, internalized, and immortalized into enduring legends that mold organizational identity. You will hear them prefaced by "I always say." Satya Nadella:

> I always say, what happened last year is what happened last year. What happens this year is what we stay focused on.[16]

Practical wisdom, boiled down to simple rules, can save companies. Banco Santander survived the subprime mess by following shrewd advice from its chairman, Emilio Botin:

> If you don't fully understand an instrument, don't buy it. If you will not buy for yourself a specific product, don't try to sell it. If you don't know very well your customers, don't lend them any money.[17]

Simple. Clear. Actionable. These little leadership phrases take many forms—simple rules, anecdotes, axioms and other -isms. They distill complex strategy, values, and principles into simple, repeatable rules that guide daily action.

They are the bread and butter of leadership storytelling.

Create a movement

Two types of power exist in an organization: organizational power and storytelling power. Organizational power comes from position and political clout. Storytelling power comes from charisma—the ability to persuade, inspire, and motivate. Neither is innate—one is granted, the other is learned. And both types of power, used in harmony, can *create a movement*.

This starts with communicating a vision.

Elon Musk, CEO of SpaceX, dreams of "making humans a multi-planetary species." Mary Barra, CEO of GM, speaks of a zero world:

> Zero crashes, to save lives; zero emissions, so future generations can inherit a healthier planet; and zero congestion, so customers get back a precious commodity—time.[18]

Satya Nadella has outlined his vision for AI:

> To create intelligent systems that augment human capabilities and experiences.

But vision is just the start. It points the movement in a direction. Coupled with vision are other tools in the charismatic leader's arsenal.

To get people to invest, you must engage in storytelling—an appeal to collective identity that fosters belonging and solidarity. At SpaceX, Musk builds a collective identity around innovation and the future of humanity. He shares stories of overcoming challenges and pushing boundaries, creating a sense of belonging for people who see themselves as pioneers and visionaries.

The leader as storyteller is emotionally expressive, letting their passion, energy, and enthusiasm shine through. As they describe challenges to overcome, their stories project confidence and optimism.

Create a movement

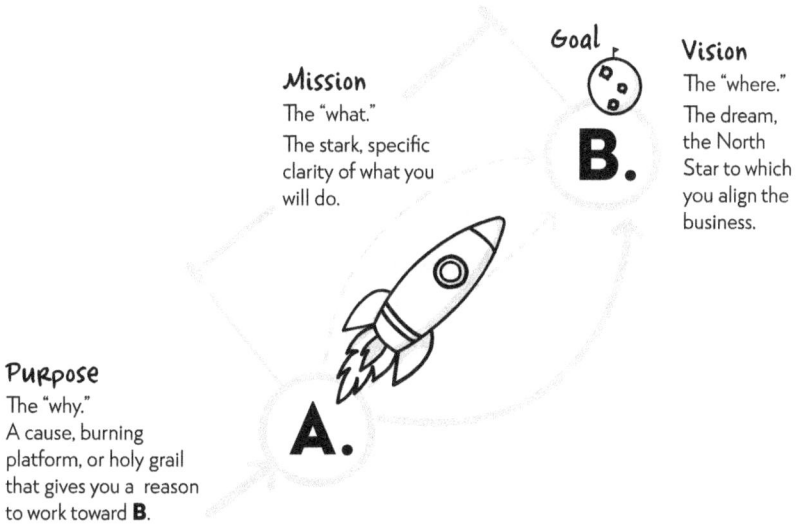

Mission
The "what."
The stark, specific clarity of what you will do.

Goal

B.

Vision
The "where."
The dream, the North Star to which you align the business.

Purpose
The "why."
A cause, burning platform, or holy grail that gives you a reason to work toward **B**.

A.

These stories are rich with rhetorical devices. Metaphors, analogies, and repetition add flavor to the recipe. Ingvar Kamprad likened IKEA furniture to a jigsaw puzzle—underscoring the simplicity and satisfaction of self-assembly. Stewart Butterfield compared Slack's impact to "taking the elevator instead of the stairs." Brian Chesky repeats the phrase of "belonging anywhere" to communicate Airbnb's mission.

The movement gains momentum through action.

A leader's role is to model what they say and live in the stories they tell. They can amplify it through symbolic action. Nelson Mandela understood this when he wore a Springbok jersey—symbolizing South African unity—to the 1995 Rugby World Cup. Business leaders use symbols too: Elon Musk launching a Tesla into orbit on a SpaceX Falcon Heavy. Yvon Chouinard donating his ownership of Patagonia to a nonprofit trust to combat climate change.

Alan Mulally refusing government bailouts as head of Ford during the 2008 financial crisis.

As soon as a movement is launched, it must be reinforced. Repetition, symbols, and shared rituals keep stories alive. The best leaders don't just tell stories—they invite others into them. Storymaking. Fan fiction. Shared authorship.

A movement sticks when people see themselves in the vision, when they take ownership of the story. You may command compliance, but you can't command belief. This is why positional power needs storytelling power—because a title may give direction, but stories create a movement.

Connect people and dots

Management divides. Leadership connects.

Management *systematically* divides things into parts—sales territories, product lines, functions—so they run more efficiently. Leadership, however, is about people, not parts. Those people, no matter where they sit—territory, line, or function—work in a system. And it's the job of a leader to think *systemically*.

The words *systematic* and *systemic* are often confused but are distinct. *Systematic* is about following a structured process, while *systemic* is about understanding the big picture: the system itself and how all its moving parts interact.

Understanding the whole system—*and* its individual parts—allows a leader to see both the bigger picture and the details. Holism is the antidote to silos, breaking people out of "my part works" thinking or the mindset that "the enemy is out there."

Systems thinking means grasping interconnections, feedback loops, outcomes, leverage points, and cause-and-effect—knowing that one domino can cause a ripple, a second can create chaos, and a third can spark a revolution.

Leadership storytelling maps these complex systems. It helps people see themselves in the picture and understand the part they play.

One dot connects to another.

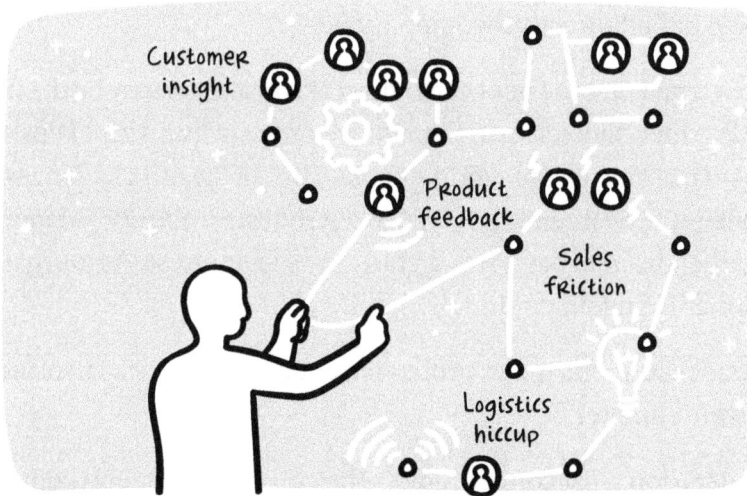

Connect people and dots

Leadership is seeing the whole picture —
and helping others see how their dot connects.

Indra Nooyi, PepsiCo's legendary former CEO, frequently demonstrated this ability. Her stories emphasized sweating the small stuff.

During a tour of Pete's Fresh Market in Chicago, Nooyi noticed a display of Aquafina water. She lifted a 32-pack off the stack and pointed out the difficulty women might have handling such a heavy package—a practical demonstration of *dot-connecting*, linking product design to customer experience to sales outcomes.

Nooyi's meticulous attention to detail, constantly raising standards, was her way of dot-connecting. On store visits she would fix misaligned logos, remove obstructive stickers, and show how small changes could have a big impact in brand performance.

This systems thinking reframed PepsiCo's product lines, and how Pepsicans thought about them. She grouped products into "fun for you," "better for you," and "good for you," aligning product innovation to a growing consumer demand for healthier food options as junk food consumption declined.

Nooyi pulled threads together publicly.

She warned that the next generation of consumers may be the first to "live for a shorter span than its predecessor," and that PepsiCo must face "one of the world's biggest public health challenges, a challenge fundamentally linked to our industry: obesity." Mapping together discrete parts was dictated by self-interest. As journalist Jennifer Reingold put it:

> PepsiCo's long-term profits would be fatter if its customers were slimmer.[19]

Leaders don't just connect dots—they make people feel them in a way spreadsheets and strategy decks never can. Through stories, they flip the abstract into action. The best leadership storytelling doesn't just explain how things fit together—it shows where people stand in the picture and gives them reason to care.

Lead change

All business, it is said, is change business.

The litany of companies that missed this is long—glittering stars that faded away or blinked out. Kodak. Blockbuster. BlackBerry. Sears. Toys "R" Us. Red Lobster.

Bankruptcy, as Ernest Hemingway's Mike Campbell notes in *The Sun Also Rises*, happens in two ways: "gradually, and then suddenly." To avoid collapse—gradual, sudden, or both—leaders must embrace change.

This is *the* balancing act of leadership.

Change is like a river—a steady current, in parts slow and meandering, in others raging through white-water rapids and plunging waterfalls. That current is swayed by external forces—competition, political shifts, economic swings, social change, and technological trends. It's also shifted by internal forces—reshuffles, new strategies, and rebudgeting. Too much change leads to chaos; too little calcifies into a slow, inevitable decline—entropy and inertia locked in stalemate.

How leaders balance change—how they lead through it—becomes their legacy. From Ben Franklin and the Revolutionary War to Satya Nadella's embrace of AI, leadership is defined by the ability to navigate what's next. That fulcrum—between too much change and too little—creates both space to work and a challenge to live into.

This is a Goldilocks zone.

Too much change—too many moving parts, too many unknowns— is a recipe for stress, burnout, avoidance, and battening down hatches. Too little change breeds bureaucracy, stagnation, and learned helplessness, creating an organization slow to react to external threats and opportunities. The job of leadership is to get this balance just right: to create pools of stillness in the roiling river of change.

How, then, do you *lead change* through leadership storytelling? By telling two stories—*Story 1* and *Story 2*.

Story 1 is the journey—the path to get there. It answers how and when:

How do I do that, and by when?

Story 2 is the destination—the vision. It answers where and why:

Where are we going, and why?

Both stories are important. And symbiotic.

Lead change

story 1
How and when

story 2
Where and why

Show both where you are going
and how to get there.

If neither story is told, leaders miss a central tenet of change: People must see themselves in the picture. When change stalls, it's because that doesn't happen. And there are a few reasons why.

Story 1, the journey, fails when the path is not clear. The roadmap is disjointed, complex, or, worse, ambiguous. The steps are too big, too overwhelming. Personal challenges and obstacles go ignored, leaving people feeling isolated and unsupported.

Story 2, the destination, falls flat when the vision is generic or unrealistic. There's no concreteness—more "motherhood and apple pie" than clear, compelling outcomes. Worse, the story is buried in business lingo. Story 2 becomes dry and boring: high on jargon and acronyms, low on relevance and emotion. Without message discipline, it wobbles. Mixed signals do their worst: On Monday, it's all rah-rah and strategy; by Friday, it's back to business as usual.

What we see most often: Story 2 is told without Story 1, or vice versa.

When it's all destination (Story 2), there is no movement. Plenty of why and where, but the how and when are missing. In the case where it's all journey (Story 1), there's spin. The classic "Are we there yet?"—lots of activity, but old ways of doing things get jumbled in with the new, causing overload and burnout.

Satya Nadella tells change stories that expertly weave both Story 1 and Story 2—where people and dots are connected. He created movements around AI and the cloud, guiding with practical wisdom, questioning the future, and, when needed, facing harsh truths. All of this was supported by one of Nadella's first moves: shaping Microsoft's culture.

Change isn't just a strategy—it's an emotional journey. Leadership storytelling—especially in times of change—doesn't just outline steps or vision; it anchors people in purpose. It gives them a simple how and when.

A leader's job—your job—isn't just to manage change. It's to make it mean something.

YOU KNOW...

...that **leadership storytelling inspires and connects people.** It creates shared context, aligns teams, and animates movements through narratives that resonate.

...that **effective leaders use stories to bridge the gap between authority and empathy.** They bridge vision and values, ensure engagement and understanding within their teams, and make the abstract concrete.

...that leadership storytelling follows six key principles:

1. **Truthtelling, not fabletelling.**
2. **Question the future.**
3. **Preach practical wisdom and simple rules.**
4. **Create a movement.**
5. **Connect people and dots.**
6. **Lead change.**

...that **truthtelling builds trust.** Authenticity and transparency are crucial for effective leadership; they foster credibility and commitment among team members and stakeholders.

...that **questioning the future** engages teams in exploring new possibilities. It sparks invention, kindles forward-thinking solutions, and ignites a culture of curiosity.

...that **preaching practical wisdom** with simple rules provides clear guidance and actionable insights. Leadership storytelling simplifies complexity, making strategy accessible and actionable.

...that **creating a movement** rallies people around a vision. It inspires a collective identity and a shared sense of purpose and fosters a sense of belonging.

...that **connecting people and dots** requires systemic thinking—mapping out individual contributions to the larger mission, ensuring everyone sees their place in the big picture.

...that **leading change** is a balancing act. It requires stability and innovation, guiding teams through uncertainty with clarity, confidence, and vision while maintaining momentum and morale.

Master these principles, and storytelling will be a tool to inspire, engage, and lead.

Leadership storytelling isn't just about conveying information, it's about shaping action. Tell the right story, and you won't just lead—you'll forge deeper connections, build trust, and orchestrate real change.

10 CULTURE STORYTELLING

Culture is the machine that creates all future things.

— BRIAN CHESKY

The invisible machine

We are our history.

This reality reflects the paradox of nature vs. nurture—one of the oldest scientific debates. Although nature might provide potential, it's nurture that guides us. One defines where we start. The other decides where we go.

German philosopher Immanuel Kant, standing on the shoulders of giants like Descartes, Locke, and Hume, coined *Weltanschauung*. Translated into English, it means "worldview"—the lens through which we intuit and interpret the world, sculpted by experience, society, and culture. Like Adam Smith's invisible hand guiding markets, our worldview invisibly overlays our narrative networks.

Culture works the same way. It runs quietly in the background, invisibly shaping decisions, behaviors, and outcomes. You don't see it, but you feel its effects. This unseen mechanism exists, widely distributed, in people's heads, filtered through their worldview, interacting with their narrative network, and influencing their actions.

In this sense, culture is *how we do things around here.*[*]

The *do* is why culture is so powerful; it can corrode and sabotage strategy or fortify and elevate it. Strategy is what we intend to *do*, but culture runs the show—deciding how we actually *do* things around here.

Culture is the invisible machine

Strategy

Cultural friction

Unspoken Rules

Norms   Habits

"The way we do things"

And here's where it gets personal.

Culture isn't just an abstract force—it's shaped by the choices of individual leaders. You decide whether to let it drift or deliberately direct it. The question is: Will you?

---

[*] Culture—as a range of behaviors and beliefs that fall inside or outside the norm—is a little like an Overton window (first discussed in chapter 5): a boundary for what the group will, or won't, accept.

Will you form culture in service of value, product, brand, sales, and your leadership? Each has its own *do*: For value, it's proving worth. For product, it's bringing ideas to life. For brand, it's building worlds. For sales, it's engaging and converting. For your leadership, it's inspiring people to *do*.

If how you *do* things runs counter to what you *intend* to *do*, the machine grinds. Gears slip. Momentum stalls.

Pushing harder won't help.

You can't force product stories into motion or jam brand messaging through a broken system. People see through it.

Any successful venture—whether a transformation, a team, or a company—works *with* culture, not against it. You must fine-tune culture's machine. Adjust the gears. Oil the mechanism. But first, you must understand it.

The mechanics of culture

How, then, do you start? How do you make the invisible visible? You have to look under the hood to understand the inner apparatus. Four key mechanics keep the machine humming: *symbols*, *discipline*, *collective habits*, and *unwritten rules*.

Symbols are the visible parts—the gears and levers you can see. They show up in the physical environment, communication styles, and work practices.

Discipline is the design philosophy—the blueprint that determines how the business model runs.

Collective habits are the software—the unconscious routines of teams that keep everything in motion.

Unwritten rules are the machine's code—the deeply ingrained norms that dictate "how we do things around here."

Symbols—the visible cues that signal how a culture works—are the levers that influence behavior and reinforce norms. Some are large; some are small. Some have an immediate, obvious impact. Others you pull, and nothing seems to happen—until later when the system shifts.

Some symbols reinforce permanence, locking routines in place. Others signal change, setting new behaviors in motion. Saying "The boss says..." reinforces hierarchy and bureaucracy; it cedes authority and stalls culture.* Not good. Selling office buildings signals a shift to distributed work and a more modern way of working.

Some symbols are built into the physical system—the office layout, materials, even lighting. A mahogany-lined boardroom signals tradition. A bare-brick open space signals transparency. A shared startup hub signals agility. Even signage—austere and formal or casual and playful—tells employees and visitors how to engage.

Other symbols are intertwined with the operating system of culture. Behavioral symbols show up in rituals, traditions, and dress codes. Communication symbols emerge in language, jargon, and the stories people tell. Procedural symbols guide how decisions get made and work gets done.

Beneath those symbols is an underlying *discipline*.

This is the core strand in a company's cultural DNA—not as easy to spot as symbols, discipline reveals itself in priorities and organization: how the business runs.

---

* You might not think this happens around here. But I'll bet it does. Replace "the boss" with the first name of your favorite C-level exec or CEO and see what happens.

Classically, organizational culture evolves around three distinct disciplines. Each mobilizes the machine in a different way:[*]

Operational excellence: Emphasizes efficiency, consistency, and streamlined processes. These companies refine their systems to run like clockwork. Think Verizon, McDonald's, Walmart, and Amazon.

Customer intimacy: Prioritizes relationships, tailoring products and services to meet unique needs. These businesses form their culture around deep customer connections. Examples include Zappos, Fifth Third Bank, and Patagonia.

Product leadership: Thrives on innovation, brand marketing, and staying ahead of the industry. These companies keep the machine moving by driving new ideas forward. Think SpaceX, Apple, and Alphabet.

Market leaders don't try to be everything at once. A company that builds around multiple disciplines invites organizational schizophrenia—a machine fighting against itself.[†]

Symbols and discipline are the visible mechanics of culture. Beneath them are the hidden systems that keep everything running—*collective habits* and *unwritten rules*.

---

[*] Although it's not treated as a cultural element in their book, I have based my concept of discipline on the work of Treacy and Wiersema, *The Discipline of Market Leaders: Choose Your Customers, Narrow Your Focus, Dominate Your Market.*

[†] Treacy and Wiersema argue that market leaders succeed by committing to one dominant discipline—operational excellence, customer intimacy, or product leadership—while maintaining competence in the others. A company that tries to master all three dilutes its strategy, confuses its identity, and grinds its machine to a halt.

Culture revolves around a core discipline

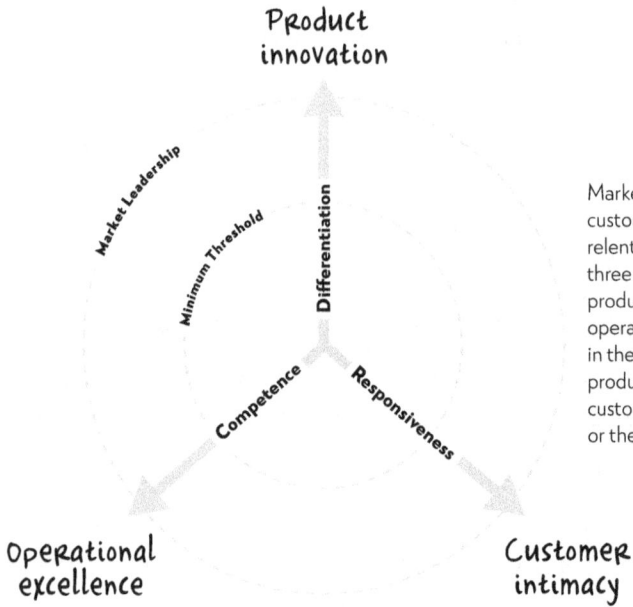

Product innovation

Market Leadership

Minimum Threshold

Differentiation

Competence

Responsiveness

Market leaders win customers through a relentless focus on one of three value propositions — product, customer, or operations—manifesting in the highest quality products, the best customer experiences, or the lowest prices.

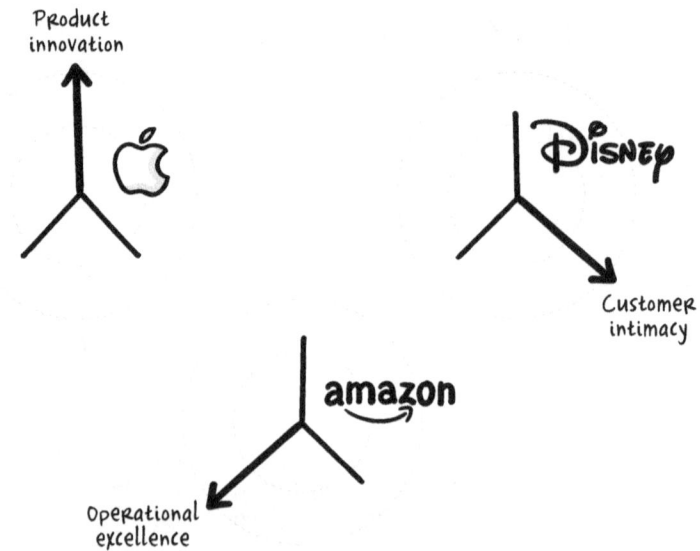

Operational excellence

Customer intimacy

Product innovation

🍎

DISNEP

Customer intimacy

amazon

Operational excellence

At the heart of culture are collective habits. They're the unconscious routines of teams, which power the machine. They're the engine of culture, the *how* in how we do things around here.

Some are innocuous—standardized email signatures reinforce a professional, brand-standard image, but don't impact outcomes. Some are useful—lean meetings tackle daily issues and keep projects moving. And some are insidious—overstuffed calendars and micromanagement.

Unwritten rules are hardwired into culture's machine—deeply ingrained implicit norms that dictate how things actually get done. They are undocumented standards—but everyone follows them.

The meeting after the meeting to clarify decisions. The social cue to sign a birthday card and eat cake. The silent expectation to respond to emails over weekends and holidays.

These unwritten rules reinforce discipline. In an operationally excellent organization, the rule might be "Inspect what you expect"—constant oversight to ensure efficiency. A customer-intimate company might "Go the extra mile," caring for relationships over standardization. In a business built around product leadership, "Fail fast" is deeply ingrained—experimentation and innovation are prized above all.

But these rules don't travel well across disciplines.

A customer-intimate company would resist the idea to fail fast, especially if it meant letting the customer down. They would go to extreme lengths to avoid it. Operationally excellent companies would push back, too—against an idea that works on paper but, in practice, might break the system.

When unwritten rules and collective habits fall out of sync, unintended consequences follow. Rigid procedures and a focus on metrics, prized in operational excellence, can breed inflexibility, incrementalism, and bureaucracy. Customer-intimate companies can over-customize, white-gloving every client to the point of losing scale. Product-led companies, risking perfectionism and internal competition, can fall for innovation for innovation's sake—and miss markets entirely.

When it's good, it's good

At Fountain Square Plaza in Cincinnati stands the Fifth Third Bank Museum. Its mission: to archive and showcase more than 165 years of company history, highlighting contributions to the City of Cincinnati and the financial services industry.

But this isn't just a museum. It tells the story of Fifth Third's identity, ensuring that its values and principles shape the company's future.

Fifth Third is a Midwest powerhouse, traded on the Nasdaq and managing over $634 billion in assets. Commercial, consumer, wealth, small business—they do it all.[1]

For employees, it's Fifth Third's culture that stands out. In its offices, a silver and green sign reads:

> WE LIVE HERE. WE WORK, PLAY AND RAISE OUR FAMILIES HERE. That's why we're committed to improving lives in all the places we serve.

More than just words, it's a symbol—a reminder of what matters. As one employee puts it, "It's easy to love what you do, when you see what it does for the place that you live."

Culture is shaped by leaders. At Fifth Third, leadership means a commitment to customers. As CEO Tim Spence puts it:

> Our ambition is to be the One Bank people most value and trust—and that trust is earned every day when our employees

do the right thing for our shareholders, our customers, and our communities.[2]

That ambition traces back to 1858, three years before the Civil War.

It was a time of wildcat banks and currency chaos, when banks issued their own money and failed often, leaving depositors penniless and notes worthless. In that climate, William W. Scarborough opened the doors of The Bank of the Ohio Valley in Cincinnati with a simple promise: People could feel secure bringing their money there.

In 1871, the bank merged with Third National and later with Fifth National, becoming Fifth-Third National. Around the same time, Jacob Schmidlapp arrived in Cincinnati, opening a liquor store and bottling whiskey. An entrepreneur at heart, he expanded, buying Clifton Springs Distillery in 1889 and founding Union Savings Bank & Trust Co. the following year. Already a millionaire, he never drew a salary during his time at the bank.

Union Savings would eventually become part of Fifth Third, and Schmidlapp's influence lives on in the bank's culture today.

Just steps away from John Roebling's Cincinnati-Covington suspension bridge, he commissioned a building to house his bank. Then, in 1901, a symbol of change: the 19-story brick and steel Union Trust Building—the city's first skyscraper.

A statement. A mark of ambition, progress, innovation, and identity.

Schmidlapp was ahead of his time.

Though Jacob Schmidlapp and IKEA's Ingvar Kamprad came from different eras and industries, they shared a vision: to make life better for the many, not just a few. Schmidlapp founded the Cincinnati Model Homes Company to build safe, affordable housing, especially for working families and African Americans at a time when segregation severely limited access.

Kamprad's IKEA took a different path, but the aim was the same—well-designed, affordable homes for everyday people.

Schmidlapp codified his philosophy in a simple rule: "One day's wages for one week's rent."[3] Kamprad echoed the sentiment: "To create a better everyday life for the many people."[4]

As Fifth Third expanded, its culture deepened, shaped by Schmidlapp's values and the leaders who followed.

He believed banking was about community. So does Fifth Third. Its culture remains rooted in a rich history of service, trust, and doing the right thing. Every innovation, every first, every bold move—it all traces back to the same gene: community and customer. This guides every generation of leadership and every employee.

During the Great Depression and World War II, John J. Rowe steered the bank through uncertainty. His tenure was marked by strength and steady decision-making. Fifth Third absorbed weaker banks, expanded its reach, and deepened its role in the community.

When trust was in short supply, Fifth Third was an anchor.

William S. Rowe Jr. picked up the baton in the 1970s, an era marked by technological change. Under his watch, Fifth Third launched JEANIE®—one of the first online shared networks in the country—a convenience that better served Fifth Third's customers.

By celebrating its roots, Fifth Third reinforces its identity, not just through policies, but through stories.

And then there are the rituals.

Every May 3rd—5/3 Day—employees across the bank take part in community service. It's not just branding. It's a habit—a way to live the values outside the office. The museum plays its role too. It's where new hires learn the company's story—and where long-timers return to see how far it's come.

Storytelling isn't just tradition—it's how Fifth Third keeps its identity alive.[5]

The six rules of culture storytelling

Culture storytelling is repeated lore.

When it's good, it's very good, a well-oiled machine pushing business forward.

Fifth Third Bank understands this well. It has built a culture around customer intimacy—its core discipline—reinforced by the stories it tells. From its corporate storyteller and historian to the stories embedded in how employees talk about their work, Fifth Third builds a culture around relationships. Employees don't just serve customers; they carry forward a tradition of service, innovation, and community building. Culture storytelling isn't an afterthought—it's how the company keeps its identity intact.

When leaders sculpt culture intentionally, it becomes an advantage. Netflix codified this in its famous Culture Deck, ensuring every employee understood the values that drove decision-making.[6] Microsoft, under Satya Nadella, moved from cutthroat internal competition to collaboration, changing the company's trajectory entirely.[7]

But when culture breaks down, it jams progress. Annoyingly, that glitch is often invisible—a gremlin in the mechanism. You don't notice it right away. At first, you feel it. Culture obstructs. Friction builds. Change drags.

It's the ghost in the machine that makes the fix so hard.

Uber's early years were defined by a toxic, unchecked culture, where aggressive internal competition and ethical lapses nearly destroyed the company.[8] No matter how strong the business model, the machine may seize. And sometimes, a shift in business model jams the machine. Take Boeing: A shift from engineering excellence to cost-cutting resulted in catastrophic failures.

At most, leaders tend to tinker with culture.

At best, they rewire it. But culture isn't something you fix once—it's a machine that needs constant tuning and oiling to keep running. And to do that, we must engage in a little culture storytelling.

Against a backdrop of symbols, discipline, unwritten rules, and collective habits, leaders make a choice: Let culture drift, or steer it deliberately.

Culture storytelling is a tool to fine-tune the machine—adjusting the mechanism, tightening the alignment, and keeping it running smoothly—through six key rules:

1. **Anchor stories in history and heritage.**

2. **Showcase core values and principles.**

3. **Connect to the broader vision.**

4. **Use symbols and rituals.**

5. **Cultivate high-trust relationships.**

6. **Intertwine work and culture.**

This is the final piece of the business storytelling puzzle. If stories pass the creative spark, build value, ideate products, create connections for brands, sell, and inspire followership, then culture storytelling informs how we *do* that at scale.

When it's bad, it's very bad

Boeing is a storied American company built on engineering excellence.

The son of an immigrant, timberman William "Bill" Boeing first became fascinated with aviation after attending an air show in 1910. He trained as a pilot, bought a seaplane, and by 1917 founded the Boeing Airplane Company—securing a US Navy contract to build fifty seaplanes.

From the start, Boeing's identity was clear: facts, precision, and engineering. A placard hung in Bill's office:

Hippocrates said:

1. There is no authority except facts.
2. Facts are obtained by accurate observation.
3. Deductions are to be made only from facts.
4. Experience has proved the truth of these rules.[9]

Boeing's story is a history of product leadership.

The company became an aviation pioneer, building the bombers of WWII, launching the iconic 707 and 747, and setting new industry standards with the 777 and Dreamliner.

The Seattle-based giant operated as an engineering-first collective. Executives held patents, spoke the complex language of aerodynamics, and reveled in the smell of aviation fuel.

During its golden era, Boeing CEOs had two things in common: an engineering degree and years of company service. They knew *how* planes were built and *who* built them.

But starting in the mid-1990s, Boeing began to lose its grip on its *history and heritage*.

The first crack came in 1997: the McDonnell Douglas merger. Engineering excellence took a backseat to financial engineering.

New leadership, trained in cost-cutting, not aircraft design, prioritized profits over product. Outsourcing, offshoring, and maximizing shareholder returns ruled.

In 2001 CEO Phil Condit relocated Boeing's headquarters from Seattle to Chicago, deliberately distancing the executive branch from day-to-day operations.

Peter Robison, author of *Flying Blind*, noted this symbol of change:

> Condit's old office had been in a gritty industrial strip of South Seattle, its windows looking directly onto the [air]field...

> Boeing's new, supposedly "leaner" headquarters had 19th-century rugs, an antique French barometer topped with a carved eagle, a glass scepter and an English Regency gilt mirror among the objects d'art dotting its leather-and-wood executive suites.[10]

The move was symbolic: Engineering excellence was no longer the company's priority.

Condit resigned two years later amid procurement scandals. His successor, Harry Stonecipher, chased RONA—Return On Net Assets.

John Hart-Smith, a senior technical fellow, warned against the new metric:

[We'll] outsource everything except a little Boeing decal to slap on the nose of the finished airplane.[11]

An outsider, Stonecipher had a rocky relationship with the old engineering culture, blasting them as "arrogant." He used leadership axioms to tilt the culture from engineering and safety to finance and profit: "A passion for affordability" and "Less family, more team."[12]

Stonecipher also fell in scandal. Another GE alum took his place—James McNerney.

With a BA in American Studies from Yale and an MBA from Harvard, McNerney was the antithesis of the old guard Boeing CEO-engineer. A stint in brand management at Proctor & Gamble, consulting at McKinsey, and a steady climb up the GE corporate ladder had defined him as a leader of numbers, not airplanes.

McNerney pushed for profitability above all else. During his tenure, Boeing's stock price doubled. The company prioritized cost-cutting, standardization, and operational efficiency.

The pursuit of value flew in the face of values.

The first warning lights blinked. In January 2013, the FAA grounded all Boeing 787 Dreamliners after multiple battery fires. By the time McNerney retired, the rust had settled into the machine.

Dennis Muilenburg was an engineer. But by the time he took over, Boeing was no longer an engineering company.

In 2018 and 2019, two Boeing 737 MAX aircraft—Lion Air Flight 610 and Ethiopian Airlines Flight 302—crashed. Fleets were grounded.

MCAS, a control software designed to compensate for the MAX's aerodynamic instabilities, was hidden from pilots to cut training costs. Boeing gambled no one would notice. Until 346 people died.[13]

Trust fractured.

Muilenburg was forced out, but his replacement, David Calhoun, was yet another GE cost-cutter, not an engineer.

One senior Boeing insider was apprehensive:

> If it's more cost-cutting, that's not what we need. We have to restore the culture of engineering excellence that has served us so well for over a century.[14]

Separating engineering excellence from culture led to a spiral of failure.

Door plugs blew off planes in flight. Boeing Starliner astronauts got stuck in orbit.

How did a company with Boeing's reputation, a pioneer in aviation, stall so badly? The answer is culture. Decisions about how we do things around here—made with good intent over decades—had ripple effects and unintended consequences. They echoed through the business. And ultimately, they destroyed value, cast doubt on products, tragically lost lives, and tarnished a once-shining brand.

Culture is never neutral. Left untended, the machine rusts, errors creep in, unintended consequences pile up. Boeing's downfall happened gradually, then suddenly.

In Story Business, culture storytelling may be the most important story of all.

Anchor stories in history and heritage

We all seek to be part of a tribe.

Social structure gives us a sense of belonging, a role, and an identity. Since the days of the Storyteller, this has been wired into our brains, an evolutionary hack for survival.

Anchor stories in history and heritage

The Storyteller

Social bonding, trust, and group cohesion

Oxytocin—the cuddle hormone—feeds bonding, trust, and group cohesion.[15] It floods our brains when we connect: holding hands, sharing a laugh, or hearing a well-told story.

That's what stories do.

They make us *feel* part of a group. Amped up by oxytocin, stories—tribal lore—foster belonging and place. It's a lesson lived at Fifth Third Bank, but they're not alone. IKEA published its origin story, *The Testament of a Furniture Dealer*, and encourages employees to read it. Under Satya Nadella, Microsoft reconnected to its engineering roots and retooled itself into a learn-it-all culture.

Great cultures don't drift—*they anchor in history and heritage.*

Alan Gardner, chief people officer of Frontier Communications, knows the power of history and heritage. He grew up in Kansas City, earned degrees in computer science and business, and spent 31 years climbing the ranks at Verizon, retiring as a Senior Vice President of HR. Frontier brought him in post-bankruptcy to help steer its turnaround—just in time for an acquisition by Verizon.[16]

Stories are a social act. For Gardner, they're also a reminder of progress: "They really do tell you who you are, and where you can go."

Storytelling framed the culture of the new Frontier:

> We have spent a lot of time talking to people because Frontier people have been so bruised and beat up, going through bankruptcy. We have used stories to paint a picture of what possibility and success can look like—so people can grab onto that and move forward to the future.[17]

Frontier is rebuilding its culture by anchoring in its new history.

A growing timeline tracks the company's comeback—emerging from bankruptcy, hitting profitability, breaking sales records. It's more than a list of milestones; it's a narrative scaffold, a visual story of resilience. The new Frontier journey is memorialized on a wall in their Dallas hub, a permanent reminder of where they've been—and where they're going.

Culture storytelling connects.

Your company's origin story—of challenges, victories, and vision—constructs identity. Success stories aren't just history; they're invitations. They bring people in—a social call that highlights achievements, reinforces shared values, and turns history into belonging.

Showcase core values and principles

If culture is how we do things around here, it's vital for the "how" to be self-evident to the "we."

The moral of the story has to show. Telling the story of *The Tortoise and the Hare* without the lesson "slow and steady wins the race" would be like telling a joke without a punchline. So it goes with culture storytelling: Core values (what a company believes to be true) and principles (the practices that animate them) must be visible.

Boeing is a cautionary tale of what happens when a company loses sight of its core values.

Its culture—once built on product leadership and engineering excellence—was slowly eroded by an obsession with cost-cutting. What started as financial discipline turned into short-term thinking, sacrificing the principles that made Boeing great.

A business must understand what makes it great—and how that greatness is encoded in its cultural DNA.

Leaders *showcase values and principles* through the stories they tell: Satya Nadella draws leadership lessons from his beloved game of cricket; Frank Slootman, Toto Wolff, and Jensen Huang extol the value of hard work and attention to detail through stories of scrubbing toilets. Even the meta-story has a tell—Bill Boeing's legendary office sign, a shrine to facts.

Leaders model behaviors. The stories they tell make the abstract concrete, putting the "how" in culture. This can't be left to a generic list of values—respect, responsibility, inclusion—each one must be brought to life.

Like values, principles often appear in shiny lettering wrapped in vague phrases and grand words: *integrity, excellence, innovation, leadership*.

Science, being science, has a branch of linguistics dedicated to measuring how abstract (language-based) or concrete (experience-based) words are. Words are ranked on a 1–5 scale. *Integrity*, *excellence*, *innovation*, and *leadership* all score low—abstract: well-known, but not well understood.

The trick is turning abstraction into action—and Netflix nailed it.

In 2009, Netflix founder Reed Hastings published a 125-page deck on Netflix's culture. It went viral. It was a master class in culture storytelling—and a trendsetting move that *showcased core values and principles* with clarity and conviction.

Every abstract principle was made concrete through specific, actionable behaviors. The guide spoke directly, often beginning with "you." As in: "*You* make time to help colleagues" (Selflessness) and "*You* take smart risks" (Courage).

At times, it's brutally blunt. At Netflix, high performance is nonnegotiable. Hastings put it plainly:

Adequate performance gets a generous severance package.[18]

But the culture deck makes room for aspiration. It quotes Antoine de Saint-Exupéry, author of *The Little Prince*, to make a simple point:

If you want to build a ship,

...teach them to yearn

for the vast and endless sea.

In other words, culture isn't built through tasks. It's built by tapping into want.

Hastings's handbook is a how-to manual for culture storytelling. Its core values and principles are tailor-made for a company built on the discipline of product leadership.

Showcase core values and principles

Now ask yourself: Are your core values and principles clear and concrete? Do they speak to you? Or are they just lofty words?

Do people in your company walk the walk *and* talk the talk? Or do they nod at the words on the wall while doing something else entirely?

Culture storytelling isn't just about what you say. It's about what people live.

Connect to the broader vision

When culture and strategy clash, strategy loses.

The machine always wins. What we set out to *do*—strategy—gets ground through the gears of *how* we do things—culture.

Companies work hard to align vision, mission, and goals with purpose. But when strategy also aligns with symbols, discipline, collective habits, and unwritten rules—they hit their stride.

Ferrari's storytelling and strategy reinforce product leadership.

Airbnb is designed around customer intimacy.

Amazon is a force, dedicated to operational excellence.

Prime delivery vans emblazoned with "Time flies when Prime delivers" and "That thing you wanted? It's right. In. Here." are symbols of Amazon's obsession with speed and efficiency. The fabled Bezos memo banning PowerPoint wasn't just a rule—it was a demand for structured thinking. Six-page memos are a ritual that cemented this operational DNA. "Frugal innovation"—an Amazon term—isn't a suggestion, it's a mandate to do more with less, to optimize relentlessly.

Leaders must configure vision to culture and culture to mission.

Alan Mulally left Boeing to become CEO of Ford in 2006. He inherited a company in crisis. The automaker's turnaround is chronicled in Bryce Hoffman's book *American Icon*, which describes how Mulally *connected culture to broader vision*.

Digging into Ford's history, Mulally found an old Henry Ford-era ad with the caption "Opening the highways to all mankind." Hoffman writes:

He grabbed a pen and a pad of paper and began writing in his usual stream-of-consciousness style: Pull all the stakeholders together around a compelling vision: Opening the highways to all mankind.[19]

Connect to the broader vision

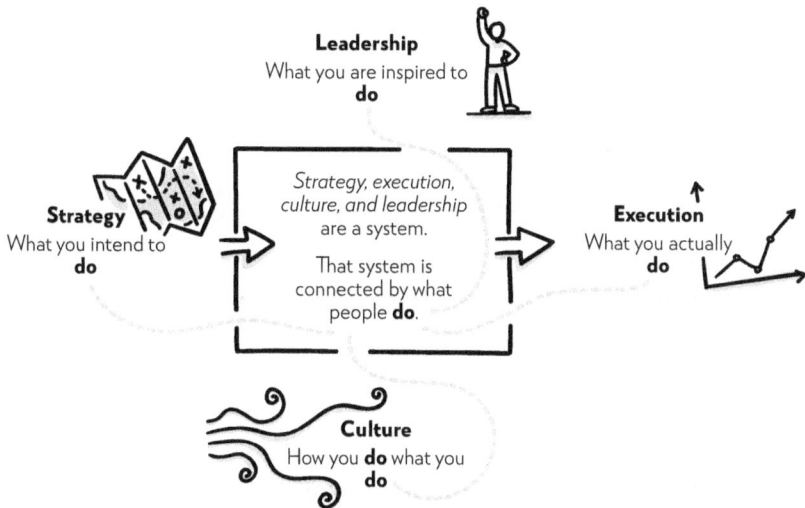

Leadership
What you are inspired to **do**

Strategy
What you intend to **do**

Strategy, execution, culture, and leadership are a system.

That system is connected by what people **do**.

Execution
What you actually **do**

Culture
How you **do** what you **do**

Halfway down Mullaly's notes: "Change the culture." What he called "auto culture," Hoffman variously described as "a culture of entitlement," "entrenched, careerist," one that "resisted all change" and "put individual advancement ahead of corporate success." It was "noxious," "poisonous," and riddled with "intrigue and backstabbing."

To fix Ford, Mulally had to first fix its culture.

He connected culture to vision with a blue card—a handy, wallet-size distillation of strategy. On it, four simple phrases: "One Ford," "One Team," "One Plan," and "One Goal." Mulally spelled out his vision:

People working together as a lean, global enterprise for automotive leadership, as measured by: Customer, Employee, Dealer, Investor, Supplier, Union/Council, and Community Satisfaction.

On the flip side were the collective behaviors that would power this vision:

Foster Functional and Technical Excellence

Own Working Together

Role Model Ford Values

Deliver Results

Alan Mulally's One Ford vision tied Ford's culture to a mission of unity and excellence. Through clear articulation and relentless communication, he aligned the company's goals, fostered collaboration, and drove cultural change.[20]

Culture storytelling must be relentless, not rigid. Like a well-worn joke, it evolves. You adapt, refine it, and weave in employee stories—making them part of your narrative constellation.

Make it concrete. Give people a way to take part.

Constantly connect stories to vision, mission, and values—not the ones in shiny letters on the wall, but the *real* ones. The ones revealed by who gets rewarded, promoted, or let go.

That's the culture people believe in. That's the story that sticks.

Use symbols and rituals

Symbols and rituals shape culture.

They reinforce values, create shared meaning, and build identity. Whether a company is thriving or in flux, symbols and rituals sync the gears, align teams, and make culture real.

But culture doesn't idle. It is swayed by the collective habits of the many people within it. Over time, unwritten rules creep in, silently steering how work gets done—for better or worse.

To break bad habits, unwritten rules must be rewritten.

Culture stories bring hidden norms into the open, exposing and reworking the friction that slows the machine down.

Used with purpose—and grounded in history, values, and principles—*symbols and rituals* are the fastest way to refine culture over time. Bob Toohey, chief HR officer of FIS, put it simply:

> Changing culture is a long game—it takes years, and you have to be very intentional every step of the way. You have to get at what's in people's heads, the way they think, the way they act, the way they behave. Symbols of change, little rituals built into the way people work, are the best way to do that.[21]

In his previous role as CHRO at Allstate, Toohey embarked on that journey, starting with connecting to their vision: to be *the lowest-cost digital protection provider*.

This reset would take one of the largest publicly held insurers in the United States, founded in 1931 as part of Sears, Roebuck & Co., and reshape its culture in pursuit of transformative growth. Tom Wilson, Allstate's CEO, captured this challenge in a letter to shareholders:

> Creating a transformative growth enterprise requires culture change, keeping the good and having the courage to stop things that get in the way.[22]

What "to stop" starts with the villains of your culture story.

Traditionally, culture villains are hard to spot, hidden by opinion and hearsay. In the age of AI, the task becomes easier. At Allstate, tens of thousands of verbatim employee comments were fed into an advanced AI model to uncover the collective habits and unwritten rules holding the company back. To avoid hallucinations, HR business partners and leaders vetted the findings. This made the code of culture—usually invisible—visible. Wilson, Toohey, and the team had hard data to act on.

Many collective habits are rooted in seemingly reasonable unwritten rules. For example, an unspoken expectation to "stay in your lane" can lead to fragmented thinking between departments. Similarly, a preference for predictable, incremental change—anchored in standardized processes—can quietly slow innovation or transformation.

Taken in isolation, collective habits often seem to offer business value. Together, they have a stifling effect. Over time, the burden builds—turning an operationally excellent company into a bureaucratic one, making a customer-intimate company struggle to scale, or leaving a product-driven one blind to the market.

Allstate embraced symbols of change. Selling its Northbrook, Illinois, headquarters signaled a shift from an office-bound culture to one that was more inviting, flexible, and agile.[23]

Where leadership gatherings were once exclusive to company officers, Allstate opened its conferences to leaders at all levels—breaking down silos and hierarchy.

As he works to reinvent HR, Toohey points to the power of rituals:

> We're working on it. How do we build operational excellence into the fabric of our work? In my organization, it's daily stand-ups, embracing agile principles, and thinking about HR as a product. We have a ritual of starting every meeting with data.

Rituals work when they are relevant and incorporate employee input.

Regular feedback helps refine them. Storytelling plays a key role. For example, a staff meeting might include sharing stories under themes like "what's better," to highlight recent improvements, or "why it's good," to showcase great work. These small storytelling rituals engage employees, raise standards, and reinforce shared values.

Culture storytelling comes to life through practice.

Flattening the Hierarchy

Use symbols

- Selling the HQ as a symbol of change
- Flattening the hierarchy

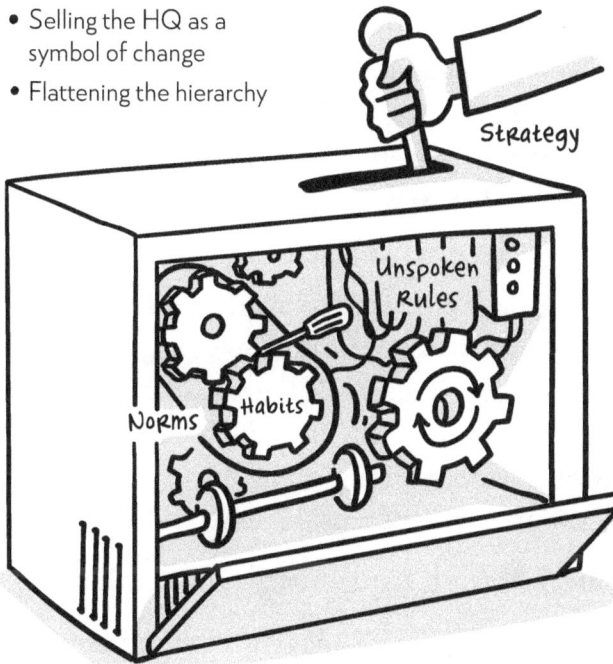

Strategy

Unspoken Rules

Norms   Habits

Use rituals to shape behaviors

- Daily stand-ups
- Team retrospectives

You make it real. Use symbols and rituals to reinforce it. Let signs guide behavior. Create social routines that build new collective habits for your team. Culture isn't just what you say—it's what you do, and the way you do it.

So, how will you guide the tribe?

Cultivate high-trust relationships

Trust is the lubricant that keeps a culture running smoothly.

When people don't have psychological safety—the confidence to speak up, share ideas, and take risks without fear of punishment or retribution—friction builds. Over time, culture grinds down its inhabitants.

In low-trust environments, rules are followed rigidly, without nuance. Command-and-control dynamics dominate. Policies and procedures balloon—covering not just what happens during daily operations, but what *might happen* on a rainy day, on a Tuesday, under a blue moon.

Trust, in a business context, is a shared understanding of standards. It is a common expectation of outcomes and behaviors—of *how we will do things.* Trust builds speed, sharpens performance, and strengthens engagement and collaboration. It's the oil that keeps any organization running, engineered for product leadership, operational excellence, or customer intimacy.

Storytelling fuels trust; transparency promotes it.

Satya Nadella embraced both, moving Microsoft from a low-trust, know-it-all culture to an inquisitive, learn-it-all one. This highlights the critical role of psychological safety in cultural transformation. By encouraging openness and collaboration, Nadella built an environment where employees felt safe to share ideas and take risks, which reinforced *high-trust relationships*.

Cultivate high-trust relationships

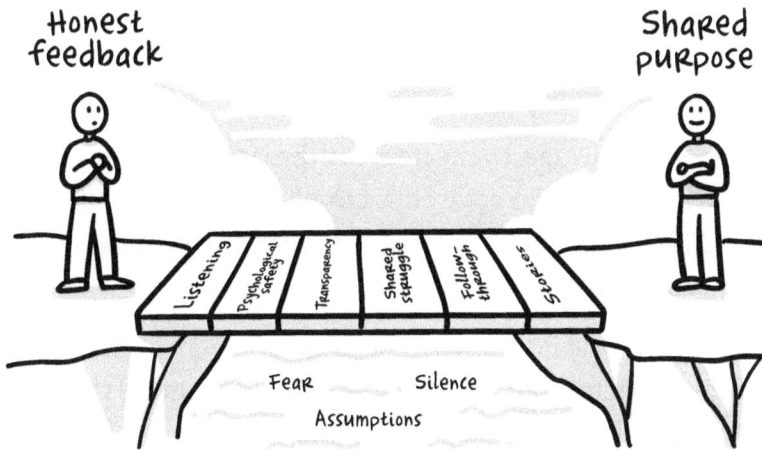

Honest feedback

Shared purpose

Listening · Psychological safety · Transparency · Shared struggle · Follow-through · Stories

Fear   Silence

Assumptions

Trust doesn't appear—it's built, plank by plank,
through shared effort and story.

Alan Mulally did the same, moving from a cutthroat corporate culture to a collaborative One Ford.

But trust is a delicate commodity, to be calibrated constantly, at every level. Boeing, the once revered brand, has lost trust. A string of high-profile failures have shaken confidence inside and out. Whistleblower reports to the Federal Aviation Administration have surged—126 in the first half of 2024 alone.[24]

Even Microsoft wobbled. In its rush to lead in AI, it launched "Recall," a feature designed to take constant snapshots of a user's activity to boost productivity. Trust glitched. Customers pushed back. Recall was recalled.[25]

Under Mulally, Ford posted a profit every year from 2009, galvanized by a culture that transformed how the company worked.

"Alan really captured the hearts and minds of our employees," said Chairman Bill Ford.[26] But since Mulally's retirement, Ford has seen a revolving door of CEOs and a declining stock price—struggling to sustain the cultural momentum of One Ford.

The role of storyteller must extend beyond the CEO.

Culture carriers—superconnectors with broad, diverse networks—play a critical role. They're well regarded, influential, and trusted beyond their immediate circles. They're go-to-people for information and insight.

To craft culture, find these superconnectors. Give them a task: Shape the operating environment. Ask them to spread the stories that define culture, repeating lore and linking everyday actions to the broader mission. Invite them to make abstract ideas concrete, real, and relatable through lived examples and daily practice.

Most importantly, ask them to connect the dots between *what* people do—the work—and *how* they do it—the culture.

Alignment is everything.

Culture carriers need a framework. Objectives and key results (OKRs), pioneered by Andy Grove at Intel, provide the scaffolding for trust, transparency, and candor.[*] They encourage open communication, give employees bounded autonomy, and create a vehicle for recognition and feedback.

Most importantly, OKRs translate strategy to concrete tactics and actions.

Google has used OKRs for decades. Team goals are visible, which fosters openness and trust. Mulally had a similar system at Ford,

---

[*] OKRs, which stands for Objectives and Key Results, are a simple way to set goals by clearly stating what you want to achieve and how you'll measure progress.

with a different name: business plan review (BPR). Strategy was distilled into key metrics and data, then reviewed collaboratively, week after week.

As described by Bryce Hoffman in *American Icon*, the process would

> shine a light into the darkest corners of the company. Everything would be illuminated.

Nadella, too, in building a learn-it-all culture, insists on

> gathering all the decision-makers in a war-room setting.

For him,

> trust is built by being consistent over time.[27]

High-trust relationships hold culture together. Trust lubricates the free flow of ideas, candid feedback, and collective learning. When employees trust their leaders—and each other—they are more willing to take the risks necessary to change and grow.

Trust doesn't come from trust falls at off-sites. It comes from working, failing, trying, and succeeding—together. It grows through open, honest conversations about decisions, goals, and obstacles.

Trust is built in the trenches of daily work. It thrives on continuous feedback, shared struggles, and hard-won successes.

Collect the stories that reinforce trust—the wins that prove it works, the failures that prove it's needed.

Then, tell them.

Intertwine work and culture

Culture is soft. Work is hard.

Perhaps that is why people hold them separately, distancing the invisible from the visible, scheduling them at different times. A two-day retreat focused on company culture. Real work for the other 363 days of the year. But to do this is to deny gravity, to scream "Earth is flat!" while flying from St. Louis to Sydney.

Narrative is a natural device to close the gap.

You must weave storytelling into the work environment, not treat it as an occasional activity. Encourage employees to share relevant anecdotes during team meetings, project updates, even informal check-ins.

These culture stories all share a theme—*how we do things around here*. They might be tales of overcoming challenges, customer wins, or personal growth.

Embedding them into daily routines keeps culture vibrant. It reinforces the "how" behind mission, vision, values, and purpose. It gives context.

Some of these stories will emerge organically. Some you can engineer.

At Allstate's 2023 leadership conference, some hundred senior executives gathered. Culture and transformative growth were center stage. In groups, they played the culture game—*once upon a time at Allstate...*

Leaders started with business scenarios, telling stories about how work gets derailed. Each group was prompted with "culture villains"—insidious collective habits and unwritten rules that fed bureaucracy.

Each villain was printed on a black card. "Let's share it when it's fully baked" slowed progress and reinforced hierarchy. "Is that data right?" questioned factual information, stalling change and keeping teams in silos. With dozens of villains to choose from, groups delighted in drawing on their lived experience—telling tales of slowed transformation, stalled projects, and fragmented work.

These stories made culture visible.

The game sparked a realization: Each of us contributes to both positive and negative aspects of our culture. It's not just horror stories. Success stories have an equal place. After teams outlined just how badly culture might derail their best efforts, they flipped the script. Anchored to Allstate's purpose and values—about how work could move forward. As one senior leader put it:

> Folks are learning to lead. They really have to come up with practical solutions to address what's going on. It's making it real.

Intertwine Work and Culture

Stories make culture visible.

Culture stories must live in the work itself. They should sit at desks, steer meetings, and guide decisions. Call out the culture villains—the collective habits that slow progress and tangle teams.

Most importantly, use culture storytelling as a tool for reflection and adaptation.

Storytelling is a safe way to complain at work—to bring the conversation from the corridor into the room. It gives teams permission to ask: "What's holding us back?" But also: "What will help us move forward?"

Make culture part of your ongoing conversation, not a side project. Because culture isn't a retreat—it's how work gets done.

YOU KNOW...

...that **culture is invisible yet powerful.** It whispers how we work, act, and lead—how we do things—guiding behaviors and decisions, often without us even realizing.

...that **culture storytelling turns the invisible into the visible.** It gives leaders a tool to sculpt and sustain culture through narrative.

...that culture storytelling follows six key rules:

1. Anchor stories in history and heritage.

2. Showcase core values and principles.

3. Connect to the broader vision.

4. Use symbols and rituals.

5. Cultivate high-trust relationships.

6. Intertwine work and culture.

...that **anchoring stories in history and heritage** connects the present to the past, creating a shared sense of belonging and continuity.

...that **showcasing core values and principles** makes culture real—not just words on a wall, but behaviors that are lived.

...that **connecting to the broader vision** aligns daily actions with the mission, keeping everyone pulling in the same direction.

...that **using symbols and rituals** embeds culture in action, reinforcing what matters through visible cues.

...that **cultivating high-trust relationships** fuels collaboration, which fosters openness, shared purpose, and a willingness to take risks.

...that **intertwining work and culture** ensures culture isn't a side project—it's how work gets done.

Strong cultures don't happen by accident. They're built, one story at a time.

Culture storytelling connects, engages, and transforms how people work, creating an environment where everyone can thrive.

THE PAYOFF

If you have read this far, thank you.

If you're one of those people who picks up a book and skips to the end, I expect you will now turn to page 1—it's a better starting place.

In writing this book, I kept returning to formative moments that have forged my *Weltanschauung*—my worldview. Conversations with clients that sparked ideas. My own struggles with logarithmic tables as a schoolboy. Visits to museums to stare in awe at Ashurbanipal's reliefs or Babbage's machines. Writing *Story Business* has been my own journey through time and ideas.

But the moment I return to most belongs to British science historian James Burke.

His 1978 show *Connections* traced surprising links between seemingly unrelated events. In one episode, "Faith in Numbers," Burke revisits the late 1800s and the game of snooker. Snooker balls were made from ivory, and demand was outstripping supply—to say nothing of the ecological impact of elephant hunting.

An alternative was sought.

Enter John Wesley Hyatt. In 1869, the American inventor set out to find a substitute. He developed celluloid—one of the first thermoplastics—by treating highly flammable nitrocellulose with camphor. A breakthrough. The first moldable plastic soon found its way into combs, buttons, and, of course, snooker balls.

Then came another problem—a volatile one.

Striking celluloid billiard balls too hard caused small explosions. Meanwhile, Alfred Nobel—he of Nobel Prize fame—was tackling volatility from another angle, trying to stabilize nitroglycerin. That spark led the Swedish chemist to produce a more powerful explosive: dynamite.

Throughout the series, Burke weaves stories into a broader truth: Progress isn't linear. It twists and turns. The search for a better billiard ball led to the invention of plastic, which in turn led to the development of explosives. A chain reaction.

Connections planted an idea in me: that history and invention are not linear creatures. They are part of a complex web, a nuanced and often surprising chain of cause and effect that determines progress.

Everything is connected.

For me, Burke was a superb packager of ideas. A storyteller. That is the central theme of this book—that it's not the best ideas that win, it's the best-packaged ideas.

Connections planted that seed in the fortified citadel of my mind.

I have, hopefully, planted a few in yours.

One is that story shapes how we see the world and, therefore, informs the decisions we make—even the seemingly rational ones.

This should lead you to a conclusion:

> In business, storytelling is not just the remit of marketing—it belongs to finance, product, engineering, human resources, change management, and sales.

More importantly, storytelling is the responsibility of leadership—your responsibility—and a powerful tool to shape the culture and the future history of your organization.

That's why *Story Business* laid out six genres of storytelling:

Value storytelling makes numbers mean something.

Product storytelling turns ideas into reality.

Brand storytelling builds worlds that attract.

Sales storytelling creates conversations that convert.

Leadership storytelling provides shared context.

Culture storytelling guides the future of an organization.

The tenets of the Storyteller give you the fundamentals. *The mathematics of story* gives you tools. *Synapse and story* explain why this all works. Hook, Meat, and Payoff not only makes you smarter, it makes your audience *feel* smarter.

Now it's your turn.

Burke's lesson is clear: No idea stands alone. And the stories you tell will frame how people understand your work. Your strategy. Your vision. Your company.

So, what's your story?

Most importantly—how will you tell it?

My wish is that you've enjoyed reading *Story Business*—and found it useful. I hope your copy is littered with scratch marks and notes—where, somehow, I've struck a chord.

Now the Payoff.

My ask? ***Try it.*** Take one thing—one notion, one tool, one anecdote—and ***use it.*** Apply it to your work. Try it with your team.

Storytelling is a cumulative skill. Once you've got the hang of one element, try another. Then another. Tomorrow, next week, next month. It all adds up.

Take your idea, and make it the best-packaged idea. Take your story, and use it to penetrate the fortified citadel of the human mind.

My mother never knew how to end stories. A trait she passed on to me. In our family, she would tell a story, get to the end, then stop—rather like the King's advice in *Alice in Wonderland*.

One of us would then pipe up and ask, "Is that the end of the story?"

It is.

Maybe.

IT TAKES A VILLAGE

Journalist Christopher Hitchens said, "Everyone has a book in them, but in most cases, that's where it should stay." Let's hope his advice isn't true. But the first part of that particular adage should come with a warning label—one with big letters and flashing lights.

Writing a book is *really hard* work.

I have wanted to write a book for years. My secret fantasy was to become a famous author the lazy way. I had even developed a fiendish five-step plan to become one:

Step 1. Invent a time machine.

Step 2. Travel forward into the future.

Step 3. "Borrow" manuscripts from really famous (but unknown in our time) authors.

Step 4. Return to my own time and pass off said "borrowed" manuscripts as mine.

Step 5. Live the glittery yet secluded life (depending on mood) of a rich, pretentious, famous author.

Of course, if you think about it, the plan has a few plot holes. Aside from a general lack of expertise in quantum physics that

Wikipedia can't solve and a few ethical considerations about "borrowing," it's a pretty terrible plan for commercializing the world's first time machine.

So I had to write this book the hard way, and I had *a lot* of help.

Thanks to:

Sheri, for listening to early drafts and not cringing. Alexandra and Quinn for unwittingly contributing phrases and stories to this book.

Fellow fforwarders: Rose, Dave, Jess, Sally, Liz, Shannon, Andreas, Amy, Pam, Frank, Jill, Michael, Peter, Eugene, Max, Cristina, Christian, Rebecca, Jim and Mike, who all contribute in thousands of ways, every day.

Eugene, especially, who collaborated on the beautiful illustrations. Jess, Giovanni, and Cristina, who shepherded this book over the finish line, have my special thanks. Stacey Ennis's nonfiction book school helped kickstart this book. Robin Bethel coached me.

Special thanks my publisher Otterpine: My editor, Amy Reed, gave me just the right amount of feedback, and Saeah Wood and her team brought an idea to life.

The people who inspired me and showed me the way in writing a book: Justin Foster, Bryce Hoffman, Stephanie Evergreen, Joe Jaffe.

Alpha and beta readers, whose comments and reactions were indispensable: Mike Andrews, Gopal Rajagopalan, Jim Gerace, Misty Balinsat, Rebecca Haarlow, Peter Watts, Nicole Hawthorne, Noreen MacMahon, Lance Mald, James Sherwin-Smith, Jess Merten, Martha Delehanty, Jonathan Green, Tom Broderick, Michael Flanagan.

Barry Wacksman shared his stories and views on innovation and invention.

Jorge Fino patented the earbud you might have dangling in your ear, and we had one of my earliest conversations about product storytelling.

PR man Lou Hoffman spun anecdotes about the power of anecdotes.

Julie Roehm and Ted Wright told me about word of mouth and their collaboration in gathering stories for SAP.

Marc Escobosa brought up the conversation about stories as units of work.

Peter Watts for numerous contributions and discussions about storytelling and his genius idea of the Hero Formula.

Simon Levin and Joel Wecksell told me of their masterstroke—the evidence stack.

Raja Rajammanar has been a friend of fassforward for years and is an inspiration in the field of marketing.

Futurist Mike Bechtel pointed me to the past and the story of Charles Babbage.

Sarabeth Stine reminded me that salespeople are really good at getting others to tell their stories—that's true.

Kevin Zavaglia is a fount of practical wisdom in business and sales.

Chris DeMaio shared his draft book on Airbnb and stories as *The Accidental Superhost*.

Abhishek Mittal and Manoj Nair told me horror stories and love stories.

Howie Waterman lent me his expertise in PR and crisis communications.

Tami Erwin talked about the necessity of leadership storytelling and truthtelling.

Ronan Dunne gave me leadership storytelling as shared context.

Amy Purcell shared the history of Fifth Third Bank.

Alan Gardner shared stories of history and heritage.

Bob Toohey and I have had many conversations about how to shape culture through storytelling.

Alexandra Band has been a generous partner in putting those ideas into practice.

Others have given their valuable time, had their brains picked, and volunteered their views on storytelling as it applies to business: Adam Levine, Ali Ahmed, Andrea Gilman, Carolyn Weiss, Derek Fetzer, Domenic D'Ambrosio, Doug Popovich, Drew Davidson, Isaac Cohen, Isabelle Guis, Janine Paavola, Jay Jaffin, Jeremy Godwin, Mary Jane Begin, Matt Yee, Ned Ehrbar, Niclas Nordensved, Paulina Davilla, Elizabeth Stuckman, Peter Laughter, Ricardo Galan, Rona Elliot, Sharman Ghio, Shelley Cavanaugh...et al.

Thank you!

GLOSSARY

Preface and Introduction

Story Business The concept that stories compel business decisions, acknowledging that it's the *best-packaged* ideas, not the best ones, that win.

Corporate pig latin Jargon and technical terms used in business communication that can be difficult for outsiders to understand.

Jargon monoxide A play on words referring to the overuse of business jargon that can "suffocate" clear communication.

Weekend speak A communication style that avoids corporate jargon and uses more relatable, everyday language.

Chapter 1

Cuneiform An early system of writing developed in ancient Mesopotamia, using wedge-shaped marks pressed into clay tablets with a reed stylus.

Hieroglyphs An ancient Egyptian writing system that used pictorial symbols to represent words, syllables, or sounds.

Rhetoric The art of persuasive speaking or writing, codified in ancient Greece as a formal discipline.

Acta Diurna An early form of daily public chronicle in ancient Rome, often considered a precursor to modern newspapers.

Cursus Publicus The state-run postal and transportation system of the Roman Empire.

Words, Pictures, and Structure The basic elements of story-telling. *Words* carry meaning, *Pictures* evoke experience, and *Structure* organizes the narrative.

Lingua franca A common language used by people who speak different native languages, often in a business or professional context.

Chapter 2

The shoulders of giants A metaphor describing how new ideas and innovations build upon the work of previous thinkers and innovators.

Mythobiome The concept that we live surrounded by stories that make us who we are, as other biomes influence our physical environment and health.

Remixing Combining or editing existing ideas to create some-thing new. In storytelling, it involves borrowing and reimagining elements from various sources to craft original narratives.

Chapter 3

Default mode network (aka the narrative network) A system of connected parts of the brain that lights up when we're awake, creates stories, but when unfocused is used for "planning, pondering, and daydreaming."

Task-positive network The brain's system that activates when we're focused on a specific task, kicking in when we pay attention.

Cognitive biases Mental shortcuts that ease hard thinking and save the brain valuable calories but can also introduce errors.

Narrative fallacy Our limited ability to look at sequences of events without weaving an explanation into them or forcing a logical link upon them.

Arrow of relationship A storytelling concept that illustrates the connection between different elements in a narrative.

Satisficing A decision-making strategy that aims for a satisfactory or adequate result, rather than the optimal solution.

Somatic marker hypothesis The idea that emotions and their associated bodily states influence decision-making.

System 1 and System 2 thinking System 1: Fast, automatic, intuitive thinking. System 2: Slower, more deliberate, and more logical thinking.

Motive Triangle A concept with three corners—Hope, Fear, and Reason—used to understand decision-making and motivation.

Chapter 4

Story A story is any piece of information, wrapped in emotion.

Storytelling Occurs in the sweet spot between framing the way people see the world and moving them to action.

T-Leaf An audience map used in storytelling to understand and address the audience's needs and perspectives.

Hero Formula "We bring X to Y to help them deal with Z," where We is the storyteller, X is the product/solution, Y is the audience, and Z is their challenge.

Hook, Meat, and Payoff A simple structure for organizing content in business storytelling.

Chapter 5

Value storytelling The mix of numbers and narrative that lift stock valuation, price, or perceived worth.

Story stock A stock valued more for its potential than its current financial numbers. The narrative explains why it will succeed in the future.

Purpose The business purpose is its "why." A holy grail, or burning platform, that motivates and binds employees in a common cause.

Meme stock A stock that rises quickly because of social media hype, not because of the company's actual performance. Example: GameStop.

Evidence stack A framework outlining different levels of evidence, from strongest to weakest.

Arrow of coherence A straight line of narrative logic that provides causality and consistency to allow the audience to make sense of their experience.

Narrative constellation Groups of stories that, while distinct, share common themes and together create a compelling, larger narrative.

Overton window The range of ideas considered acceptable or mainstream in public discourse.

Chapter 6

Product storytelling The science fiction that conceives products and brings ideas to life.

Jobs to be done A framework focusing on the specific goals and outcomes a customer is trying to achieve with a product.

Use cases Detailed descriptions—step-by-step scenarios that demonstrate functionality—of how a product or feature will be used.

User stories Short narratives (often encompassing multiple use cases) giving context for how a person interacts with a product in real life.

Wicked problems Complex, interconnected challenges that are difficult to define and have no straightforward solution.

Comparator An element in product naming that compares the new product to something familiar.

Descriptor An element in product naming that describes a key feature or attribute of the new product.

Backers, builders, and buyers Key audiences for product stories. Backers fund the idea, builders help develop it, and buyers are the purchasers and users of the product.

Chapter 7

Brand storytelling The worldbuilding that attracts a deeply invested audience.

Iceberg theory Hemingway's approach to storytelling, suggesting that the deeper meaning of a story should be implicit.

Sub-creation Tolkien's term for worldbuilding, the process of creating an internally consistent and believable fictional world.

Show bible A comprehensive reference document used in television and film production that outlines the characters, settings, storylines, and rules of a fictional universe.

Blandscaping Le Guin's critique of creating generic, interchangeable settings in worldbuilding.

The IKEA effect A cognitive bias where consumers place a disproportionately high value on products they partially created.

Lagom A Swedish philosophy and design approach meaning "just the right amount" or "in perfect balance."

Fan fiction Stories created by fans based on existing fictional universes, characters, or real-world brands.

Storymaking The process of enabling, creating, and curating experiences for consumers to be part of the story.

Chapter 8

Sales storytelling The conversations that engage and convert prospects to customers.

Dark funnel The part of a buyer's journey occurring without the seller's knowledge, where they research and form opinions on what to buy without ever speaking to a prospective seller.

Supercommunicators People who are exceptionally skilled at creating meaningful connections through conversation.

Emotional reciprocity A sales technique where the salesperson acknowledges and reflects the customer's emotions to build rapport and trust.

Looping Asking clarifying questions, restating responses, and aligning perspectives to ensure mutual understanding.

Love stories In a sales context, anecdotes or mini case studies that highlight positive customer experiences with what you're selling.

Horror stories Cautionary tales used in sales to illustrate the potential negative consequences of not choosing a particular product or solution.

Grandma language A communication approach using simple, relatable terms to explain complex concepts, making them accessible to a wide audience.

Chapter 9

Leadership storytelling A leader's use of stories to inspire, guide, and motivate their teams or organizations.

Shared context A common understanding of situations, goals, and values within an organization, created through leadership storytelling.

Truthtelling The practice of honest and transparent communication by leaders, even when sharing difficult information.

Beautiful question An ambitious yet actionable question that can shift perceptions or thinking.

Anecdote A short, interesting story about a real incident or person, used to illustrate a point.

Aphorism A concise, memorable statement of a general truth or observation.

Axiom A statement or principle that is generally accepted to be true without proof.

Chapter 10

Culture storytelling The history and lore that shapes collective habits and lays the path to the future.

Weltanschauung Our intuition of the world—our worldview; the complex interplay of our lived experiences through which we interpret the world.

Values What an organization believes in. The core beliefs that shape its identity, culture, and decision-making.

Principles How an organization puts its values into action. The guiding behaviors that turn beliefs into everyday decisions and practices.

Symbols Observable elements of organizational culture, such as physical environment, communication styles, and work practices.

Discipline The core strand in the cultural DNA of a company, guiding the business model's function.

Operational excellence A discipline emphasizing efficiency, consistency, and streamlined processes in organizational culture.

Customer intimacy A discipline focusing on building strong relationships with customers by tailoring products and services to meet unique needs.

Product leadership A discipline prioritizing innovation, brand marketing, and being at the forefront of the industry.

Collective habits The unconscious routines of teams that act as the engine of culture.

Unwritten rules Deeply ingrained implicit norms that dictate "how we do things around here" in an organization.

Culture carriers Trusted storytellers scattered throughout an organization who influence through tales of culture.

Goldilocks zone In the context of change management, the balance between too much change (leading to stress and burnout) and too little change (leading to stagnation).

Psychological safety The belief that one can speak up, express ideas, and take risks without fear of punishment or retribution.

Story 1 The journey or path to get to a destination in change management.

Story 2 The destination or vision in change management.

ENDNOTES

Introduction

1 Ronan Dunne, former CEO, Verizon Consumer Group, chairman, Six Nations Rugby, interview by the author.

2 Brian Fugere, Chelsea Hardaway, and Jon Warshawsky, *Why Business People Speak Like Idiots: A Bullfighter's Guide* (New York: Simon and Schuster, 2005).

Chapter 1

1 Annemieke Milks et al., "A Double-Pointed Wooden Throwing Stick from Schöningen, Germany: Results and New Insights from a Multianalytical Study," *PLOS One* 18, no. 7 (2023): e0287719, https://doi.org/10.1371/journal .pone.0287719.

2 Elizabeth Knowles, *What They Didn't Say: A Book of Misquotations* (Oxford: Oxford University Press, 2006).

3 Natalie Thaïs Uomini and Georg Friedrich Meyer, "Shared Brain Lateralization Patterns in Language and Acheulean Stone Tool Production: A Functional Transcranial Doppler Ultrasound Study," *PLOS One* 8, no. 8 (August 30, 2013): e72693, https://doi.org/10.1371/journal.pone.0072693.

4 Maxime Aubert et al., "Earliest Hunting Scene in Prehistoric Art," *Nature* 576, no. 7787 (December 11, 2019): 442–45, https://doi.org/10.1038/s41586 -019-1806-y.

5 The British Museum, "I Am Ashurbanipal: King of the World, King of Assyria," accessed August 20, 2023, https://www.britishmuseum.org/exhibitions /i-am-ashurbanipal-king-world-king-assyria.

6 David H. Tucker, George Unwin, and Philip Soundy Unwin, "History of Publishing," *Encyclopedia Britannica*, July 26, 1999, https://www.britannica.com/topic/publishing.

7 Pew Research Center, "Demographics of Mobile Device Ownership and Adoption in the United States," January 31, 2024, https://www.pewresearch.org/internet/fact-sheet/mobile.

Chapter 2

1 John of Salisbury, *Metalogicon* (1159), fol. 217r.

2 Shnayer Z. Leiman, "Dwarfs on the Shoulders of Giants," *Tradition*, Spring 1993.

3 Science Museum, "How Was Penicillin Developed?," accessed August 26, 2023, https://www.sciencemuseum.org.uk/objects-and-stories/how-was-penicillin-developed.

4 Science History Institute, "Howard Walter Florey and Ernst Boris Chain," June 2, 2016, https://www.beckmancenter.org/education/scientific-biographies/howard-walter-florey-and-ernst-boris-chain.

5 National WWII Museum, "Making Penicillin: Thanks to Penicillin...He Will Come Home!," 2020, https://www.nationalww2museum.org/sites/default/files/2017-07/thanks-to-penicillin-lesson.pdf.

6 Shauna O'Brien and Sam Bourgi, "How Does Apple Stock React to Product Releases?," *Dividend.com*, March 8, 2018, https://www.dividend.com/how-to-invest/how-does-apple-stock-react-to-product-releases.

7 Julia Kollewe, "Apple Stock Price Falls on News of Steve Jobs's Death," *The Guardian*, October 6, 2011, http://www.theguardian.com/technology/2011/oct/06/apple-stock-steve-jobs.

8 Gary Wolf, "Steve Jobs: The Next Insanely Great Thing," *WIRED*, February 1, 1996.

9 Steve Jobs, "Stanford Commencement Address," YouTube, 2005, https://www.youtube.com/watch?v=UF8uR6Z6KLc.

10 John Schroter, "Steve Jobs Introduces iPhone in 2007," YouTube, 2011, https://www.youtube.com/watch?v=MnrJzXM7a6o.

11 Daniel Hillis and Bran Ferren, *Touch Driven Method and Apparatus to Integrate and Display Multiple Image Layers Forming Alternate Depictions of Same Subject Matter*, US Patent No. 7724242B2, issued May 25, 2010.

12 Kevin Ashton, *How to Fly a Horse: The Secret History of Creation, Invention, and Discovery* (New York: Anchor, 2015).

Chapter 3

1 Judson A. Brewer et al., "Meditation Experience Is Associated with Differences in Default Mode Network Activity and Connectivity," *Proceedings of the National Academy of Sciences* 108, no. 50 (November 23, 2011): 20254–59, https://doi.org/10.1073/pnas.1112029108.

2 Friederike Fabritius and Hans W. Hagemann, *The Leading Brain: Neuroscience Hacks to Work Smarter, Better, Happier* (New York: Penguin, 2018).

3 Nassim Nicholas Taleb, *The Black Swan: The Impact of the Highly Improbable* (New York: Random House, 2009).

4 Jonathan Gottschall, "Why Storytelling Is the Ultimate Weapon," *Fast Company*, May 2, 2012, https://www.fastcompany.com/1680581/why-storytelling-is-the-ultimate-weapon.

5 Dan Ariely, *Predictably Irrational: The Hidden Forces That Shape Our Decisions* (New York: HarperCollins, 2008).

6 Michael M. Grynbaum, "In New York, Taxi Revenue and Tips From Credit Cards Rise," *The New York Times*, November 7, 2009, https://www.nytimes.com/2009/11/08/nyregion/08taxi.html.

7 Ariely, *Predictably Irrational*.

8 Herbert A. Simon, "Rational Decision Making in Business Organizations," *American Economic Review* 69, no. 4 (1979): 493–513.

9 Donald B. Calne, *Within Reason: Rationality and Human Behavior* (New York: Pantheon Books, 1999).

10 Jonathan Cohen, "What Is Neuroeconomics?," *Yale Insights*, January 15, 2010, https://insights.som.yale.edu/insights/what-is-neuroeconomics.

11 Antonio Damasio, *Descartes' Error: Emotion, Reason, and the Human Brain* (New York: Penguin, 2005).

12 Steve Twomey, "Phineas Gage: Neuroscience's Most Famous Patient," *Smithsonian Magazine*, January 1, 2010, https://www.smithsonianmag.com/history/phineas-gage-neurosciences-most-famous-patient-11390067.

13 Daniel Kahneman, *Thinking, Fast and Slow* (New York: Farrar, Straus and Giroux, 2011).

14 Brian Fugere, Chelsea Hardaway, and Jon Warshawsky, *Why Business People Speak Like Idiots: A Bullfighter's Guide* (New York: Simon and Schuster, 2005).

15 UK Research and Innovation, "A Brief History of Climate Change Discoveries," accessed January 19, 2025, https://www.discover.ukri.org/a-brief -history-of-climate-change-discoveries/index.html.

16 Steve Sternberg, "How Many Americans Floss Their Teeth?," *US News & World Report*, May 2, 2016, https://www.usnews.com/news/articles /2016-05-02/how-many-americans-floss-their-teeth.

17 Meta, "Meta Reports Third Quarter 2024 Results," October 30, 2024, https://investor.atmeta.com/investor-news/press-release-details/2024 /Meta-Reports-Third-Quarter-2024-Results/default.aspx.

18 Stacy Jo Dixon, "Facebook: North America MAU 2023," *Statista*, April 26, 2024, https://www.statista.com/statistics/247614/number-of-monthly -active-facebook-users-worldwide.

19 Benedict Carey, "This Is Your Brain off Facebook," *The New York Times*, January 31, 2019, https://www.nytimes.com/2019/01/30/health/facebook -psychology-health.html.

Chapter 4

1 Marc Escobosa, interview by author, n.d.

2 Shigeru Miyagawa et al. "Linguistic Capacity Was Present in the *Homo sapiens* Population 135 Thousand Years Ago," *Frontiers in Psychology* 16 (2025), https://doi.org/10.3389/fpsyg.2025.1503900.

3 Jean M. Twenge and W. Keith Campbell, *The Narcissism Epidemic: Living in the Age of Entitlement* (New York: Free Press, 2009).

4 Brady Butterfield and Janet Metcalfe, "Errors Committed with High Confidence Are Hypercorrected," *Journal of Experimental Psychology: Learning, Memory, and Cognition* 27, no. 6 (2001): 1491–94.

5 Fiammetta Marini et al. "Three's a Crowd: Fast Ensemble Perception of First Impressions of Trustworthiness," *Cognition* 239 (October 2023), https: //doi.org/10.1016/j.cognition.2023.105540; Janine Willis and Alexander Todorov, "First Impressions: Making Up Your Mind After a 100-Ms Exposure to a Face," *Psychological Science* 17, no. 7 (2006): 592–98, https: //doi.org/10.1111/j.1467-9280.2006.01750.x; Microsoft Canada, "Attention Spans: Consumer Insights," *Microsoft Advertising Research Report*, Spring 2015, https://dl.motamem.org/microsoft-attention-spans-research -report.pdf; SWNS Digital, "First Impressions Do Count and It Takes

Less Than 30 Seconds to Form an Opinion on Someone," April 3, 2023, https://swnsdigital.com/uk/2023/04/first-impressions-do-count-and-it-takes-less-than-30-seconds-to-form-an-opinion-on-someone; Paul W. Eastwick and Eli J. Finkel, "Sex Differences in Mate Preferences Revisited: Do People Know What They Initially Desire in a Romantic Partner?," *Journal of Personality and Social Psychology* 94, no. 2 (2008): 245–64, https://doi.org/10.1037/0022-3514.94.2.245.

6 Anne Trafton, "In the Blink of an Eye," *MIT News*, January 16, 2014, https://news.mit.edu/2014/in-the-blink-of-an-eye-0116.

7 Allan Paivio, *Imagery and Verbal Processes* (New York: Holt, Rinehart and Winston, 1971).

8 John Sweller, "Cognitive Load Theory, Learning Difficulty, and Instructional Design," *Learning and Instruction* 4, no. 4 (1994): 295–312.

9 Richard E. Mayer, *Multimedia Learning* (New York: Cambridge University Press, 2001).

Chapter 5

1 J. Clement, "Topic: Video Game Industry," *Statista*, November 6, 2024, https://www.statista.com/topics/868/video-games.

2 David Floyd, "Buffett's Bet with the Hedge Funds: And the Winner Is …," *Investopedia*, June 25, 2019, https://www.investopedia.com/articles/investing/030916/buffetts-bet-hedge-funds-year-eight-brka-brkb.asp.

3 Mike Dash, *Tulipomania: The Story of the World's Most Coveted Flower and the Extraordinary Passions It Aroused* (New York: Crown, 2001).

4 Aaron Patrick, "Elizabeth Holmes May Be a Fraud, but She Knows Leadership Psychology," *Australian Financial Review*, January 14, 2022, https://www.afr.com/work-and-careers/management/elizabeth-holmes-may-be-a-fraud-but-she-knows-leadership-psychology-20220112-p59nm3.

5 Roger Parloff, "This CEO Is Out for Blood," *Fortune*, June 12, 2014, https://fortune.com/2014/06/12/theranos-blood-holmes.

6 Ariana Eunjung Cha, "Theranos Blood Test: The Insanely Influential Stanford Professor Who Called the Company Out for Its 'Stealth Research,'" *The Washington Post*, July 3, 2015, https://www.washingtonpost.com/news/to-your-health/wp/2015/07/03/the-insanely-influential-stanford-professor-behind-biotech-firms-push-to-get-fda-approval-it-probably-doesnt-need.

7 Bobby Allyn, "Elizabeth Holmes Has Started Her 11-Year Prison Sentence. Here's What to Know," *NPR*, May 30, 2023, https://www.npr.org/2023/05/30/1178728092/elizabeth-holmes-prison-sentence-theranos-fraud-silicon-valley.

8 "Ferrari, via libera dei soci Fiat al divorzio: Marchionne, 'Facciamo leva su Maranello per ridurre debito,'" *Il Fatto Quotidiano*, December 3, 2015, https://www.ilfattoquotidiano.it/2015/12/03/ferrari-via-libera-dei-soci-fiat-al-divorzio-marchionne-facciamo-leva-su-maranello-per-ridurre-debito/2274040.

9 Kevin Harris, "Professor Aswath Damodaran on Valuation," *Forbes*, July 17, 2018, https://www.forbes.com/sites/kevinharris/2018/07/17/professor-aswath-damodaran-on-valuation.

10 Aswath Damodaran, "The Ferrari IPO: A Price Premium for the Prancing Horse?," *Musings on Markets*, October 15, 2015, https://aswathdamodaran.blogspot.com/2015/10/the-ferrari-ipo-price-premium-for.html.

11 Aswath Damodaran, *Narrative and Numbers: The Value of Stories in Business* (New York: Columbia University Press, 2017), Kindle edition, 8–9.

12 Peter F. Drucker, *The Practice of Management* (New York: Harper & Row, 1954).

13 The Week Staff, "BP CEO: His 'Unbelievably Callous' Remark," *The Week*, June 2, 2010, https://theweek.com/articles/493915/bp-ceo-unbelievably-callous-remark.

14 Chris Malone, "Why Tylenol Got a Pass and BP Didn't," *Harvard Business Review*, September 15, 2010, https://hbr.org/2010/09/why-tylenol-got-a-pass-and-bp.

15 Howard Waterman, founder and CEO of The Waterman Group, interview by author, n.d.

16 Rob Stumpf, "Ferrari Hit with Ransomware Attack, Customer Data Stolen," *The Drive*, March 21, 2023, https://www.thedrive.com/news/ferrari-confirms-ransomware-attack-exposed-customer-data.

17 Soroush Vosoughi, Deb Roy, and Sinan Aral, "The Spread of True and False News Online," *Science* 359, no. 6380 (March 9, 2018): 1146–51.

18 N. Craig Smith and Erin McCormick, "Volkswagen's Emissions Scandal: How Could It Happen?," *INSEAD Publishing*, May 28, 2018, https://publishing.insead.edu/case/volkswagen-scandal.

19 Karen McIntyre and Cathrine Gyldensted, "Positive Psychology as a Theoretical Foundation for Constructive Journalism," *Journal of Media Ethics* 34, no. 2 (2019): 66–78.

20 Paula Moya and Matt Abrahams, "Telling Good Stories: How to Use the Elements of Narrative to Keep Listeners Engaged," *Think Fast, Talk Smart* (podcast), Stanford Graduate School of Business, February 4, 2022, https://www.gsb.stanford.edu/insights/telling-good-stories-how-use-elements-narrative-keep-listeners-engaged.

21 Robert J. Shiller, *Narrative Economics: How Stories Go Viral and Drive Major Economic Events* (Princeton: Princeton University Press, 2019).

Chapter 6

1 "The Tables of de Prony Are Finally Published Ninety Years After They Were Compiled," *History of Information*, accessed February 24, 2024, https://historyofinformation.com/detail.php?entryid=643.

2 Riche de Prony, *Notice sur les Grandes Tables Logarithmiques et Trigonométriques: Adaptées au Nouveau Système Métrique Décimal* (Paris: Didot, 1824).

3 De Prony, *Grandes Tables Logarithmiques et Trigonométriques*.

4 Bruce Collier and James MacLachlan, *Charles Babbage: And the Engines of Perfection* (Oxford: Oxford University Press, 2000).

5 Fast Company, "Why People Don't Buy Products—They Buy Better Versions of Themselves," January 28, 2014, https://fastcompany.com/3025484/why-people-dont-buy-products-they-buy-better-versions-of-themselves.

6 Samantha Cole, "Slack's Founder on How They Became a $1 Billion Company in Two Years," *Fast Company*, February 4, 2015, https://www.fastcompany.com/3041905/slacks-founder-on-how-they-became-a-1-billion-company-in-two-years.

7 Kaitlyn Tiffany, "'Slack' Is an Acronym," *The Verge*, September 28, 2016, https://www.theverge.com/2016/9/28/13098164/slack-is-an-acronym.

8 Tiny Speck, "Slack: Be Less Busy," Slack, January 14, 2014, https://web.archive.org/web/20140113184636/https://slack.com.

9 Internet Archive, "Slack.com," Wayback Machine, accessed February 19, 2024, https://web.archive.org/web/20190101000000*/slack.com.

10 Slack, "Dear Microsoft," *Slack Blog*, accessed February 19, 2024, https://slack.com/blog/news/dear-microsoft.

11 Harvard Business Review, *HBR's 10 Must Reads on Strategic Marketing* (Boston: Harvard Business Review Press, 2011).

12 Stewart Butterfield, "We Don't Sell Saddles Here," *Medium*, August 30, 2021, https://medium.com/@stewart/we-dont-sell-saddles-here -4c59524d650d.

13 Kevin A. Wilson, "Worth the Watt: A Brief History of the Electric Car, 1830 to Present," *Car and Driver*, March 31, 2023, https://www.caranddriver .com/features/g43480930/history-of-electric-cars.

14 Donna Tam, "Flickr Founder Plans to Kill Company E-Mails with Slack," *CNET*, August 14, 2013, https://www.cnet.com/tech/tech-industry /flickr-founder-plans-to-kill-company-e-mails-with-slack.

15 Butterfield, "We Don't Sell Saddles Here."

16 Jon Fingas, "Samsung Officially Delays Galaxy Fold Launch," *Engadget*, April 22, 2019, https://www.engadget.com/2019-04-22-samsung-officially -delays-galaxy-fold-launch.html.

17 Mark Roberge, "When and How Fast to Scale Your Business," *Stage 2 Capital*, accessed February 19, 2024, https://www.stage2.capital/science-of-scaling.

18 Everett M. Rogers and Ronny Adhikarya, "Diffusion of Innovations: An Up-to-Date Review and Commentary," *Annals of the International Communication Association* 3, no. 1 (1979): 67–81.

19 Ron Adner, *The Wide Lens: A New Strategy for Innovation* (New York: Portfolio Trade, 2012).

Chapter 7

1 Seth Godin, *All Marketers Are Liars: The Power of Telling Authentic Stories in a Low-Trust World* (New York: Portfolio, 2005).

2 Ernest Hemingway, *Death in the Afternoon* (New York: Scribner, 1932).

3 J. R. R. Tolkien, *The Return of the King* (New York: Del Rey, 1986).

4 J. R. R. Tolkien, "On Fairy Stories," in *The Monsters and the Critics and Other Essays*, ed. Christopher Tolkien (London: George Allen & Unwin, 1983), 109–61.

5 The Walt Disney Company, "Disney to Acquire Marvel Entertainment," August 31, 2009, https://thewaltdisneycompany.com/disney-to-acquire -marvel-entertainment.

6 Gene Roddenberry, *The Star Trek Guide*, Desilu Studios, 1967.

7 Henry Jenkins, *Convergence Culture: Where Old and New Media Collide* (New York: NYU Press, 2006).

8 FOX News, "IKEA Shares Recipe for Swedish Meatballs with Customers on Coronavirus Lockdown," *FOX 13 Tampa Bay*, April 21, 2020, https://www.fox13news.com/news/ikea-shares-recipe-for-swedish-meatballs-with-customers-on-coronavirus-lockdown.

9 The IKEA Museum, "The Road from Trading Pens to Furniture."

10 The IKEA Museum, "IKEA Culture According to Ingvar Kamprad."

11 Michael I. Norton, Daniel Mochon, and Dan Ariely, "The 'IKEA Effect': When Labor Leads to Love," *Journal of Consumer Psychology* 22, no. 3 (2012): 453–60.

12 The IKEA Museum, "The Story of a Beloved IKEA Bag."

13 *Jimmy Kimmel Live*, "Ryan Reynolds & Rob McElhenney on First Time They Met, Their Height Difference & Owning a Team," YouTube, August 10, 2022, https://www.youtube.com/watch?v=eMtbc6R16oI.

14 Lou Hoffman, interview by author, n.d.

15 Simon Sinek, *Start with Why: How Great Leaders Inspire Everyone to Take Action* (New York: Portfolio, 2009).

16 The IKEA Museum, "Restaurants That Make Customers Happy."

17 Mark Sweney and Catherine Shoard, "Apple Does Not 'Let Bad Guys Use iPhones on Screen,'" *The Guardian*, February 26, 2020, https://www.theguardian.com/technology/2020/feb/26/apple-does-not-let-bad-guys-use-iphones-on-screen.

18 The IKEA Museum, "The Art of Naming IKEA Products."

19 Akash Sriram and Hyunjoo Jin, "Elon Musk's Embrace of Advertising at Tesla Grabs Marketers' Attention," *Reuters*, May 18, 2023, https://www.reuters.com/business/autos-transportation/elon-musks-embrace-advertising-tesla-grabs-marketers-attention-2023-05-17/.

20 Ted Wright, interview by author, n.d.

21 Raja Rajamannar, *Quantum Marketing: Mastering the New Marketing Mindset for Tomorrow's Consumers* (New York: Harper Business, 2021).

22 Deloitte and *The Wall Street Journal* CMO Today, "Mastercard's Shift from Storytelling to 'Storymaking,'" *CMO Today*, November 29, 2016,

https://deloitte.wsj.com/cmo/mastercards-shift-from-storytelling-to
-storymaking-1480482146.

23 Julie Roehm, interview by author, n.d.

24 Raja Rajamannar, "How Can Brands Cut Through the Digital Noise?",
Mastercard Perspectives, June 10, 2021, https://www.mastercard.com/news
/perspectives/2021/how-can-brands-break-through-the-digital-noise/.

25 Mastercard, "Touch Card," accessed April 20, 2025, https://www
.mastercard.us/en-us/personal/find-a-card/touchcard.html.

26 IKEA, "Live Lagom Community," accessed January 19, 2025, https://
www.ikea.com/gb/en/this-is-ikea/sustainable-everyday/ikea-live-lagom
-community-pub8d845141.

27 D&AD, "Case Study: It's a Tide Ad Campaign," *D&AD*, accessed April
20, 2025, https://www.dandad.org/en/d-ad-tide-ad-campaign-case
-study-insights.

Chapter 8

1 Daniel H. Pink, *To Sell Is Human: The Surprising Truth About Moving Others*
(New York: Riverhead Books, 2012).

2 6sense, *The 2023 B2B Buyer Experience Report*, December 11, 2023,
https://6sense.com/resources/research/2023-b2b-buyer-experience
-report/.

3 *The Incredibles*, directed by Brad Bird (Burbank, CA: Pixar Animation Studios,
2004), film.

4 Yves Jeffcoat, "Meet the Conman Who Sold the Brooklyn Bridge—Many
Times Over," *HowStuffWorks*, July 26, 2022, https://history.howstuffworks
.com/historical-figures/conman-sold-brooklyn-bridge.htm.

5 *The Brooklyn Daily Eagle*, "A Bridge Across the East River," February 25, 1892,
https://www.nyshistoricnewspapers.org/?a=d&d=tbd18920225-01.1.6.

6 David McCullough, *The Great Bridge: The Epic Story of the Building of the
Brooklyn Bridge* (New York: Simon & Schuster, 1972).

7 Kevin Zavaglia, interview by author, n.d.

8 Leigh Gallagher, *The Airbnb Story: How Three Ordinary Guys Disrupted an
Industry, Made Billions...and Created Plenty of Controversy* (Boston: Houghton
Mifflin Harcourt, 2017).

9 Erick Schonfeld, "AirBed and Breakfast Takes Pad Crashing to a Whole New Level," *TechCrunch*, August 11, 2008, https://techcrunch.com/2008/08/11/airbed-and-breakfast-takes-pad-crashing-to-a-whole-new-level/.

10 Gallagher, *Airbnb Story*.

11 *TechCrunch* headlines.

12 OxfordUnion, "Brian Chesky," YouTube video, April 13, 2017, https://www.youtube.com/watch?v=LBGfjt2g2i4.

13 Airbnb, "Form S-1 Registration Statement," filed November 16, 2020, US Securities and Exchange Commission, https://www.sec.gov/Archives/edgar/data/1559720/000119312520294801/d81668ds1.htm.

14 Annie Murphy Paul, "Your Brain on Fiction," *The New York Times*, March 17, 2012, https://www.nytimes.com/2012/03/18/opinion/sunday/the-neuroscience-of-your-brain-on-fiction.html.

15 Jennifer Kingson, "'Multisensory branding' lets you sniff, taste, hear, see and touch a company," *Axios*, June 14, 2024, https://www.axios.com/2024/06/14/multisensory-marketing-mastercard-branding-priceless.

16 Sarabeth Stine, interview by author, n.d.

17 Zavaglia, interview.

Chapter 9

1 Microsoft News Center, "Satya Nadella Email to Employees on First Day as CEO," February 4, 2014, https://news.microsoft.com/2014/02/04/satya-nadella-email-to-employees-on-first-day-as-ceo.

2 Microsoft News Center, "Nadella Email to Employees."

3 Satya Nadella, Greg Shaw, and Jill Tracie Nichols, *Hit Refresh: The Quest to Rediscover Microsoft's Soul and Imagine a Better Future for Everyone* (New York: HarperCollins, 2017), Kindle edition.

4 Microsoft, "New CEO Satya Nadella Says Microsoft Will 'Move Faster, Push Harder and Continue to Transform,'" *The Official Microsoft Blog*, February 7, 2014, https://blogs.microsoft.com/blog/2014/02/07/weekend-reading-feb-7th-edition-new-ceo-satya-nadella-says-microsoft-will-move-faster-push-harder-and-continue-to-transform-and-windows-azure-being-used-to-live-stream.

5 *The Wall Street Journal*, "Satya Nadella: 'The Learn-It-All Does Better than the Know-It-All,'" *WSJ Video*, 2019, https://www.wsj.com/video/satya-nadella-the-learn-it-all-does-better-than-the-know-it-all/D8BC205C-D7F5-423E-8A41-0E921E86597C.

6 Ars Staff, "Microsoft 'Loves Linux' As It Makes Azure Bigger, Better," *Ars Technica*, October 21, 2014, https://arstechnica.com/information-technology/2014/10/microsoft-loves-linux-as-it-makes-azure-bigger-better.

7 Nadella, Shaw, and Nichols, *Hit Refresh*.

8 Tami Erwin, interview by author, n.d.

9 Microsoft, "Subject: Focusing on Our Short- and Long-Term Opportunity," *The Official Microsoft Blog*, January 18, 2023, https://blogs.microsoft.com/blog/2023/01/18/subject-focusing-on-our-short-and-long-term-opportunity.

10 Warren Berger, *A More Beautiful Question: The Power of Inquiry to Spark Breakthrough Ideas* (New York: Bloomsbury, 2014).

11 Ronan Dunne, former CEO, Verizon Consumer Group, chairman, Six Nations Rugby, interview by the author.

12 Microsoft, "Full Keynote: Satya Nadella at Microsoft Inspire 2023," YouTube, July 18, 2023, https://www.youtube.com/watch?v=RhwVMt_XCUE.

13 Lou Hoffman, interview by author, n.d.

14 Frank Slootman, *Amp It Up: Leading for Hypergrowth by Raising Expectations, Increasing Urgency, and Elevating Intensity* (New York: Wiley, 2022).

15 Jenny Luna, "Jensen Huang on How to Use First-Principles Thinking to Drive Decisions," *Stanford Graduate School of Business*, April 25, 2024, https://www.gsb.stanford.edu/insights/jensen-huang-how-use-first-principles-thinking-drive-decisions.

16 Surabhi Agarwal and Archana Rai, "Exclusive Q&A: We in the US Don't Take Anything for Granted, We Need to Compete, Innovate: Microsoft CEO Satya Nadella," *The Economic Times*, January 8, 2025, https://economictimes.indiatimes.com/tech/technology/indias-human-capital-its-biggest-satya-microsofts-ceo-satya-nadella/articleshow/117033486.cms.

17 Jerome Socolovsky, "Spain's Banco Santander Weathers Crisis—for Now," *NPR*, October 9, 2008, https://www.npr.org/2008/10/09/95517447/spains-banco-santander-weathers-crisis-for-now.

18 General Motors, "Mary Barra," accessed April 21, 2025, https://www
.gm.com/company/leadership.detail.html/Pages/bios/global/en/corporate
-officers/Mary-Barra.

19 Jennifer Reingold, "PepsiCo's CEO Was Right. Now What?," *Fortune*, June 5,
2015, https://fortune.com/2015/06/05/pepsico-ceo-indra-nooyi/.

Chapter 10

1 Fifth Third Bancorp, *2024 Annual Report*, accessed April 21, 2025, https:
//s23.q4cdn.com/252949160/files/doc_financials/2024/ar/FITB-12-31
-2024-Annual-Report-Final.pdf.

2 Fifth Third Bank, "Fifth Third Named One of the World's Most Ethical
Companies by Ethisphere for the Fifth Time," news release, March 4,
2024, https://ir.53.com/news/news-details/2024/Fifth-Third-named-one
-of-the-Worlds-Most-Ethical-Companies-by-Ethisphere-for-the-fifth
-time/default.aspx.

3 Walnut Hills Historical Society, "Jacob Schmidlapp," *Walnut Hills Stories*,
accessed April 21, 2025, https://walnuthillsstories.org/stories/jacob
-schmidlapp/.

4 Ingvar Kamprad, *The Testament of a Furniture Dealer* (Leiden: Inter IKEA
Group, 2018), accessed April 21, 2025, https://www.inter.ikea.com/en/-
/media/InterIKEA/IGI/Financial%20Reports/English_The_testament
_of_a_dealer_2018.pdf.

5 Amy Purcell, interview by author, n.d.

6 Reed Hastings, "Netflix Culture: Freedom & Responsibility," *SlideShare*,
August 1, 2009, https://www.slideshare.net/slideshow/culture-1798664
/1798664.

7 Dawn Kawamoto, "Culture Transformation at Microsoft: An Ongoing
Journey," *HR Executive*, December 5, 2024, https://hrexecutive.com
/why-microsofts-culture-transformation-is-continuous.

8 Brian Tayan, "Governance Gone Wild: Misbehavior at Uber Technologies,"
Harvard Law School Forum on Corporate Governance, January 20, 2018,
https://corpgov.law.harvard.edu/2018/01/20/governance-gone-wild
-misbehavior-at-uber-technologies.

9 Boeing, *Aerospace Pioneers: Boeing Leaders through the Years*, accessed April
21, 2025, https://www.boeing.com/content/dam/boeing/boeingdotcom
/history/pdf/Boeing_Founders.pdf.

10 Peter Robison, *Flying Blind: The 737 MAX Tragedy and the Fall of Boeing* (New York: Doubleday, 2021).

11 *The Seattle Times*, "A 'Prescient' Warning to Boeing on 787 Trouble," February 6, 2011, archived at https://seattletimes.newsbank.com/sign-up?docref=doc/news/1354908534C9BBA0.

12 Useem, Jerry. "How Boeing Lost Its Bearings." *The Atlantic*, November 20, 2019. https://www.theatlantic.com/ideas/archive/2019/11/how-boeing-lost-its-bearings/602188.

13 M. Durgut, "Maneuvering Characteristics Augmentation System (MCAS): Function, Controversy, and Safety Enhancements," *AviationFile*, December 15, 2024, https://www.aviationfile.com/maneuvering-characteristics-augmentation-system-mcas-function-controversy-and-safety-enhancements.

14 Dominic Gates, "What Insiders Say New Boeing CEO Must Do," *Chicago Tribune*, January 13, 2020, https://digitaledition.chicagotribune.com/tribune/article_popover.aspx?guid=aaaee4c4-0198-43fb-9e2c-b8041bad789e.

15 Robert Sapolsky, *Behave: The Biology of Humans at Our Best and Worst* (New York: Penguin Press, 2017).

16 Verizon, "Verizon to Acquire Frontier," press release, September 5, 2024, https://www.verizon.com/about/news/verizon-to-acquire-frontier.

17 Alan Gardner, interview by author, n.d.

18 Patty McCord, "How Netflix Reinvented HR," *Harvard Business Review*, January–February 2014, https://hbr.org/2014/01/how-netflix-reinvented-hr.

19 Bryce G. Hoffman, *American Icon: Alan Mulally and the Fight to Save Ford Motor Company* (Three Rivers Press, 2012).

20 Hoffman, *American Icon*.

21 Bob Toohey, interview by author, n.d.

22 Allstate, *Notice of 2024 Annual Meeting and Proxy Statement: 2023 Annual Report*, accessed April 21, 2025, https://www.allstateproxy.com/proxy-statement/?p=182&v=false.

23 Allstate, "Allstate Reaches Agreement to Sell Northbrook Campus," news release, November 29, 2021, https://www.allstatenewsroom.com/news/allstate-reaches-agreement-to-sell-northbrook-campus.

24 Hugh Cameron, "Boeing Crisis as More Than 100 Whistleblowers Contact FAA," *Newsweek*, July 4, 2024, https://www.newsweek.com/boeing-whistleblowers-contact-faa-news-1921081.

25 Samantha Kelly, "Microsoft's AI Recall Tool Faces Another Delay Amid Privacy Concerns," *CNET*, November 1, 2024, https://www.cnet.com/tech/services-and-software/microsofts-ai-recall-tool-faces-another-delay-amid-privacy-concerns.

26 Greg Migliore, "Takeaways from the Executive Shakeup at Ford," *Autoblog*, May 22, 2017, https://www.autoblog.com/news/ford-ceo-jim-hackett-mark-fields-takeaways.

27 Hoffman, *American Icon*.

INDEX

ABOUT THE AUTHOR

Gavin McMahon is the co-founder and CEO of fassforward, a leadership and storytelling consultancy that helps companies build capability, shape culture, and turn strategy into action. An engineer by training, a consultant by trade, and a storyteller at heart, Gavin has spent 30+ years working across industries—automotive, defense, publishing, and tech—in roles spanning engineering, strategy, and product development. His work lifts teams, leads change, and creates impact—all through the power of story. His client list is a who's who: Allstate, American Airlines, Commvault, Estee Lauder, FIS, IPG, Mastercard, Microsoft, S&P, SpaceX, Verizon, and Yahoo.

Gavin holds a B(Eng) Hons. in mechanical engineering from UCLAN and is a Sainsbury Fellow of the Royal Academy of Engineering. After serving as a platoon commander in the British Army, a stint in the defense industry, and a chapter in Africa, he pivoted to business, earning an MBA in innovation, strategy, and information technology from the Institute Theseus in France.

He believes the world isn't a meritocracy—it's not the best idea that wins, it's the best-packaged idea. Ideas don't stand alone; they need a story. For three decades, Gavin has helped leaders connect the two—using storytelling to sharpen strategy, lift performance, and inspire action.

Ready to put *Story Business* into action? Scan the QR code or visit story-business.com to access exclusive tools and bonus resources.